MODERN GIRLS, SHINING

STARS, THE SKIES OF TOKYO

5 JAPANESE WOMEN

"Modern Girl" and "The Odor of Pickled Radishes" first appeared in *The New Yorker*.

Photo Credits
Matsui Sumako: The Tsubouchi Memorial Theatre Museum, Waseda University
Takamura Chieko: Nihonmatsu-shi Kyōiku Iinkai
Yanagiwara Byakuren: Miyazaki Fuki and Tomoo
Uno Chiyo: Estate of Uno Chiyo
Takamine Hideko: Takamine Hideko

Columbia University Press
Publishers Since 1893
New York   Chichester, West Sussex
Copyright © 1999 Columbia University Press
All rights reserved

Library of Congress Cataloging-in-Publication Data
Birnbaum, Phyllis.
     Modern girls, shining stars, the skies of Tokyo : five Japanese women / Phyllis Birnbaum.
          p. cm.
     ISBN 0–231–11356–0
          1. Women—Japan—Tokyo—Biography. 2. Tokyo (Japan)—Biography. I. Title.
HQ1762.5.A3B57 1999
305.4′092′252135—dc21   98–15268

∞
Casebound editions of Columbia University Press books are printed on permanent and durable acid-free paper.
Printed in the United States of America
Designed by Linda Secondari
c 10 9 8 7 6 5 4 3 2 1

MODERN GIRLS, SHINING

STARS, THE SKIES OF TOKYO

5 JAPANESE WOMEN

PHYLLIS BIRNBAUM

COLUMBIA UNIVERSITY PRESS NEW YORK

FOR ASHOK

CONTENTS

PREFACE

THIS COLLECTION OF BIOGRAPHICAL essays began as journalism assignments and, looking back, I see those first forays as an innocent time in my adventures as a biographer. Equipped with the latest in compact Japanese tape recorders and many elaborate introductions to the famous and their associates, I roamed around Tokyo in search of information about my subjects. My problems at the time seemed formidable: Would I be able to arrange the necessary appointments with those I wished to interview? How would I find that critic's camouflaged residence? And why didn't anyone turn on the heat?

But as I nervously checked to make sure that my tape recorder hadn't failed and scanned house numbers in Setagaya, I didn't know yet that I had underestimated my difficulties. I had put too much faith in electronic equipment and the certainties of maps, failing to realize that my journalism projects faced greater obstacles: my work would be hindered by my impatience with the truth. Before I set off, I had read many of the personal essays, fictional works, and autobiographies that my subjects had written. By temperament, I seem to prefer the life of a reader of books rather than the life of a busy reporter, and so I placed much trust in those Japanese volumes. From them, I had formed a very precise picture of the person I was soon to meet, could hear her voice and imagine exactly how she approached a bowl of noodles. If I had been writing a novel, I would have been able to supply this person with dialogue that would bring her quickly and wholly alive.

But journalism is not fiction, and editors tend to take a dim view of reporters who fabricate quotations out of thin air. The subjects of interviews get to speak for themselves.

My subjects did not disappoint me. They were just as extraordinary in real life as their autobiographical writings had promised. I was impressed by their courage, their talent, their tenacity, and also their patience in tolerating my questions. Yet it grieved me to note that their every utterance insisted upon the existence of people completely different from those I had been creating. The discrepancy between the person I had imagined from the writings and the flesh and blood being before me was almost too much to bear. More seasoned reporters have perhaps learned to steel themselves against such daunting developments. Stubbornly, these real live people proclaimed opinions that contradicted the views I had so carefully fashioned for them. Their strong words, their certainties, and most of all their solid presences put a dismaying damper on my imagination. So great was my reluctance to part with my inventions that I would not be surprised if stray details of my own creation crept into my written portraits.

Those encounters will make me forever wary of biographers who re-create their subjects only from written materials. I now know too well about the enormous gap between the main figure in one of those long, carefully researched autobiographies and the person who really dined at home in, say, western Tokyo each evening. Researchers on Murasaki Shikibu—author of the eleventh-century novel *The Tale of Genji*—base their portraits solely on the memoirs and autobiographical materials that have survived the centuries. Consider the outcome if a biographer had a chance to interview Murasaki Shikibu in a Kyoto coffee shop. Certainly a totally different portrait would result if Ms. Murasaki had bawled out the waitress for serving lukewarm tea or had confessed to a lifelong battle with stuttering.

Because of these experiences, I changed my approach for my next portraits. When it came time for me to write more biographies of Japanese women, I decided to take the easy way out and not interview anyone. I would write only about the long dead, who had been immortalized in their own writings and in the works of others, and would then be free to create my subjects' lives from the printed word alone. More important, I would not have to be jarred again by the disconcerting reality of the actual person. With this in mind, I set up my research headquarters in the Tokyo suburbs. By day, I hardly ventured out since I had no interviews scheduled. Instead, I stayed inside with my books and communed with my safely deceased subjects. They were the same kind of women I had selected for my live subjects—women with an artistic bent and a penchant for drama in their personal lives. It is a commonplace that biographers become their subjects, and this seems most true when the author has a choice of whom to write about. By instinct, I chose only those dead women whose lives I could easily inhabit, and perhaps much about me can be deduced from my inability to get inside a Japanese opera star or a literary anarchist, and my contrasting sense of ease in the skin of a hot-tempered actress or a moody artist.

Seeking a smoother journey this time around, I began to acquaint myself with the basic facts about my (dead) subjects' lives. No need to interview anyone, no trips to the other end of town, no anxiety about whether my tape recorder was broken. In choosing these women, I had every intention of presenting their cases fairly, of weighing the evidence and coming forth with an admirably balanced portrait. But I could not restrain my sympathies once I began to read about the hardships these women endured. Divorced because *he* gave her venereal disease? Forcibly married off to an idiot? Ended her days out of her mind? Reading alone there on the floor of my Tokyo apartment, I caught the feeling of those moments when my women had stared glumly at the dirty sky or considered desperate strategies to fight off unemployment. I felt stirred to do my utmost to convey these women's efforts to survive in a harsh universe.

It was not only the trouble in my subjects' lives that made my objectivity quiver as the fall days gave way to winter. What swayed me also was a certain kind of secondary material. Since these were my first attempts at research on dead subjects, it was the first time I had ever depended so much on books written by eyewitnesses. Here again, I got a great shock. Many times, I put down one of these books and closed my eyes in distress. The first part of the shock was that in certain cases, these chroniclers clearly detested my subjects. They hardly had a good word to say. This did not go well with the admiration I intended to express in my biographies.

The second part of the shock came when I realized that I was tempted to ignore these opinions. I had gone to Tokyo to write about my subjects in peace and quiet. In creating my portraits, I sought the freedom to live within my imagination, to fashion nothing but the truth itself—but at home, where I would commune only with the mist and my muse. Instead, I found myself slogging through the mud, reading page after page of disdainful criticism. One woman sliced up her lover's hat, contemporaries reported; another procured a mistress for her husband; another lacked even a smidgen of talent. In the face of these onslaughts, I could barely make out the glorious women I had envisioned at the outset. They were being overshadowed by those less attractive creatures created by their detractors.

I was surprised at how ready I was to adjust to this setback. I should have incorporated the negative testimony with gratitude, humbly accepting those eyewitnesses' authority and their views. Instead, I found myself prepared to interpret what they said about my women more to my tastes. I looked between the lines of those derogatory biographies and always found my dear girls peeping through. In many cases, the critics were so preposterously prejudiced that I had much leeway to fiddle and mold. In other instances, the charges against my women didn't leave me much room to maneuver. There were times—I admit this with much reluctance—when the critics might have been correct in their damning assessments. Still, I was surprisingly eager to stick to my guns and my views despite these disparaging accounts.

The matter of the commandeered telephone is my most shameful example. The very day after her lover died, one of my women wiped away her tears and strode off to get the rights to his telephone transferred to her own name. To some of her contemporaries, this at the very least amounted to crass scheming during a solemn mourning period; at the most, it constituted theft of a valuable possession. I concede that I saw a certain amount of indelicacy in going down to the telephone office several hours after the love of your life has died and filling out the forms for the phone line. Yet I could convince myself that my subject deserved credit for demonstrating practicality and quick thinking in a crisis.

These biographical essays reflect my astonishment at the skewed vision biographers bring to their work. In the end, I made furious attempts to see my subjects from every which way in order to obey the stern commands of accuracy. Having peered at these women upside down and from the right and left, I am left with only the humble feeling that the truth about another person is as hard to grasp as a single autumn leaf rushing down a swollen river.

A biographer may not be a novelist, but the methods of both writers are more similar than I had thought. I once believed that novelists drew their characters from the endless colors of the imagination—infinite shades of red and blue and green—while a biographer was stuck with only a couple of dented buckets filled with the facts. But now I see that the biographer may add more blue to a subject's portrait if so moved, or leave yellow out entirely. It is surprising how a splatter of red can change the final picture. Before the paint hits the biographer's canvas, many things can happen.

This collection of essays considers the lives of five women who, in their day, did their best to stand up and cause more trouble than was considered proper in Japanese society. They came of age during periods of great change in Japan, and new modes of thought had much influence, especially on the urban populace. They were all born after the 1868 Meiji Restoration, when Western ideas of freedom and equality came to Japan. Japanese women had every reason to believe that the modernization of their country would also bring about changes in their subservient role, long ago allotted to them by custom and law. But as the decades passed, no sweeping reforms improved the position of women in Japanese society. Increasingly, female voices could be heard speaking out against the assumptions and inequities that had kept women in their place.

The five women in this collection were not ideologues or movement activists; they did not go to the gallows for their revolutionary beliefs or rouse the masses with fiery speeches. They were all noted more for their beauty, their artistry, and their love affairs than for any association with politics. Still, through the fearlessness of their art and their private lives, they influenced large sections of the population and alarmed defenders of the status quo. Glamorous and intelligent, rebellious and talented, they helped to bring a new kind of woman to Japan, and along the way changed the lives of many.

Some readers will no doubt applaud the courage these women displayed in facing down opposition; others will deplore their willful insistence on getting their way. In my current chastened mood, I can say that both views are probably correct. Since I have now spent a number of months in the company of each of these women, I feel qualified to speculate about what it would be like to live with them at close quarters. If any of them took up residence in my neighborhood, I believe that I would welcome their coffee-hour conversations about their latest triumphs. A burst of high-powered talent in the late afternoon might just stimulate me to work more diligently. In certain of these women, I detect a no-nonsense approach to the vicissitudes of life that I might find bracing. In others, I see another response to a wretched fate. Some, contradicting our idealized view of the bravely enduring Japanese female, could not summon amazing reserves of inner strength and "make the best of it." They did not rise above their sorrows by stoicism or by going out into the villages to build huts for the poor. Saintly altruism simply did not suit their temperaments. Instead of succoring the needy, they complained and brooded and let the world know about their discontents. I also have no difficulty warming to this kind of mentality.

If these women lived down the street, they would stimulate me, certainly, but they might also wear me out, since their energies— for work, mischief, love—were immense. I might enjoy their company, but after some time I might also start to worry about the price exacted for their accomplishments. Their struggles often began in melancholy and did not always end in bliss. Along the way, the lives of those close to them were often disrupted and ruined. There is much in these pages about the Japanese interest in the self and the lure of individualism. Clearly, the more individualistic my subjects became, the more serious the charges that they behaved selfishly and without consideration for others. Their lives make us ask the old questions about human goodness, human achievement, and just how much of one gets sacrificed in pursuit of the other; this leads to the grander question about just exactly what we live for. Finally these life stories force us to remember that the self, so often analyzed, is not just a literary notion evaluated by the experts but a vibrant presence, both marvelous and disturbing.

As I mentioned at the outset, these essays began as journalism assignments, and I have written throughout with the general reader in mind. I would of course be pleased if specialists found these writings of some use as well. Readers in search of a continuum may be disappointed because these five women are perhaps connected only by their taste for independence, their talent, and my affinity for them. Since I make no promises about binding themes, I feel uneasy at the thought that anyone would read these life stories all at one go, without a breather in between. If I close my eyes and imagine these five gathered together at a party, the room fills with too much noise; the illustrious guests speak all at once, with too much urgency, and I never get to try the hors d'oeuvres. Better to receive each woman alone on a different day, when she will have the leisure to pronounce her name clearly and play with her napkin. Then she can explain why she deserves your attention.

As I look at the pile of five essays, I remember the excitement I felt in trying to organize these women's biographies. The very idea that I might be able to bring them to life tells me of the distance I have traveled from those long-ago days when I first began to study Japanese. By a trick of fate, Japanese took me out of the small world where I grew up and introduced me to other complicated places far away from my old haunts. Even though much time has passed since I first tried to read a Japanese book, I still feel the wonder of entering the minds of those whose writing moves vertically down a piece of paper. It is my hope that some of this wonder has touched these essays.

MODERN GIRLS, SHINING

STARS, THE SKIES OF TOKYO

JAPANESE LITERATURE HAS MORE
than its share of male authors who
have ruined themselves with drink,
courted breakdowns, or chosen to
end their sufferings through suicide.
While ordinary readers may puzzle
over the reasons for these destruc-
tive tendencies, to a contingent of
Japanese men the explanation is
obvious: the women are to blame.

There is the case of the eminent
writer whose suicide looks suspi-
cious. Some maintain that he did not
drown himself voluntarily, but was in
fact held underwater by his female
companion. She then supposedly
drowned herself in order to gain
notice as the partner in his double
suicide and a place in literary history.
The male chroniclers also like to
mention the pure and gentle author
who was led to his doom by a scheming female journalist. "For at least a
year and a half he kept refusing her,"
a literary friend fumed afterward,
"but he was stuck to her and like a

male spider caught in a female spider's entanglements, he was completely consumed by her in the end."

On the list of women who have singlehandedly wrecked the lives of Japanese literati, Matsui Sumako has been given a prominent place. Now dead and unable to speak a word in protest, Matsui has long been at the mercy of her lover's writer friends, who have written denunciations of her in numerous biographies and reminiscences. Over the years, Matsui has been held responsible for the bouts of fever her beloved suffered, his financial dilemmas, the lonely look in his eye. It is said that she put impure ideas into the mind of her unfortunate partner, Shimamura Hōgetsu, whose only indulgence had been drinks at a second-floor noodle shop.

Matsui achieved fame as Japan's first Western-style actress, and she surely would have preferred to be mentioned, first and foremost, for her skills onstage. The critics raved about her Salome ("Sumako has performed this role with tremendous skill, and her Salome is at once egotistical, driven, and willful"); Matsui's powerful Nora caused a sensation; hypnotic and seductive in other roles, she brought the house down. Yet despite these theatrical triumphs, some only remember her for her alleged role in the downfall of a decent man. One contemporary wrote,

Sumako's fierce selfishness put relentless pressure on the weak-willed Shimamura-sensei. . . . We members of the troupe worried constantly that he would have to shoulder the evil consequences of Sumako's behavior and that the troupe would eventually collapse. . . . It pained me to think that he would certainly be unhappy. And as might be expected, he was no longer able to read books or think about things. Instead, he wore himself out with worry, spending his days and nights keeping her in line and seeing to trivial matters that kept cropping up.

Such comments make one wonder whether Matsui truly deserves to go down in posterity as another woman who snuffed the life out of her lover. Certainly Matsui was vigorous and emotional, with an ability to maintain her intensity in performance after performance. She was also impossible to abide at close quarters if crossed in any way. But while her power and determination may have impelled her to hog the stage at every opportunity and nag Shimamura constantly, these same traits allowed her to break free of convention and claim a right to live as she wished. There was also a tragic side to Matsui's life that had nothing to do with her dire effect on a male companion.

Anyone who has read the historical documents soon realizes that few view Matsui Sumako in a positive light. As is by now obvious, she is not flattered by the portraits of her that remain in the literary annals. She did, however, enjoy better luck in other matters: she lived in a period perfectly suited to her talents. Matsui embarked upon her acting career during the early part of the twentieth century, when the Japanese theater world was in the process of moving away from traditional forms like Kabuki and No. The modern impresarios were introducing more up-to-date creations to Japanese audiences, and these made good use of Matsui's obstreperous temperament. At that time, Western drama was being imported at a rapid pace, and translations of Ibsen, Maeterlinck, and Hauptmann, among others, flooded the market. Matsui had the opportunity to show off her hotheadedness as an outspoken German singer with family problems and a medieval Italian wife who tries to stop a war all by herself.

While many of her colleagues struggled to adjust, Matsui seems to have taken easily to the new and disconcerting conventions. Reality, most of all, didn't daunt her in the slightest. As soon became clear, the newly popular Western playwrights described their world with a certain amount of accuracy, but the true-to-life had not been a staple of the Japanese theater, which banked on impossible coincidence and supernatural intervention to push the plots along. Kabuki and Nō, in particular, had a large supply of fantastic ghosts and wily animal spirits to hold the attention of the audience. In contrast, scenes from the realistic modern plays could dwell on the hero merely eating breakfast. Although her colleagues may have hesitated, Matsui was capable of eating a perfectly acted, absolutely plain breakfast, lunch, and supper onstage as if she had been dining in front of packed theater halls all her life.

Matsui also had no trouble speaking naturally in public, and she thus escaped another pitfall. Many Japanese actors, trained for the traditional stage, were more adept at the stylized chanting and unnatural cadences of Kabuki and Nō. For the new works, they had to change their techniques drastically and speak the everyday dialogue in an ordinary manner. Matsui never wavered in her ability to deliver lines—onstage and off—with spontaneity, conviction, and power. "As the play unfolded," a critic wrote of her, "I took great, great pleasure in being able to hear the dialogue spoken naturally for the first time by an actress born in Japan."

Another piece of good fortune was that Matsui started out at a time when directors badly needed genuine women to act in their stage productions. Long before, government moralists had forbidden women from appearing on the stage, and female roles had since been played by men. This had given rise to a whole new specialty of female impersonators who, to this day, are idolized for their grace and charm. Audiences may have enjoyed the make-believe of such a male *onnagata*, decked out in a wig and gorgeous kimono, playing the loyal courtesan in an old Kabuki tale like *Yoshitsune and the Thousand Cherry Trees*, but the producers of the new theater felt that the push for realism would be ill-served if that same male actor walked across the stage in a Western dress and pearl earrings playing Nora in *A Doll's House*.

Even though Matsui eagerly fulfilled requests to perform, a real woman playing a real woman, she had to win over opponents who still had doubts about the need for females onstage. Some people simply could not tolerate the spectacle of a woman immodestly displaying herself in front of a theater audience; actresses were held in such low esteem that the brother of a female star killed himself because of the disgrace her profession had brought upon the family. There were other objections. "Women are incapable of the hard dedication art requires"; "Women artists are nothing more than a bunch of performing monkeys." In addition, female impersonators rightly saw the use of real live women onstage as a threat to their job security.

In this environment, Matsui Sumako caught the acting bug. Her character, either passionate or deranged, depending on your point of view, helped her overcome broken marriages and the terrors facing a woman unskilled and alone. Passion and derangement also marked her acting, and she became known for her portrayals of forthright, headstrong heroines who cried a lot. She also played a few very modern women who, for the first time on the Japanese stage, made stunning declarations about independence and the imperfections of the female situation. A master of reality in all its high-pitched glory, Matsui stirred audiences when playing characters who suddenly comprehended the whole truth of their lives.

In her private life, Matsui lived out another drama of female strife and transformation. After failed attempts at more conventional arrangements, she began to live publicly with a learned and married stage director. Later, when the scandals surrounding Matsui's private life boosted her popularity, there was gossip about how she had brought disaster to a good man. As she began to be typecast, many thought that it was not much of a stretch for her to play Salome, whose allures caused the death of a saintly male.

Historians' grudges against Matsui involve more than her supposed mistreatment of her lover. She has been upbraided for the time she assaulted a rival actress by thrashing her with a fancy

Japanese robe ("Quite a vocabulary on her," a witness commented. "Suddenly it was like some fishwife's brawl backstage") and for her astonishing stinginess ("That's not something actors usually do," a colleague muttered about one of her tight-fisted practices. "That's not something human beings do," his friend replied). Other members of her troupe protested that success had gone to her head, and that she took her fans at their word when they called her "The Queen of the Japanese Theater." Her temperamental outbursts caused whole brigades of actors to quit in outrage; she treated those who remained behind like her personal servants. Moreover, men have pilloried Matsui for lacking the magic of femininity—*onna-rashisa* in Japanese. In any language, this absence of femininity is often at the heart of many men's complaints against forceful women, but in Japan the question of whether the woman possesses *onna-rashisa* or not is debated so solemnly and shamelessly that femininity seems recognized as a concrete skill, with qualifications and rankings. Just as a man without thumbs cannot hope to be a carpenter, so a Japanese female without *onna-rashisa* can never succeed as an adult woman.

A wild and impetuous nature is probably not high on every man's list of feminine virtues, but this certainly swept Matsui Sumako out of Matsushiro, the country village where she was born in 1886. To this day, Matsushiro seems a blessed locale only for those who can tolerate monotony. Boredom in the countryside is well-known to readers of Japanese literature, since a category of fiction focuses upon this very problem. In such writings the protagonist—who is usually a stand-in for the male author—spends many pages cursing the fate that has exiled him to the slow and backward provinces. The theme most often hinges on how to get out immediately.

Now several hours from Tokyo and a dusty bus ride from the nearest city, Matsui Sumako's birthplace could easily serve as one of those oppressive fictional settings. This village does offer the pleasures of lush mountain ranges sprinkled with wildflowers and pine groves. Yet amid such natural beauty are tightly packed houses and the certainty of hidebound, nosy neighbors who make sure that no untoward behavior misses their notice or censure. In Matsui's day, the village of Matsushiro was probably just like those novels about the Japanese countryside, offering no drama, no hope of a different future, no resolution of daily conflicts.

Matsui grew up surrounded by the mountains, and her excessive energy did not go unnoticed. Later her detractors would seize upon this vigor as the deadliest of her traits. ("Sumako, who was hardiness itself, survived of course"—one can imagine them grumbling—"but Shimamura caught her cold and died"). Much has been made of the location of her hometown, which the surrounding mountain range deprived of sunlight for half the day. Romantic biographers like to surmise that the continuous darkness in this "Half-day Village" affected Matsui deeply and that her tumultuous later life was nothing more than a search for sunnier surroundings.

Matsui briefly lived in Tokyo, where she studied sewing, but soon was married off, in the traditional manner, to a husband selected by her relatives. Since she was the last of nine children, Matsui's betrothal must have come as a relief to her family. Her father had already died by the time of her marriage, and this left her bereft of important family protection. Later, as a famous actress writing her memoirs, *Makeup Brush*, she would make much of these early sorrows, depicting her youthful self as a piteous heap of tempestuous emotions that were all the time waiting to be unleashed onstage. "Death parted her from her father during her girlhood," Matsui wrote of herself. "She went through sadness unimaginable to an ordinary girl and spent many of her days crying."

She had high hopes for this marriage, which would serve as a substitute for the family she had left behind. Her new husband's family ran an inn in another town, and after her marriage Matsui moved there and set to work. She wrote that she enjoyed her new circumstances and was thus astonished when after only a few months her husband's family declared her an unsatisfactory wife. With cruel briskness, she was divorced. Matsui claimed that she never understood what happened. "She spent two or three months dreamily enjoying the intimacy and warmth of this second home," she wrote. "But when she thinks about it now, she suspects that there was either some strange disagreement among the people around her or some other reason unfathomable to a naive woman like herself. No one said anything or agreed to anything. The connection was simply severed."

Here, the coarse edges of Matsui's character never come into question. Later on, of course, others would take her to task for throwing hot soup at her suitors or feeding them too many dinners of smelly beans. After this divorce, however, she does seem to have been deeply wounded and frightened. The speculation is that her in-laws considered her too weak for the work at the inn; others say that she was divorced because she had contracted a venereal disease from her husband. Devastated and disgraced, the eighteen-year-old Matsui returned to Tokyo in 1904, where she helped out in her sister and brother-in-law's pastry shop. As she toiled, lacking even the talent to wrap a package, Matsui was so forlorn that she attempted suicide. "It was just when the plums were coming into bloom," she wrote.

She could hardly eat as she sat in the sunny second-floor room with a southern exposure and veranda that her sister allowed her to use. She just stared at the paper screens, crying her eyes out on the pillow. She would think about things and cry; then she would cry and think about things. Finally she decided to die and stopped crying, perhaps because no more tears remained.

A new man turned up soon after.

It is essential to come to grips with Matsui's allures, for she was never short of male admirers. The photographs show that she was not a Japanese beauty in the conventional sense; on the contrary, her face was too full and robust for perfection. In a kimono, she did not sparkle; the paddings in her Western clothes did her a disservice; and the flowing robes, wood-sprite costumes, and feathered helmets she wore in her various stage parts failed to accentuate her best features. Yet there is no doubt that she possessed a raw and fervent energy that served her well on stage and also captivated the men. She could claim a number of conquests among the intellectual and artistic set, though some later hated themselves for succumbing to her frank sensuality. As they look back, most of these men refuse to express downright admiration, since they may have at one time been spurned by her and/or been members of groups dedicated to removing her from her position of eminence. Thus the compliments emerge in a fashion that is indirect, even by Japanese standards. "She didn't have any appeal to us," one contemporary reports; his colleague continues, "I mean, it's a different story if you have a taste for the uncouth or enjoy a glimpse of the maid's flesh. She was a country bumpkin, you see, with many rough spots." Another says: "I wouldn't go so far as to say that she was like the mythical flying horse soaring through the heavens, oblivious of all obstacles, but if Sumako wanted to go down a certain path, nothing got in her way. I mean, she had no idea what the word 'hesitation' meant. She just forged innocently ahead." From these comments one can at least conclude that Matsui provided the exhilarations of sexuality and decisiveness to the abstracted, melancholy males who were her favorites.

Four years later, in 1908, she married a literary youth named Maezawa Seisuke, who felt drawn to the uneducated but lively young pastry store clerk. Observers never considered the couple perfectly matched: "Maezawa was just twenty-six, but looked about forty," Tanaka Eizō wrote in *Reminiscences of the New Theater.* "He had a second-degree black belt in judo and the broad, sturdy body and the wide shoulders to go with it. On that big square face of his, he'd grown an old-style mustache that twirled up at the tips. . . . Reminded me of a police chief. Not at all the type women go for." Maezawa became a history teacher at the newly established Tokyo Acting School and pursued his interest in drama, both old-style and new. He joined a group of traditional storytellers and at the same time sought friendships with members of more modern acting troupes. For Matsui, who had never before seen a play performed, the heady talk with budding actors and directors about their plans for new theatrical productions was inspiring. She would give up Fūgetsudō, the sweet shop, and become an actress.

Later, she wrote about acquiring her first acting skills when studying her brother-in-law's way with his customers. With a true sense of discovery, she notes that his polite way of speaking encouraged people to purchase more of Fūgetsudō's offerings. "The first part of his 'thank you,' " she explained in her memoirs,

was spoken in a low, thick voice, and with a strength that emanated from the depths of his stomach. The next syllable was somewhat blurred, and the last part was spoken in a higher tone and lightly trailed off. This was truly a proprietor's dignified way of speaking. . . . Later, as a customer was leaving, she was this time able to say 'Thank you' very naturally. She said it exactly as her brother-in-law had done just a moment ago. She felt that she had become a professional very quickly and had mastered her first role.

Matsui had all sorts of other chances to hone her acting skills informally. She had to learn, for example, how to put on a decorous demeanor in front of the neighbors the morning after one of her many stupendous squabbles with Maezawa. In the course of these conflicts, objects were pitched out of windows and her language was not that of a budding ingenue. Maezawa remained devoted to her despite these noisy disagreements, and he cast about for ways to train his wife as an actress, particularly after he had secured his teaching post at the Tokyo Acting School. Although Maezawa would live to regret the ambitions he had fostered in his touchy spouse, more than one memoirist remembers his sincere and earnest appearance the day he stood before officials of another acting school and declared, "I'd like to make my wife an actress. Would you come and meet her? Tell me if she is qualified or not."

By then, the distinguished critic, dramatist, and translator Tsubouchi Shōyō had been persuaded to set up an acting school within what would become Tokyo's Waseda University. Tsubouchi had first earned a place in the history of modern Japanese literature in 1885 when, at age twenty-four, he started to publish *The Essence of the Novel*. This influential study urged writers to abandon the cardboard characters and stock situations familiar to traditional fiction and instead to depict human life in its slippery complexity. Thus Tsubouchi Shōyō made his mark early as a staunch partisan of realism. Among his many other achievements, Tsubouchi translated the complete works of his adored Shakespeare into Japanese.

A man of exalted ambitions, Tsubouchi was not content to set up a mere trade school for the training of actors; he also sought to elevate the cultural level of the nation, to whose service he was committed. As suited a serious man of letters, he established a regular drama research center. At Tsubouchi's school, acting students learned the history of drama; they took demanding courses on such subjects as Shakespeare, modern drama, psychology, and English. Coed classes were still a rarity in those days, but Tsubouchi acknowledged the need for trained actresses. Perhaps because of his reputation for extreme probity, he dared to admit women acting students along with men; strict rules forbade extramural socializing between the sexes. Maezawa hoped to enroll Matsui in this school, called Bungei Kyōkai (Literary Arts Society).

"When a husband comes to you and says that he wants to make his wife an actress, you expect him to show you a real beauty," wrote Tanaka, who was one of the officials of the school.

So we went over to meet her. Maezawa had just got married a month before. He and his wife lived together on the second floor of Suzuki's Stationary Shop in Mita. They were both from the same town in Shinshū. "This is my Ma-chan," he said, introducing a woman to us. I thought his way of introducing her extremely affectionate, but I was more surprised to have a look at this person who wanted to become an actress. She could not even say the proper words of greeting when she met us for the first time. In fact, she could hardly get a decent sentence out. Not quite standing up, she bowed at us just once in a most perfunctory manner. She looked like just a common fishwife, wearing her short coat with short sleeves and somewhat soiled green tabi socks (in those days, I really hated women who wore colored tabi).

No question about it, her looks were below average and none too good. Her face and body were big, and there was roughness and agitation in the way she moved around. On top of that, she had an ugly, flat nose. I started to have real doubts about Maezawa's eye for beauty. There wasn't even a trace of any learning or manners. All told, she seemed vulgar and coarse and had an extremely crude way of talking. Whenever she said anything, her country dialect came flying out, even when she uttered the simplest words (you could always hear this dialect when she spoke her lines on stage later, and until the day she died, she was never able to get rid of it). No way around it, she was a country bumpkin through and through. . . . "And this woman wants to became an actress," I thought. "Press her somewhere, and she'll make that sound, I suppose."

This description sounds like an exaggeration, but others confirm that Matsui's flat nose worried her supporters. The nose was apparently too much of a flaw to overlook, especially if she was to play Western women, who were envied throughout Japan for their high nasal bridges. A professional storyteller in Yūrakuza had found a solution for this same defect by undergoing an operation. Impressed by these results, Matsui underwent the same nose job herself. The techniques of this operation were still primitive and painful, employing some kind of paraffin injection to achieve the desired effect. In cold weather, this substance turned an ugly violet and caused Matsui embarrassment; after the procedure, she avoided posing for photographs in profile. From the front, however, the operation was judged a success. Just a few months later, Matsui appeared before Tsubouchi Shōyō and others for the crucial audition at Bungei Kyōkai.

Her prospective teachers did not much care for her rustic manner or her obviously meager education. Only Matsui's large size and hardy appearance worked in her favor. "As far as her qualifications as an actress go," Tsubouchi is said to have declared, "there's only that sturdy body of hers." It is assumed that Tsubouchi sought Japanese women of more than average physical proportions to play substantial Western heroines. Upon acceptance, Matsui was required to attend classes from six to nine in the evening.

Matsui could more than match the two other female students in looks and enthusiasm, but she faltered badly in her studies. In fact, her complete ignorance of English conversation nearly caused her expulsion from the school, since students, following Tsubouchi's orders, had to study many scripts (by Shakespeare and selected modern dramatists) in English. Only special intervention by Maezawa and other supporters, her promise that she would study harder, and her pathetic outpouring of tears earned Matsui a reprieve. Reportedly, her husband Maezawa was served a steady diet of odorous *nattō* beans during this period when Matsui Sumako set out to conquer Shakespearean English.

Matsui's battle with *The Merchant of Venice* went beyond merely deciphering the meaning of the major speeches. She could not read even a single English letter, much less worry over Elizabethan verb forms. Her diligence in overcoming this difficulty has earned her the respect of her most virulent critics.

Determined not to be exiled to the sweet shop again, she studied Shakespeare by using two copies of the play. In one, she transcribed the pronunciation of every single syllable into Japanese sounds; in the other, she carefully noted the translation of every sentence. She also inveigled tutors to come to her shabby home, and they later complained about the provincial food she served them while she tirelessly practiced her day's lines. "She was the only student who so speedily had to go from learning the ABCs of English to reading Shakespeare in the original," Tanaka writes. "It was a pitiful situation, as if an elementary school student had suddenly entered college." A student who sat next to Matsui in class kindly offered assistance whenever he found her studying with the English texts upside down.

It is just about here that a biographer may seek to point out the most attractive aspects of Matsui Sumako's life. Reading many pages of invective against her produces a strong impulse to present her as a misunderstood and winning figure. Therefore, her story becomes a cautionary tale for the biographer. Where those who hated her paint a picture of vulgarity, a conniving nature, and lunatic fits, a warmer approach can come up with ebullience, honesty, and the behavior required to survive. This pleasant image is based upon Matsui's decision to establish a career in Tokyo, far from her country home, and the perseverance she displayed in her attempts to pronounce Shakespearean English at drama school. In a certain light, her saga can seem a very rousing study of how to seize a moment and make the most of it: clearly, Matsui was not one to let any of her moments pass by without giving them their due. In addition, the creeds of self-help and self-improvement have a special meaning in our present age. There is the hope that her story can—if handled adroitly—inspire the fainthearted to carry on, to remain undaunted in the face of rain, winter, or wind.

In this mood, a biographer approves of Matsui's pressing forward with her ambitions. While English would never become her strong suit, Matsui must have seen that mastery of a foreign language was merely the pet project of overly fastidious teachers. No one would be able to complain about her if she dazzled audiences with her acting, which, after all, would be in Japanese. She had faced the terror of being dismissed from the school for her academic failings and had been allowed to continue only after hardwon negotiations. These humiliations fortified her to fight back; from this time forward, witnesses say, she made no bones about her dogged commitment to her career in front of her husband, her fellow students, and her teachers. It must be conceded that the stories of Matsui's rude and pushy behavior—later to grow into a mountain of caustic accounts—began to accumulate during this period. "For the sake of 'art,' she stripped herself bare and pressed forward, casting off everything else," Tanaka wrote.

Such an attitude did not bode well for domestic harmony with Maezawa, who had so loyally stood by his wife as she embarked upon her new career. The couple moved closer to the acting school, renting a tiny second-floor apartment accessible only via a crude rope ladder. Busy with her classes, Matsui had no time for interior decoration and so their home did not boast any feminine touches. Visitors have recalled the scant furnishings in the apartment.

Matsui was tireless in her efforts, practicing alone on stage for hours and then forcing fellow students to join her for some more hours of rehearsal. These habits remained with her, and even after she had achieved great fame, Matsui was not the sort to join a friend or fellow student for a cup of tea and chitchat when she could be using the time for rehearsal. Her marriage to Maezawa ended amid rough squabbles and, on at least one occasion, her assaulting him with a lighted gas lamp. Finally ordering him out of her life forever, Matsui threw Maezawa's belongings from the

second-floor window onto the street. In the drama histories, Maezawa Seisuke later earned mention as the man who hit upon acting as a career for his wife and thereby found a healthier outlet for Matsui Sumako's tumultuous nature than the mutilation of his favorite hat. He died during the Great Kantō Earthquake of 1923.

At this point, a sympathetic biographer experiences some discomfort in moving forward with the story. Matsui's status as a besieged and unfairly censored heroine never feels very secure. Once her next lover arrives, the problem becomes more acute, since at this juncture her detractors grow more eloquent and vociferous. These critics would probably take Matsui more to task for her harsh treatment of Maezawa if they were not so busy damning her for every misfortune that befell the great love of her life, Shimamura Hōgetsu. They pillory her for destroying Shimamura's noble nature. They claim that she practically committed murder by not taking him to the hospital during his last illness. As if that were not enough, she had the gall to transfer his telephone line to her own name the day after his death. The critics do allow that she brought Shimamura immortality, though admittedly not of the dignified, academic kind he had once sought. Without her, Shimamura would not have become a main character in countless Japanese ballads, sordid novels, hallucinatory dance productions, and modern Nō plays, all meticulously dissecting his private life.

Shimamura Hōgetsu, who was fifteen years older than Matsui, had gone through much struggle in his youth. First his mother died, and then his father, a financial ruin, perished when the house caught fire while he was drunk. A local benefactor saw the young Shimamura's promise, adopted him, and paid for his education. In 1890, Shimamura took that thrilling journey—chronicled by so many members of Japan's future elite in those days—from his home in the countryside to Tokyo, where he attended the future Waseda University. His talents were recognized, and he became a prized student of the august Tsubouchi Shōyō. Praised for his graduation thesis, which established him as an incisive theorist on aesthetics, Shimamura became a lecturer in the literature department and worked as an editor of a prestigious literary journal at Waseda before going to Europe on a scholarship. There he was to educate himself on cultural trends in the Western world.

Shimamura went on to become a prolific and influential critic (particularly of Japanese Naturalism), scholar, novelist, and translator. His brilliance and his learning were by all accounts prodigious. For three and a half years, Shimamura studied psychology and aesthetics, among other subjects, in England and Germany. He also found the time to immerse himself in the artistic offerings of these foreign cities. The theater in particular enthralled him, and it is said that Shimamura saw some eighty plays during one year in England.

Shimamura's apparent professional success and promise of more achievements to follow did not come without a price. He later complained that the hardships he had suffered had robbed him of a carefree childhood: "I was separated from my mother and father when I was eleven or twelve, and until I entered college, I had to fight all the vicissitudes of the world myself." In addition, he was constantly aware of his obligations to the adoptive father who had lifted him out of the destitution of his family home, enabling him to learn about Dante at Waseda and to hobnob with the literary lights of Tokyo. In recognition of this debt, which he was expected to repay by lifelong obedience and service, Shimamura agreed to an arranged marriage to a close relative. The couple increased Shimamura's burden of responsibilities by eventually producing seven children.

In the films later made about Matsui's life, Shimamura's wife always receives dreadful treatment. Usually dressed in dark cloaks, she is portrayed as dour and reproachful; with a child or two close by, she repeatedly berates Shimamura, in a most unmodern fashion, about his family responsibilities. Were such speeches deemed filmic, she would be the one to speak of Confucius and quote one of his wise sayings about the need to maintain a moral social order. In written accounts Mrs. Shimamura fares no better, for she does not even merit the kind of malice heaped on Matsui. Usually the male chroniclers mock this wife's pesky persistence in keeping track of her husband and her intemperate reactions when he disappears for days at a time. The men rise in chorus to dismiss her as "hysterical." A wife nowadays might well dispute this assessment, imagining the vehement emotions she might summon if her husband had gone off on a leisurely tour of Europe's cultural capitals for several years, then, upon his return home, had become preoccupied with his own ennui or with a hale young actress from Matsushiro, leaving his spouse behind to tend a brood of children.

In spite of this, Shimamura Hōgetsu is a man difficult to dislike. Japanese literature provides abundant examples of men like him who are dreamy weaklings before the wiles of tough and crafty women. Heroes as far back as Prince Genji in *The Tale of Genji* have demonstrated great refinement of feeling and a lack of willpower when it comes to managing their love lives. Time and time again such men foolishly risk everything for love, but frequently their incompetence about the simplest details of everyday life (they are cheated out of money, they forget to hide a telltale kimono) crushes all hopes for happiness; the couple may be next seen chanting poetry about how life is as fleeting as the cherry blossoms while they trundle off to their double suicide. Japanese literature would contain far fewer love suicides (and far less wonderful poetry) if, from the outset, women had been put in charge of organizing the lovers' escape.

In a certain sense, Shimamura fits in well with this parade of frail and dithering heroes. After his return from Europe, he fell into the doldrums and could not tolerate the tedium of his academic life. He resumed his teaching duties at Waseda, but became known for yawning if visitors stayed too long. His classes also failed to hold his interest, and he once said, "It's a wonder that I don't feel guilty about repeating the same lectures year after year." His despair went beyond his classroom duties, and he began to see his whole existence as a pointless exercise. In one of Shimamura's gloomy writings of that period, he described a hero who "sat in front of his desk all morning, his hands crossed against his chest, just staring into space for two hours or more. He didn't feel like doing anything. He picked up one or two of the new magazines and books strewn on the side table, but they didn't hold his interest."

Where the other professors must have set an example of diligence and fortitude, Shimamura did not disguise his own despondency, keeping his students well informed about what he called "the grayness of this world." Scholars at Waseda University today still have not forgiven Shimamura for his behavior. "The fellow was a wastrel," one Waseda professor told me recently. "I don't know what they do in the United States, but around here a professor only puts up a notice when he's going to be absent from his classes. Shimamura was absent so much that he would put up a notice when he was going to be present. When he did appear, I've heard that he would leave in the middle, telling the students that he had forgotten to shut the door of the bird cage or something and had to go home."

Turning forty proved unbearable to Shimamura. His health, never robust, worsened, and although he was committed to translating Henrik Ibsen's *A Doll's House* for Waseda's literary journal, he had to take time off to recuperate from a serious lung ailment. Upon his return, his students found him weak and more downcast. In addition, his home life gave him no peace, what with his wife's "hysterical" outbursts and the deaths of two beloved children. He did not relish the prospect of facing his teaching responsibilities once more: "When I look back at the past, it seems all emptiness, and even when I look to the future, I come up with only vague thoughts."

This morose mood, familiar to forty-year-olds of either hemisphere, contained particularly Japanese elements. In those days, Japanese men at midlife could not easily go off to explore new marital arrangements or give up an established way of life for a new career. The traditional family system, based on principles of obligation and hierarchy, demanded that each member sacrifice personal desires for the greater good of the clan. The family was the target of many writers whose fictional characters were constantly badgered and thwarted by imperious relatives. "The well-being of the family gives rise to all bad things," Dazai Osamu wrote in 1948, thirty years after Shimamura's death.

And so, as his eye begins to wander toward Matsui, Shimamura Hōgetsu retains our sympathy. He eventually left his wife and abandoned his children, but perhaps Shimamura wins us over because he tried to be true to himself throughout a terrible and genuine human conflict. He also looked upon his own selfish emotions with much horror. In gaining some pleasure for himself, Shimamura had to wound a number of people he cherished, and such brutality gave him no peace. In fact, this future leader of the modern Japanese theater was caught in the same monumental conflict between love and duty that old-style dramas had often depicted. "I have inexcusably neglected my obligations to my brother and to society," a character in one of Shimamura's short stories concedes, "but the truth is that I can't get the one I love out of my mind."

Shimamura wrote those words during the first decades of this century, when Japanese were still mulling over many ideas recently imported from the West. Among them, few would require so much thought as individualism. As Sharon K. Nolte explains in *Liberalism in Modern Japan*, "The concept of the individual hardly existed before the Meiji Restoration. Until then, proper behavior was defined by class status and gender." In the West, individualism had been stressed for centuries, but for Japanese of those days, the idea of the individual had more freshness and vitality than we can imagine. In a famous speech to students in 1914, the renowned author Natsume Sōseki described his own efforts to establish his individuality. As a young man, he said,

I completely depended upon others and was like a rootless weed that floats about aimlessly. but then I finally realized that this was not good. When I say I depended on others, I mean that I imitated them, in much the same was that a man has another person taste some sake, asks for an opinion, and then, whether that judgment is good or not, takes that opinion as his own. . . .

[But after some years of struggle] I came to believe that I was in charge, while others were merely guests. This belief has given me great confidence and peace of mind.

For much of his life, Shimamura too strove to make the change from rootless river weed to a person in charge of himself. Like many other Japanese, he does not seem to have found this an easy transition. Shimamura let the public know about his difficulties when he advocated asserting one's "true self." This quest for an identity liberated at last from falsity and from society's rules is a frequent theme of Shimamura's writings. While being pummeled into obedience, he could at least still dream about free and honest individuals. He did not for a moment see the Japanese self as an immaculate white bird soaring off into a sunny sky if given the chance. On the contrary: the Japanese self, in Shimamura's view, was more on the order of a beleaguered magpie, swatted down by social customs and crushed by demeaning responsibilities. Yet according to Shimamura, even that poor creature deserved a few moments to stagger forth into the open air. "Human beings are animals adorned with falsities," he writes.

The difficulty involved in finding one's true self is no less than the difficulty involved in achieving the religious ideal of selflessness. I sincerely wish to be a person who displays his true self. An individual may have a cold, warm, or passionate spirit, but that is all right as long as this spirit is the person's true self. The difficulty comes in expressing that coldness as coldness, the warmth as warmth, and the passion as passion. There is no reason to be passionate and speak of coldness or to be cold and speak of passion.

Like many thinkers of the period, the idea of such freedom both exhilarated and intimidated Shimamura. "For every hundred people in this present-day world, there are a hundred different kinds of individuals. It is futile to seek a common ground among such people. Each person has no choice but to go forward in silence, each in a separate way."

In the field of drama also, Shimamura championed the cause of the individual. He and many others wanted to get away from traditional Japanese stage creations that did not describe people struggling to assert their true selves, but instead told of social forces shattering even the smallest traces of individuality. It is not surprising that Shimamura, in his struggle to break free, turned to the dramas of Ibsen for solace. In Ibsen's plays, Nora leaves her husband, Gregers causes a child's suicide, Brand dies in an avalanche. Here are individuals ready to risk all for ardent though questionable beliefs. In the preface to his translation of A *Doll's House*, Shimamura praises this play and others like it "for asking agonizing questions like 'What should we do with our lives?' 'How are we to live?' This approach does not look at social issues, but instead struggles to examine the problems of life itself." Shimamura saw the risks that Ibsen's characters faced; about the somber outlook in those works, he wrote, "The powerful individualism of the hero of *Brand* prevents his emerging as a victor, and in the end, he faces destruction." Still, he insisted on the self's ultimate responsibility: "Your self is a god and the Buddha."

Shimamura could not miss the contrast between Ibsen's determined characters and his own flailing state. No wonder that the time he spent translating A *Doll's House*, coupled with his debilitating illness, left him exhausted and demoralized about his own future. While Japanese audiences interpreted A *Doll's House* as a statement about the liberation of women, Shimamura went beyond gender to take Nora's plight as his own. In the final scene, Nora's husband informs her that she has sacred duties to her family. Nora spoke for her Japanese translator when she replied: "I have other duties just as sacred. . . . Duties to myself."

The scene now shifts back to the aspiring young Japanese actress who is about to memorize the lines of a play by Henrik Ibsen. Her brooding lover will remain close by her side until the finale. At this moment between acts, the biographer seeking to revamp the image of Matsui Sumako cannot help noticing other chroniclers' similar desire to interpret the facts to suit higher purposes. Most commentators recoil at seeing the alliance between Matsui and Shimamura as just a romance between a philandering husband and an ambitious actress. Instead, it is far more satisfactory to conjure up a human encounter of grander significance that illustrates the major conflicts of the period. When writing about Shimamura's life, the writer Tayama Katai saw the relationship as nothing less than a great struggle between traditionalism and modernity; between the crowd and the individual; teacher and disciple; society and the self; the wife versus the other woman; the pleasures and sorrows of romantic love—and all this while great literature was being performed in the background.

Such writings emphasize the connection between Shimamura's actions and the books he read, studied, and translated. They even tend to stress the literary aspects of Shimamura's attraction to Matsui. "In a home in the strange and distant land of Norway, Nora walked out on her family," writes a Japanese drama historian. "Therefore, in Japan, Shimamura Hōgetsu, the head of a family and a university professor, had to walk out on his family." In these and other comments, his love becomes the logical conclusion of his scholarly pursuits. "Basically, his conflicts stemmed from the secret impatience and agony that developed when his literary theories could no longer stand up to the pressures of reality." Consequently, Shimamura had little choice but to test his aesthetic principles by abandoning his family, his job, and his superiors and running off with his lover. (In these interpretations, Shimamura gets all the poetry and the torment, since Matsui Sumako usually does not rate any such conflicts between mind and heart.)

Although it is possible to begin with the great books in describing their affair, the fact remains that it was a very fleshy business. During their courtship, she had him apply makeup to her back ("If you have never experienced it," a sage observer notes, "you can never understand the intense pleasure of brushing a woman's skin with greasepaint and gradually entering into her very pores"); they met secretly in déclassé locales ("In those days, Toyamagahara was a parade ground covered by thick grasses. I'd heard that Waseda students used the sand pits there to meet with the girls and maids from their rooming houses, but I never dreamed a respected person like Shimamura-sensei would do such a thing"); one night Shimamura's wife trailed the lovers to an assignation and provoked an undignified scene that few biographers can resist recounting ("I hate to intrude upon Hōgetsu's privacy by writing about this, but to make his behavior over the next five or six years understandable," one author writes, "I cannot conceal this important starting point").

Still, while the strictly carnal aspect must get full due, those writings about being trapped, breaking free, and living as an individual do deserve a major role in the story of the actress and her scholarly lover. Such ideas were so real, so alive at that time that they become another character in the drama—a character driving the action toward its climax. Shimamura once wrote of his admiration for *The Quilt*, a fictional work by Tayama Katai that describes a teacher's pathetic, unrequited love for his pupil. In the last scene of this novella, the teacher's beloved student has returned forever to her distant country home, and so he can only console himself by sniffing her quilt for any scents she has left behind. "This work boldly records the repentance of a man of flesh," Shimamura enthusiastically wrote in his review, "a human being in all his nakedness." Matsui and Shimamura surely understood, as if they were holding the quilt to their own faces, the hero's craving for affection, fulfillment, liberation—those human longings that are commonplaces of our present day. Some years later, when they lived out the sequel to this tale of yearning between teacher and pupil, society was still pondering the agony of that intense protagonist and his beloved's bedding.

Even so, more time would pass before Matsui and Shimamura did anything too drastic. Shimamura spent many days fretting, while Matsui Sumako continued her drama studies at Bungei Kyōkai. It is of no small importance to the history of twentieth-century Japanese drama that he held a prominent post at this institution. For her public debut, Matsui appeared in her graduating class's *Hamlet*, a production that received generally unenthusiastic notices in the press. The critics complained about Tsubouchi's stilted translation, the awkward acting, and the old-fashioned, Kabuki-esque touches throughout. Matsui's Ophelia, the first of her powerfully executed stage heroines, was one of the few positive features in an exercise generally deemed amateurish. Her performance also helped to settle the issue of whether genuine women played female roles better than men. "The ordinary Kabuki female impersonator," one critic wrote, "would be absolutely unable to perform Ophelia's mad speech to such an effect." After graduating from Bungei Kyōkai, Matsui and the other students became professional, modestly salaried members of the school's troupe. At about this time, younger members were growing increasingly unhappy about Tsubouchi's emphasis on Shakespeare and pressed for more modern dramas. In response, Shimamura and another member of the troupe assumed the directorial duties for the staging of his translation of A *Doll's House*. New to directing, Shimamura and his colleague did not immediately rise to the demands of their job. According to witnesses, they just sat back and silently observed the rehearsals. Had they spoken, it surely would have been to express astonishment at the industry of their lead actress, Matsui Sumako. Not only was Nora Matsui's first big role, this character remained onstage for much of the play. Matsui proved herself diligent, arriving to rehearse early in the morning before anyone else. Within three days she had memorized all her lines, and soon the other characters' lines also. Her prompting of forgetful fellow actors during rehearsals probably did not increase her popularity.

Many noted a distinct improvement in Shimamura's mood, and it is assumed that the alliance between the married director and his young star began during this period. The public's reaction to this 1911 production of A *Doll's House* was overwhelming, more of a stir than anyone had dreamed, and Matsui Sumako instantly became the talk of Japan. Her portrayal of the coddled wife who walks out of the house to seek her independence—slamming the door on her husband and children—forever blurred the distinction between her and Nora. "I don't think I'm going overboard," a critic wrote, "when I say that this actress's Nora won't be soon forgotten as a first in Japan both for solving the actress problem and for showing the liberation of a woman onstage." The play caused similar uproars throughout the world.

While the rave reviews lavished praise on Matsui's natural and convincing delivery of her lines, the audience's response to her debut can only be imagined. For many, the performance by a real woman, not a Japanese man in drag, must have come as a great shock. And furthermore, that genuine female did not, like a classical, self-sacrificing Kabuki heroine, speak in a stylized falsetto about selling herself off as a geisha to save her family from ruin. In *A Doll's House*, the heroine conducts a serious conversation with her husband in the final scene and talks to him in the natural, true-to-life phrasings of everyday speech. She says that she's leaving him and her three children in order to educate herself as a human being.

The alarm soon sounded at the drama's social message. In newspapers and magazines, and on street corners, Japanese discussed Nora's sudden comprehension of the true, rotten nature of her married life, giving currency to the word *jikaku*, which means "self-awakening." Experiencing *jikaku* soon became the mark of a modern woman. Much of the debate predictably focused upon whether liberation and wider career choices for women were necessary. As when the play was performed in other parts of the world, many women took a stand against Nora's actions. "She's leaving her house because Helmer got mad at her and because she wants to become a human being?" one married woman in the audience scoffed. "You'd have to be a really odd, impertinent woman to behave like that. Tell me, what is the true beauty of a woman? Even if she doesn't manage to become a human being, Nora should first think about that." For these theatergoers, a Japanese woman's "beauty" still could be found in her traditional, unawakened role at home.

The discussions show how Japanese had taken the realism of the new-style theater to heart. The old plays had assumed suspension of disbelief, and thus the audience did not object when a fox spirit transformed itself into a warrior onstage. But once *A Doll's House* purported to present life as it was truly lived, the audience needed to get a few mundane details straight before they could go on to assess the psychic awakening of the heroine. Exactly how would Nora live afterward? Where would she get money, job, a change of clothes? Nora's abandonment of her children appalled many, including the feminists, since few could excuse such heartless behavior in a mother. This was too irresponsible for a Japanese woman, even one who forged on toward liberation.

The groundbreaking women's journal *Seitō* devoted a special issue to the controversy, and its contents show how progressive women struggled to make sense of Nora's decision to walk out. Theoretically, *Seitō*'s writers might have agreed that a woman had to stalk off on her own in order to break free, but they shuddered to see the consequences of such behavior before their very eyes. For these women, customs of consideration for others and mutual obligation still counted for much. Nora, thinking only about her own difficulties as she departed, was not a pretty sight. "Nora's awakening," a female educator wrote,

is the awakening of all the world's women, or so we would hope. . . . Her future is the future of all women . . . but Nora has lived up to now in a small narrow universe, thinking of herself alone. Narrowly preoccupied with her own emotional problems, she has been unable to comprehend all of life, that is, the whole wide world beyond herself.

Hiratsuka Raichō, the editor-in-chief of *Seitō* and a great name in the history of Japanese feminism, addressed a blistering open letter to the heroine. She took Nora to task for responding to her own raw emotions and not seeing the broader causes of her discontent:

Nora-san:

Japanese women are unable to believe that a woman—unless she is just a young girl of fourteen or fifteen—acting out of such completely blind instinct could be the mother of three children. . . . You told your husband "I am a human being just like you," but in fact you are mistaken about your husband, since he, too, is nothing but a doll. He is a doll controlled by man-made laws and is in no way independent. You have not understood the basic situation at all. The sound of the door you slammed shut was for both of you. . . . One day you will understand that the husband and children whom you have abandoned are all yourself. Indeed, you will start to see that all things in this world have been created by your own heart.

These writers are noteworthy for seeking an awakening that went beyond the Woman Question. A true awakening, in their view, moved from ignorance to knowledge in all spheres of life— knowledge of one's own self, one's place in society, the feelings of others. To become an awakened being entailed responsibility, required more than slamming doors and walking out.

Matsui did not respond to the brouhaha until three years later, in 1914. She admitted that when reading *A Doll's House* for the first time, she had only worried about what on earth the English meant and had not sought deeper meanings. Since then, she had entered into a public relationship with Shimamura. In her autobiography, she reflects upon her firsthand experience of defying society and the cruel choices required. She stands in contrast to the others when she speaks out, unequivocally, on behalf of selfishness:

Finally after we put on the play, everywhere you went, these women's issues became a popular topic of discussion. People had various opinions about Nora's departure from her home. When I thought about it then from various angles, I couldn't sympathize with a woman who had sacrificed the love of her three children just to clear a new path for herself. But even then, I wondered what would come of her intention to educate herself if she stayed there, restrained by her love for the children and always under Helmer's thumb.

Now, however, looking at it from the point of view of the person I am today, I am sad to say that I have come to sympathize with Nora's position. I believe that holding herself back out of love for her children would have meant the sacrifice of her whole life. She had to be resolute about sacrificing her children in order to establish a life for herself. Nora's self-awakening was but the first step in her journey. She must go on. A self-awakening that is not a result of much floundering and fumbling through the cold, dark world is not a true, very powerful self-awakening.

In her next hit play, Matsui went on to consolidate her reputation as dangerous, awakened woman. The Ministry of Home Affairs came up with its own form of drama criticism when it condemned her all-too-persuasive acting as a menace to society. *Magda*, Shimamura's translation of Hermann Sudermann's *Die Heimat*, also took aim at traditional social mores. The play could be seen as an attack on patriarchal family systems worldwide. Chosen to provide a vehicle for the now much-talked-of actress Matsui Sumako, *Magda* was translated freely into Japanese by Shimamura. He drew upon his studies of how Sarah Bernhardt and Eleanora Duse had played the role in Europe when directing Matsui's performance.

Magda is the daughter of a conservative military officer who expects to wield absolute control over his family. Some years previously, she fled her home to avoid marrying a man her relatives had chosen for her. After establishing herself in the big city as a singer, she returns to her hometown for a concert. Magda's racy past includes an illegitimate child secretly fathered by the very man her family selected for her. In her baggage are new ideas about selfhood and the tyranny of families. Back home, she preaches the value of sin as essential for personal growth ("And one thing more, my friend, —sin! We must sin if we wish to grow. To become greater than our sins is worth more than all the purity you preach"), and in addition, she refuses to bow to her family's authority when they ask her to discard her bohemian habits. Her lover urges her to give up her child so that they can finally wed and live in unblemished married bliss. Magda refuses him, decisively.

In other scenes, Magda heartily expresses the same derogatory views of family life then current in advanced Japanese circles. "See how much the family with its morality demands from us!" Magda upbraids her relatives. "It throws us on our own resources, it gives us neither shelter nor happiness, and yet, in our loneliness, we must live according to the laws that it has planned for itself alone." During the climactic scene Magda clings to her principles, and her father becomes so enraged that he attempts to shoot her. Overly excited, he collapses from what will be a fatal apoplectic fit. Before he dies, Magda takes a moment to sum up her position regarding the evil wrought by contact with one's closest relatives:

You blame me for living out my life without asking you and the whole family for permission. And why should I not? Was I not without family? Did you not send me out into the world to earn my bread, and then disown me because the way in which I earned it was not to your taste? Whom did I harm? Against whom did I sin? . . . Leave art out of the question. Consider me nothing more than the seamstress or the servant-maid who seeks, among strangers, the little food and the little love she needs. . . .Gag us, stupefy us, shut us up in harems or in cloisters—and that perhaps would be best. But if you give us our freedom, do not wonder if we take advantage of it.

The widely circulated photograph of Matsui Sumako in the role of Magda has her posed in a long dark dress. Buxom and stalwart, she appears unrepentant as she stares into the camera, ready to take on the social systems of several world civilizations. "This kind of powerful artistry is truly rare in today's theater," a critic wrote of her performance. "To the very end, I watched it, enthralled."

The messages in the play advocating selfhood, the end of patriarchy, and economic independence went down better this time than in *A Doll's House*. Nora had left her children behind to seek

independence, but Magda sacrificed the promise of a proper marriage to protect her child. Such resolute and maternal behavior pleased Japanese women, who could warm to this kind of freedom. In a 1912 *Seitō* essay one woman writer reflected the positive reaction:

> Magda resonated within me much more strongly than Nora. . . . I leave aside the issue of morality and say that while everyone has not come to the same end shown in the play, everyone alive today has been affected one way or another by such clashes between the new and the old ideas on family life. All the more so for women who love the arts since they will have experienced this kind of torment.

The Ministry of Home Affairs, however, did not similarly rejoice in the production values. Officials determined that the play—with a finale that showed Magda still defying her father's wishes and posed beside his corpse—violated the basic morality of the country. They closed the theater and forbade further performances. Since the drama troupe was desperately strapped for cash, Shimamura bowed to government pressure. He added a scene in which Magda apologizes for her unfilial behavior ("It's all my fault").

The ruckus vastly increased ticket sales.

While Matsui received accolades from every quarter for her portrayal of a unwavering female artist who refused to compromise just to please proper society, the star herself was in real life facing down opposition to her love affair with Shimamura Hōgetsu, another woman's husband and the father of a number of children. The drama troupe toured several Japanese cities with *Magda*, promoting the cause of selfhood. ("I am myself, and through myself I have become what I am"). Matsui and Shimamura took the opportunity to see the sights and enjoy each other's company, acting, according to contemporaries, as if they were on their honeymoon. Again, one wonders whether literature had exerted an undue influence on the principals' emotions. How could anyone immersed in Nora's and Magda's lines night after night ("There is another task I must undertake first. I must try and educate myself"; "But I must live out my own life. That I owe to myself,— to myself and mine") not be moved to extreme behavior?

Certain witnesses, however, looked beyond the spoken and written word to form other theories about who had instigated this shocking turn of events:

I'd have to say that the power pulling Sensei on this far came from Matsui Sumako. There may have been something romantic that the two were not fully conscious of, but Sumako's own strong life force was crucial. This life force, which would stop at nothing to claim anyone she set her sights on, exerted itself on Shimamura-sensei and firmed up his lax, lethargic nerves day after day.

Perhaps here, as the romance gets into full gear, is a good place to take a closer look at the attitudes of the male memoirists and drama historians who castigated Matsui so relentlessly. The intensity of the men's dislike for her may frighten the unprepared. Their attitudes, of course, threaten any friendly portrait. We can imagine these opinions being hashed and rehashed in assorted Tokyo drinking establishments where sake and wrath commingled fulsomely. We can hear the derogatory views confirmed after Matsui pulled off yet another of her miserly exploits (she used to commandeer all the fruit baskets the troupe received as gifts on tour and later sell these stale goods for personal profit to Tokyo theatergoers). Some of these men despised Matsui because of sheer personal antagonism; no doubt she inspired many resentments. Others probably thought her beneath respectful notice because of her lowly status as an actress. One also gets a very definite sense that the male memoirists wrote from fear and shock. They had watched, horrified, as one of their own—a supremely literate, clear-thinking, ambitious man—cast away a stellar career out of love for a crude, uneducated actress. Here was reality up close and awful, human life in all its irrationality—romantic love triumphing over reason, wisdom no match for a desire to take the needs of the self seriously. It was a spectacle that these male witnesses clearly found unbearable.

Perhaps the most memorable of the chroniclers is the playwright Kawamura Karyō. After a long and varied career on the Japanese stage, he wrote his memoir, *Notes on Matsui Sumako*. To his credit, Kawamura never makes any claims to objectivity, since Matsui's insolent behavior clearly blighted his days and he took Shimamura's infatuation with her as a personal affront. This does not incline him to formulate respectful evaluations of Matsui in particular or of women in general. As a result, Kawamura's account of those days is a consummately venomous document in which he discerns the basest motives behind Matsui's every action, whether she is buying noodles or jockeying her way in or out of a role. A reader soon becomes wary of any of Kawamura's statements that even venture in the vicinity of a compliment: he will surely come back swinging in another couple of sentences with a damning explanation of her (momentarily) benevolent behavior. "I wouldn't call her selfish," he wrote in one of the expressions of intense loathing that ensure his memoir an eternal freshness,

but Sumako had this idea in her head that as far as men were concerned, she could ask them for anything and that whatever she said or did was acceptable. Sumako of course respected Shimamura-sensei, but when it came to dealing with him as a man, she treated him no differently than her former husband, Maezawa Seisuke. . . . After she started to live with Shimamura-sensei, she would give him a tongue lashing, grab hold of him tightly, and have unbridled hysterics. . . . Anyone who stood in her way, she'd just brush aside. She showed absolutely no consideration for others and gave no heed to public opinion.

Kawamura cannot contain his satisfaction when he describes her relationship with her first husband, Maezawa Seisuke:

That marriage is supposed to have been a love match, but this was love only if "love" is what you call it when a man and a woman like each other and are physically intimate. Perhaps this is old-fashioned of me, but a true love affair requires some spiritual element. This was nothing more than a very common kind of male-female relationship. . . . Maezawa was a gentle, ordinary person. He'd tell me about Sumako's wild behavior, rolling up his sleeves to show me the burn marks on his arm. "This morning she threw boiling miso soup at me again," he would say. "Look at this."

Kawamura concedes that his memoir was inspired by Matsui's performance in *A Doll's House*. "Since my youth, I had seen any number of good plays, but I had never been so stunned as I was by the Nora in Bungei Kyōkai's workshop production of *A Doll's House*." Any suspicion that Kawamura has got carried away with rapture at Matsui's talents is dispelled by reading on a few pages to discover the true genius behind everything. "In *A Doll's House*, Shimamura-sensei transformed himself into Sumako's Nora. That Nora was entirely Sensei's conception. Sumako made herself a blank and performed onstage as Sensei's puppet." About *Magda* also, Kawamura has an opinion:

She always repeated the same actions, the same positions, the same smiles. Everything was always exactly the same, and when I saw this I thought that she wasn't performing a role, only hurling her whole self into some kind of body attack. . . . Sumako wasn't consciously acting, but rather, as a result of her many hours of rehearsal, she looked as if she were mechanically doing her calisthenics.

Kawamura forges on, always shaking his head over Shimamura's folly in falling for such a woman. Kawamura sees himself on the side of refinement, sensibility, civilization, and Hamlet-like reflectiveness. He stands opposed to Matsui who, in his view, represents ambition, greed, tactlessness, and downright evil. With a playwright's gift for the telling anecdote, Kawamura delights in presenting the evidence. Yet as is the case with so many opinionated narratives, the scenes he describes often give a vivid picture of the couple that is perhaps not the one he intended. In his memoir, Kawamura tells a perfectly plausible love story of a vacillating man of letters who is desperate to taste real life before death has its way with him. The man receives much-needed help in this project from a rowdy, uncomplicated woman.

"I can't even meet you as I want," Shimamura supposedly complained to Matsui. "When I meet you, what do I do anyway? We just see each other and talk about artistic matters. Is there anything wrong with that?"

"Sensei," she told him, "you really make me mad sometimes. If you like something, you like it. You should do exactly as you please."

In commenting on this interchange, Kawamura blames Matsui for lacking the delicacy of mind to understand the terrible qualms racking Shimamura. A less involved reader sees that delicacy may not have been her forte, but she had just the temperament required to hustle Shimamura toward freedom.

These interludes make for jolly reading, but the enormous effects of Matsui and Shimamura's love affair cannot be exaggerated. Slamming the door on respectability in Japan in those days was no small matter. Matsui was reminded of her disgraceful status at every turn, snubbed by teachers she esteemed, shunned by relatives, and gossiped about in the newspapers. Shimamura not only had to leave his wife, his children, and his other family obligations, but he also had to break off relations with his mentor Tsubouchi Shōyō. This was an act of grave disloyalty that would dog him forever after. "I've really burned my bridges behind me now," Shimamura used to mutter.

Modernization had changed some aspects of Japanese society, but the feudal mores demanding obedience and fealty retained their sting. As part of the ordeal facing those who betrayed their clan, Shimamura had to defend his behavior to students and colleagues at various gatherings. During these confrontations Shimamura was interrogated with breathtaking directness about his intentions. The disrespectful probings about Matsui reflect her inferior status and destroy all preconceptions about Japanese reticence. "Do you love Matsui Sumako?" Shimamura was asked. "Are you having sexual relations?" By indulging his fancy for a mere actress like Matsui, Shimamura was openly putting his own desires before the needs of the drama troupe. Ibsen's heroes might have proclaimed their right to private pleasure, but such audacity was more acceptable in Norway.

Being Japanese was not a complete disadvantage for Shimamura, since the vagueness of his native language served him well. His answer to a question about the exact nature of his relationship with Matsui is still savored by Japanese for its delicate phrasing.

"There are a lot of rumors floating around about you and Sumako," went the inquiry. "I know this may be impertinent of me, but I would like you to enlighten me on this point."

To this, Shimamura made the shimmering Japanese reply:

"There is a certain flow of feeling between Sumako and me. But certainly the rumors now circulating regarding a physical relationship are not true. However, I can't predict what will happen in the future."

Eventually, Tsubouchi Shōyō could not overlook these goings-on. From the beginning he had demanded strict separation of the sexes in Bungei Kyōkai; at least twenty members were expelled for violating these rules. Tsubouchi had given Shimamura much leeway as the rumors regarding the romance with Matsui spread. Finally he fired Matsui in May 1913. Shimamura resigned soon after, but not before he wrote a tortured, thirty-page letter of explanation that had been "composed in blood and tears."

The dejected Tsubouchi disbanded Bungei Kyōkai and retired to the safety of Shakespearean research. After much turmoil, Matsui and Shimamura, along with other rebellious refugees from Bungei Kyōkai, united to form a new acting troupe. The younger members had always seen the love affair as an opportunity to break with Tsubouchi and his conservative approach to drama. The new troupe took the name Geijutsuza, and vowed to produce modern plays of lofty literary quality. "We will do research on all kinds of new theater movements," declared the new troupe's statement of purpose, "as well as on related theater arts, and will promote their development." Prominent in the repertory over the next five and a half years would be modern plays—many by Western playwrights—about social problems and the struggle for individual freedom; these alternated with more lucrative, more popular—and less worthy—productions.

Few doubted that Matsui would be indispensable, in her professional capacity, if the new troupe were to succeed. Shimamura himself realized that failure was inevitable without her to attract the public. Almost from the moment of Geijutsuza's founding, Matsui clashed with the male actors, but everyone managed to control their tempers for the first productions. As a start, Shimamura selected two plays by Maurice Maeterlinck whose views about human life spoke to his own situation. Featuring a pragmatic heroine, Maeterlinck's *Monna Vanna* tells a story of love's endurance in fifteenth-century Pisa. The play bursts at the seams with florid declarations of affection and must have succored Shimamura's throbbing emotions. ("Is it not strange," the male lead says, "that a beloved image can live thus in a man's heart? For yours lived so in mine that each day it changed as in real life—the image of today replaced that of yesterday—it blossomed out, it became always fairer.")

Thanks to the romantic scandal, the drama played to full houses; the front seats sold out first because the crowds wanted to get a good look at the heroine. New to theater management, Shimamura took some time to learn the basics of his job. According to witnesses, his scholarly training had not honed his business instincts, and he lacked a rudimentary understanding of profitable theater practices. Despite full houses, Geijutsuza still teetered at the brink of financial disaster. The troupe's precarious situation made Matsui's presence onstage even more crucial and her behavior more disruptive. Here the memoirists detail the changes in Matsui's demeanor since her stage debut as Nora. Her confidence in her own acting ability grew, but where she "had once behaved like a little lamb," notes Kawatake Shigetoshi in *The Tragedy of Shōyō, Hōgetsu, and Sumako*, she became a vain and egotistical monster.

Reviewers always praised the wildness in Matsui's acting, and as many point out, she did shine portraying rash, instinctual women like Carmen, Salome, and Katusha (in Tolstoy's *Resurrection*). These roles required a commanding personality that she could muster without undue strain. "I'd like to become a beautiful woman with a beautiful disposition," Matsui used to say, but the critics took her to task any time she dared to attempt such a role. Playing a temptress with a swagger and a flower in her teeth, she triumphed repeatedly, berating those sensitive, hesitating boys into obedience.

As these roles pushed her career forward, still more complaints were voiced. People said that she used her theatrical gifts too often in her daily life. Especially galling to many was her propensity to cry at the drop of a hat, onstage and off. Some members of the troupe felt that Matsui had turned a genuine expression of grief for her sorrows into a habit of instant sadness. As *Resurrection*'s Katusha, her most popular role, she wept profusely and convincingly at the ends of hundreds of performances. Her tears flowed copiously in the theaters of Japan, Korea, Taiwan, and Manchuria where the troupe toured. This crying played a part in offstage professional crises too. Before a performance of Maeterlinck's *Home*, her adamant refusal to play the mother's role caused much argument backstage. To emphasize her decision, Matsui shed countless tears. ("In the end she resorted to crying, her great specialty," Kawatake reports. "There was nothing further we could do"). Finally a male writer agreed to shave off his prized mustache and play the mother's role. These crying jags reduced Shimamura to helplessness; Geijutsuza actors fumed each time he acceded to her whims.

In her autobiography, Matsui is at pains to address the source of this hated teary habit. When at last she comes forward to explain her motives, she temporarily subdues her critics and cheers up her demoralized supporters. In extremely convincing passages, she describes how she had endured much suffering in life—married, divorced, and scorned by society. Writing of herself in the third person, she says that when she played struggling, outcast women who were forms of herself onstage, "She wanted to appeal to the sympathy of the world at large. Certain roles she played reflected her exact feelings in times past. So while she was recalling this onstage, she just cried and cried and cried. This made her feel a little better."

In the wake of this testimony come the literary witnesses to argue back that the crying jags were not the only problem. In addition, they say, Matsui Sumako had other, earthshaking defects. As they speak, spreading thick and poisonous fumes, it is almost impossible to see Matsui solemnly organizing her explanations. She did venture to write a few other words in her own behalf in *Makeup Brush*, but the experts emphasize that this collection of autobiographical writings shows every sign of Shimamura's collaboration. Still, the voice of a furious, maligned woman emerges, loud and clear, from its pages.

Makeup Brush sold out its 40,000 copies upon publication in 1914, and the book was also distributed to patrons as a souvenir when the troupe toured the provinces. These essays show that Matsui, confirming all accounts, probably knew something about speaking up for herself. "Compared to the pride I have felt for my work as an actress," she explosively begins one chapter, "my feelings of humiliation have in fact been more numerous." She then goes on to take a stand against the common ideal of feminine behavior:

Is what they call a "woman" someone who is supposed to curry favor with people all the time? Is she always supposed to remain silent and just do what people tell her? This has been considered a traditional womanly virtue in Japan since ancient times. And it is perhaps for this very reason that people laugh at the work and art of us women.

Proceeding in this vein, she wonders why she is not allowed, for example, to offer any suggestions when a play is being rehearsed. Everyone pays lip service to equality of the sexes, she writes, but when you come right down to it only a man's opinion counts. If ever she dares to make suggestions about a performance, the men ignore her contributions and call her foul names. Furthermore, when wounded by these reprimands, she sometimes cannot contain her hurt and bursts into tears—a natural reaction that her readers will understand. But when she tearily expresses her misery, the men admonish her by saying, "I can't stand these sneaky women who try to get their way with crying."

She recognizes that she may not live up to ordinary notions of gentility, delicacy, or tact, but Matsui insists that she needed this very firmness to attain success.

If I were an artist who gave up easily, I would have given up art without a second thought and sought consolation elsewhere. But for my art, I renounced my parents. I renounced my brothers and sisters. I traded everything the world has to offer for this one precious treasure. . . . But to what extent can a weak woman's heart triumph in these battles? How long can she put up with this before she goes mad?

In another section, she argues that she would have been looked upon differently if she were a man:

Look, I'm the kind of person who isn't happy unless she speaks her mind to everyone. I feel things more deeply than the ordinary person and wasn't born with the kind of temperament that lets me hide this and pretend and make bland remarks. . . . S-sensei often tells me that in my personality, I'm like a cross between the writers Masamune Hakuchō and Ogawa Mimei. I've never met Masamune-san or Ogawa-san, but I imagine that they're both emotional and outspoken. Everyone knows that they're both not saints, but no one criticizes their characters. On the contrary, don't people think that such quirks are just proof of their literary superiority? It's just because I'm a woman that everyone takes me to task for the way I behave. It's really unfair.

These passages do put a whole new light on the issue. For an instant Matsui Sumako, up to now portrayed as an absolutely incorrigible woman, transforms herself into a feminist stalwart who, like Nora and Magda before her, has sacrificed ordinary happiness to open up a new frontier for the female sex as a whole. For the few moments it takes to read these sentences, she is no longer playing the abominable prima donna. For a few moments under the spell of Matsui's own words, her role takes on another look entirely. Matsui suddenly seems to be standing by a monument to generations of downtrodden, long-suffering, dutiful women, crying her eyes out over what men have done to her and her sisters.

At such a moment we are receptive to those few bit players who view her with some sympathy. According to her niece, "My aunt was a nice person, capable of deep feelings. She was very affectionate to children and wasn't at all deceitful." Another observer takes up Matsui's cause when he speculates:

In particular, she was often criticized for her "arrogance" and her "selfishness," but these were perhaps an expression of her unconscious rage. With this rage, she insisted upon the equality that should exist between men and women, indeed among all human beings. In all honesty, was not this one of the big charms that attracted Hōgetsu to her? . . . Matsui's so-called wild behavior may have been her instinctive resistance to an old morality.

Still another supporter walks down the middle of the stage, recognizing that Matsui, though good and agreeable at times, also had her defects. But try to imagine—this contemporary asks us— her situation in Japanese society at the time. She could not trust the many intellectuals around her, and this certainly bred insecurity, which in turn may not have brought out her gentlest qualities. In addition, she was a pariah to respectable society and therefore dependent on Shimamura. Losing him would have left her desperate. It is perhaps understandable that, in order to shore up her position, she did her utmost to control his very soul. This observer then wonders whether perhaps Shimamura himself was partially responsible for the negative traits she later developed: "Perhaps Shimamura also had some bad points. He can't be blamed for everything, but her character did worsen, and she was not at all a bad person to begin with."

Here, just when Matsui sheds many tears by the shrines to female pain and these few friends plead her case, other contemporaries seek to challenge these opinions. While they speak, these men gaze off in the opposite direction, perhaps at a memorial to their dead colleague Shimamura, who wasted his genius over such a woman. One such observer, who has come up with a less charitable analysis of her character, sees a completely different play unfolding before him. He feels that Matsui resembled no one more than Anisha, whom she had portrayed in Tolstoy's *The Power of Darkness*. The unscrupulous and vulgar peasant Anisha murders her husband and has a hand in the killing of a newborn baby, among other acts of barbarousness.

After Geijutsuza's production of Maeterlinck's *Monna Vanna* and *Home* played to packed houses, Matsui went on to triumph in the title role in Oscar Wilde's *Salome*. Murderous and irresistible, Matsui struck a new, hotter note in this production that other Japanese actresses soon tried to equal. The troupe did brisk business in souvenir "Salome hairpieces," and Matsui went on to make a new specialty of gutsy gypsy types with knacks for bloody finales. This success did not sustain the troupe for long since Shimamura, seeking impeccably literary works, next chose to produce Chekhov's *The Bear* and Ibsen's *The Lady from the Sea* on a double bill. These were box office failures. Idealistic and nearly bankrupt, Geijutsuza quickly solicited emergency loans.

Tolstoy's ideas were then in vogue among the young, and Shimamura decided to make the most of this with Geijutsuza's production of *Resurrection*. It is often said that this play resurrected the troupe. Matsui made sure that no one overlooked her importance as she rehearsed this tale of a wronged Russian prostitute and the prince determined to save her. During rehearsals she constantly fought with the actors, and Shimamura, faced with firing only her or firing eleven actors, chose to get rid of the men. Opposing parties summarized these developments on mimeographed sheets that were circulated throughout the theater world.

Nonetheless, *Resurrection* became a huge success throughout Japan, boosted by a hit song that Matsui sang twice in the play. Students in Tokyo copied the lyrics of this catchy "Katusha's Song" from billboards that had been put up in the lobby and helped spread them when they returned to their country homes over vacations. A recording of the song sold 20,000 copies — roughly equivalent to the number of record players in Japan at the time — and counts as Japan's first pop single. To this day, older Japanese can readily oblige with a rendition of the famous tune and lyrics: *Kachusha kawaii ya, wakare no tsurasa* ("Katusha is sweet, and parting is bitter"). Soon Japan was awash with fans of *Resurrection* wearing Russian peasant attire, the Katusha hairstyle, Katusha combs, and headbands that are still known as *"Kachusha-maki."* Matsui played Katusha on tours across the nation and to Manchuria and Vladivostok, performing a total of 444 times in four years. This great success bolstered the troupe and replenished depleted cash reserves. Of her performance, one critic wrote:

The hospital scene in the fourth act is the most affecting. It brings us the tender Katusha who touches everyone's heart. But also in this scene, one can detect in Sumako's performance traces of a prickly selfishness, temper, and coldness that have yet to achieve a true mellowing. When she puts on the same red ribbon she wore when she first met her lover and gazes into the mirror in search of her former innocent self, one would have liked to see a deeper sadness over being betrayed so senselessly. Still the scene, inadequate though it may be, seems to have enchanted the audience.

More disturbed were sober leaders of the drama world, who saw this simplified version of *Resurrection* as pandering to popular tastes and also betraying the high literary standards of the modern theater movement. In bringing the play to the Japanese stage, Shimamura had relied on previous adaptations to cut a very long novel down to its essential plot. The production became bare-bones Tolstoy, almost entirely stripped of the original novel's social critiques, beauty, and nuance. Mere Russian soap opera, purists jeered, going so far as to blame the mass-market *Resurrection* for the modern theater movement's deterioration. By way of an answer, a Geijutsuza member felt obliged to offer a weak rebuttal: "The light from the original novel shines like the sun through the small narrow window of this script."

Wounded by the disapproval, Shimamura declared that he was offering a "two-dimensional approach" to the theater, focusing on both plays with mass appeal and high art. His detractors retorted that his approach focused strictly on the one dimension of making money. More savvy now to the commercial side of the theater business, Shimamura could not afford to cultivate only the literary aristocrats. He sounded a democratic note when he said that he was presenting important and accessible productions to the general public, "by taking what is usually kept in a lacquered box sprinkled with gold and placing that on a plain plate for the masses to savor."

Because of *Resurrection*, Geijutsuza finally accumulated enough cash to make ambitious plans for the future. Under Shimamura's guidance, the troupe began to build a permanent headquarters. There were also plans for a theater research center and an acting school that would one day have whole departments of music, literature, and the visual arts. Trying to give acting a more respectable, professional status, Shimamura paid salaries to the troupe on a regular basis, which was almost unheard of in the world of the new theater at that time. Touring, building, placating his critics, his actors, and Matsui Sumako, he proved himself an agile leader. One observer has called Shimamura's achievements with Geijutsuza "miraculous."

To finance their projects, the troupe went on many tours to Japan's big cities, the provinces, and abroad. No other troupe in the new theater movement performed in so many parts of the country, and historians give some credit to Geijutsuza for helping to spread the humane thoughts of Tolstoy (*Resurrection*) and Turgenev (*On the Eve*) to the hinterlands. The strains of travel told on everyone, including the lead actress and the troupe's leader. On one occasion, when they were on tour with *Resurrection*, a geisha with literary interests asked a favor of Shimamura. She wanted him to inscribe a souvenir poem on her kimono jacket in his own hand. Once he had finished dashing off this spontaneous creation ("Compared to the love that smolders in my heart, / the smoke from Sakurajima Mountain / is but a wisp") a jealous Matsui kicked over Shimamura's dinner tray, got his clothes out of the bamboo traveling case, threw them around the room, ripped them to shreds, and then began assaulting him.

MATSUI: You may be Japan's most important literary person, but I'm Japan's most important actress.

SHIMAMURA: Listen, you upstart, just tell me, who do you think is responsible for making you what you are today?

MATSUI: You're nothing but an upstart yourself. And you'll have to excuse me for saying so, but there's samurai blood in my family.

Back home in Tokyo, the troupe still had to pay the bills for its costly new headquarters, a two-story building including offices, reception area, dressing rooms, prop room, kitchen, baths, and a large theater. To make the most of every bit of income, Geijutsuza staged cut-rate shows at a public exposition. After the exhibition was dismantled, they purchased cast-off building materials and used them for the new headquarters. On another occasion the troupe performed in Asakusa, the old working-class section of Tokyo, which the intelligentsia held in low esteem. Three times a day, budget tickets were available for Geijutsuza performances of *Resurrection* and *Salome*. "We tend to think of the new theater [*shingeki*] as very heavy and difficult," one newspaper article declared, "but there was no sense of a mismatch between *shingeki* and performing in Asakusa. Sumako played to full houses, and the Tokiwa Theater was packed."

By 1918, Geijutsuza had established itself in its new Tokyo headquarters. Early in the year the troupe went on tour across Japan, helped by a partnership agreement that gave it greater financial security. In September, Matsui performed with a popular female impersonator at Tokyo's Kabuki Theater, and two months later she rehearsed her role as the madwoman in Gabriele D'Annunzio's *The Dream of a Spring Morning*. In 1918 also, the highly contagious Spanish flu swept through Japan. Even the hardy Matsui, who had not come down with as much as the sniffles when the troupe toured Russia, caught a light case and had to take to her bed. After Shimamura nursed her back to health, he fell ill himself. Matsui wanted to skip rehearsals to tend to him, but he refused to allow it. "The stage is no different from a battleground," he told her from his bed. "You must go. Don't worry."

Very late that November night in 1918, he took a turn for the worse and died in his poorly heated room on the second floor of Geijutsuza's headquarters. Still rehearsing, Matsui had not been informed about the seriousness of his condition, and by the time she returned home Shimamura Hōgetsu was dead. "We promised each other that we would die together. Why did he have to go and die alone?" she exclaimed. Matsui began crying then, and wept almost continuously for the next two months.

Shimamura's male colleagues did not go so far as to say that Matsui slashed his throat or strangled him, but they did hold her responsible for his death. "Hōgetsu had a weak heart to begin with," Kawatake writes,

and knew all about the Spanish flu. He wanted to go into the hospital, but Matsui feared that if he were hospitalized, his wife and daughters would come to take care of him, and steal him away from her. She stren-

uously opposed the move and started crying until he gave up on the idea.
. . . If he had been hospitalized quickly, Shimamura might not have died,
and so, in one respect, you might say that by not letting him go, Matsui
killed him with her selfish behavior.

Soon Shimamura's wife and several of his children turned up to
pay their respects in the room where his dead body lay. "Matsui-
san," several troupe officials warned her, "just today, do us a favor
and don't work yourself up into a state, no matter what happens.
Sit there quietly, and don't say anything you'll be sorry for later."
In the biographies and the films, this is a hushed, formal moment
when the dark-robed and homely Mrs. Shimamura views her wayward husband for the last time. Kawatake remembers:

"We haven't met for a long time," Matsui said to Shimamura's wife in a
proper, unfaltering voice and bowed her head. "Please forgive me for
causing you so much worry."
    "No, you're not the one who is at fault. Once Shimamura left our
house, I considered him a stranger. Whatever happened afterwards was
no concern of mine." Mrs. Shimamura had probably thought about what
she was going to say beforehand, since this sentence came out like a very
practiced line of dialogue.

At the time of Shimamura's death, Matsui's relations with the
other members of the troupe were nothing short of atrocious.
Although she was appointed to replace him as the troupe's head,
intrigues doomed her from the first day. Matsui cried day and
night in her room, in the streets, and in the rehearsal hall. When
appearing in The Dream of a Spring Morning, she also cried her
eyes out during a performance and had to be reprimanded by her
co-star, "Matsui-san, you're on stage now."
    Shimamura was no longer alive to write defenses of her or to
compose lists of chores to be completed before going out on tour.
Moreover, it was too late for her to improve her interpersonal relationships, as she tried to do when she gave presents of salmon to

her colleagues. ("In the extended period that I knew Sumako, those five slices of salmon were the only gifts I ever received from her," Kawamura wrote). The men are pleased to note that at long last her femininity blossomed. "After Sensei's death, I had more chances to discuss scripts and other things with her," one colleague observed. "I was surprised to discover that she had many innocent, pure, pliant, and moreover, femininely gentle traits." So pitiful was her state—lover gone, prestige lost, good will nonexistent—that the memoirists take a moment to express their sympathy. "When she lost Shimamura, who was her sole source of support, she had to wander through the fog like a lamb. . . . It was like that line from *Hamlet*, 'Frailty, thy name is woman.' " But such a mood soon passes. "Geijutsuza ceased to exist this year," a diarist noted. "Only the flesh of that fool of a woman Matsui remains."

Did she really try to seduce another member of the acting troupe immediately after Shimamura's death, try to lure him into helping her? And what exactly was on her mind when she asked him to repeat a sentence Shimamura had once spoken to her? The facts leave room for interpretation. It appears clear that Matsui found managing the troupe without a man impossible and that she sought assistance from a certain capable member of her staff. It also seems clear that the principal male members did not rush in to support this restructuring of her executive team. Nor does she emerge blameless from accounts of this period. Once the others heard about her approaches to their colleague, they held another of those extended meetings—to which she was not invited—and effectively prevented the defection of this potential ally to her side.

On January 5, 1919, two months after Shimamura's death, she performed the starring role in *Carmen*. (She had taken to humming the lines from one of the production's songs: "It's all smoke, all smoke. Nothing but smoke"). Upon returning home to Geijutsuza headquarters, she wrote several letters and placed two photographs of herself to flank Shimamura's on the Buddhist altar. After carefully applying her makeup, Matsui Sumako went into the prop room and hanged herself.

Many of the obituaries saw Matsui's life as a romantic drama, with the heroine choosing to die at the end rather than live without her beloved. The great love story has been so interpreted in countless popular books, ballads, and plays. Others disagreed and refused to attach much importance to her passing. The suicide gave some commentators the chance to reflect upon the harmful effect of Matsui's life on public morals. There was sadness too, as the obituarists imagined her state of mind at the time of her death. "The first few shoots of a New Woman's soul can be seen in Matsui Sumako's life," one observer wrote later, "but for the most part, she bore the burdens and sorrows of an old-fashioned Japanese woman." Since feudal times, underlings had killed themselves upon the deaths of their lords, and Matsui's suicide was also seen as a variation on this old custom. In her case, she had performed the rite later than usual.

"I have felt his death penetrate my flesh like a heavy frost," cries the madwoman in *The Dream of a Spring Morning*, the role Matsui was rehearsing at the time of Shimamura's death. "And I have felt my bones bend beneath the weight." In the end, Matsui Sumako's tale seems significant for precisely what it is not. Her life never became a paean to traditional Japanese values; she suffered too much at the hands of society and of those who tried to rein her in. Her biography also does not illustrate the beneficial effects of modernization and Western ways of thinking, since imported ideas enticed the principals and tore their lives apart. Nor does Matsui qualify for the leading role in a tale of women's liberation: no woman who so hounded her rivals—male and female—can make the grade as a feminist heroine. Yet at the same time, Matsui was a twice-divorced woman in a world where only "good wives and wise mothers" received any respect. A woman who had to claw and scratch to survive under such circumstances deserves a little consideration. Refusing to identify good and evil, pulling our sympathies in all directions, Matsui's story leaves us with the very confusion of life itself.

The last scene belongs to Shimamura's wife, who still had to take care of her children and household after the deaths of her husband and his lover. This wife, whom the films and memoirs demean for her plain appearance and nagging nature, would spend the rest of her days living down many humiliations. When informed that Matsui had hanged herself, Mrs. Shimamura said: "Those who can die are better off."

MANY JAPANESE CAN QUOTE A LINE
or two from *Chieko's Sky** (*Chieko-shō*), Takamura Kōtarō's well-known
poetry collection. "I just hate think-
ing / that you will leave," begins the
very first poem, announcing the
arrival of a fervent and forthright
poet. "Do me a favor and forget that
illogical, unnatural decision," Kōtarō
goes on to plead. "I feel like crying /
when I imagine you, with your distinctive handwriting, / and an ordinary husband." The poet manages an
honesty that Japanese still find exhilarating. "My heart rushes toward you
as if propelled by a great wind, / my
dearest," he openly proclaims in
another work. "I wish you a peaceful
sleep in your suburban home / A
child's honesty is in everything you
do."

Kōtarō celebrates his love for his
wife throughout *Chieko's Sky*, which
has enjoyed great popularity among
Japanese since the publication of the
first poem in 1912 (the complete vol-

*This title is from Furuta Sōichi's English
translation of the collection (Kodansha
International, 1978). *Chieko-shō* literally means
Chieko: Selections.

ume was published in 1941). Muse, lover, force of nature, the poet's Chieko gambols on the beach in tune with the tides or contentedly weaves cloth at home. For many Japanese readers, Takamura Chieko never will be anything but the childlike female essence created by her poet-husband. The frankly sensual descriptions of the lovers at play fueled the popularity of the collection. Passages like "Our skin wakes up with a tremendous power / Our innards thrash with the pleasures of life / Our hair gives off great sparks / and our fingers, throbbing with a life of their own, feel their way around body flesh" shocked readers when the poems were first published and received widespread praise.

This was no mere joyous love affair, since Chieko eventually went mad. Kōtarō also chronicles her mental disintegration without flinching. He writes of Chieko's vague melancholy in the poem that begins with the famous line, "Chieko says that Tokyo doesn't have a sky / She says she wants to see a real sky." He goes on to describe the times when her emotional problems intensified and reality eluded her grasp: "Chieko sees what can't be seen / hears what can't be heard," reads another oft-quoted poem. Some Japanese find such frankness astonishing, and to this day—even though his reputation has been bruised in recent years—Kōtarō still merits respectful attention. "He really loved her," a Japanese professor told me a while ago with a wistful sigh.

He really loved her. This declaration went unchallenged for about fifty years, and during that period, Japanese gave copies of *Cheiko's Sky* as wedding gifts in the hope that the affection evident in the poetry would also bless the newlyweds. Only very recently did Takamura Kōtarō and his collection start to receive the kind of critical attention that has, for twenty years or so, bedeviled many male literary figures in the West. Biographers have always known that the poems do not tell an accurate story of the couple's love, but recently some Japanese—mostly women—have been asking more probing questions about the character of the man who wrote them. In the past, most commentators saw Chieko's mental illness as the result of an unfortunate, inherited defect, but now these women are in the process of fashioning new versions of her life, particularly in regard to her marriage to Kōtarō. Dark theories are being proposed about his role in her mental collapse. Is *Chieko's Sky* truly a record of Kōtarō's great love for Chieko, who is cursed by an unstable mind? Or does this poetry collection show how an egotistical husband crushed his wife's ambitions? These are not safe times for men who have earned their greatest fame on their wives' troubles, and Kōtarō now faces harsh reassessment.

It was not supposed to end in a Tokyo hospital with the weak, psychotic wife cutting out brightly colored pieces of paper and shaping them into rabbits, carnations, and dust brooms. There were not supposed to be terrible scenes in which the wild patient had to be locked up in the studio or stood out on the street shouting, "Citizens of Tokyo, assemble!" Nor was she supposed to take her husband for a devilish fiend out to poison her. On the contrary, Takamura Kōtarō and Chieko were to be a "modern" man and wife in a world where modernity counted for everything. Kōtarō, who began his career as a sculptor, was to work in his well-appointed studio, toiling with the dedication of Rodin. He would discard the commercial motives of the crafts-man to follow the noble creed of the true artist. In another room, Chieko would paint in the new Western mode. More than that, she would throw off the old female shackles. "The customs of this world have been fashioned by human beings anyway, and it would be dull to be bound by them or live out my life false to what is in my own heart," she proclaimed one day in an utter-ance worthy of the intrepid female breed she wished to join. "I want to make my own decisions about my life, since we only live once."

While she could equal the activists' fervor in her revolutionary slogans, Chieko's style of delivery was definitely unique. Painfully shy, Chieko spoke little, and when she did say anything her way of talking was often too peculiar to understand. Later, with the onset of her mental illness, these garbled communications took on a more ominous cast. Her determination and intelligence never were disputed, nor was there any doubt about the competitiveness she exhibited in her college tennis games (a most daring sport for women in those days). But it was the speaking style that struck most observers: "She spoke very slowly, and the words seemed to roll off the top of her tongue. That, taken together with her faint voice, meant you couldn't make out what she was saying."

This reticence delighted Kōtarō. They were married in 1914; Chieko had come to study in Tokyo from the countryside, where she had lived in comfort as the oldest daughter of a sake brewer. This lucrative profession brought the family much financial benefit, but not the wholehearted respect of their neighbors. It must have been to prepare their daughter for marriage to an educated husband that Chieko's family allowed her to go to college in Tokyo. To her parents' dismay, she did not return home after graduating and marry the doctor they eventually selected for her, but instead made her own choice with Takamura Kōtarō, a promising poet-sculptor of eminent lineage. He was also known for his tall stature and big feet. In the spirit of the times, this couple disdained the ages-old custom of officially entering her name in his family register, since they considered such feudal claptrap beneath their very up-to-date way of thinking.

But somewhere between her marriage and her suicide attempt in 1932, Chieko broke down; she lost her confidence and even her sanity. Perhaps longing for the security that the old customs promised, Kōtarō placed her name in the official family register the following year. By then it was too late: Chieko was already destroying the lilies she had nurtured on her window ledge and reciting historical ballads in a man's voice for all the world to hear.

Without the success of her husband's poetry collection, Takamura Chieko would have been forgotten by history. Those of Chieko's paintings that survive are clear imitations of the Impressionists. Her works show some flair, but are timid in the use of color. Kōtarō would say later that she never got color down quite right. There is the art deco cover illustration of a bold "New Woman" that she drew for the first issue of *Seitō*, the progressive journal for women of those days. She also achieved posthumous renown for the lively paper collages she created in the hospital. But these were not enough to earn her the prominent role she now plays in numerous biographies and reminiscences. It is only as Takamura Kōtarō's beloved, blighted heroine that Chieko attracts close scrutiny. His fans have sought to know more about the real woman whose moods are so gorgeously described in *Chieko's Sky*, and dutiful biographers have rushed forward to provide whatever background information they have dug up.

Not that many facts about Chieko are available for analysis; Kōtarō, who maintained a tight rein over her personal and professional legacy, never sanctioned the release of news about their domestic life. Even after Kōtarō's death his friends remained loyal to him, and despite the clamor to learn more, no gossipy books have appeared to reveal the truth of what went on in that household. Assorted versions of Takamura Chieko now exist. There is the Chieko of the poems, who always keeps in touch with the truth of things and radiates a natural verve despite her mental anguish; the troubled, secretive Chieko, whose fits wreaked havoc on her husband's professional and personal life, a creation of Kōtarō's male contemporaries; and a third Chieko, only recently known since she is the masterpiece of those who are now hard at work bringing her back to life. This Chieko suits our age: she is gifted but hesitant, submissive but furious, thwarted in her efforts to emerge into the world by the maneuvering of a vain male.

Chieko's tale must begin with the poetry, and even today, readers of *Chieko's Sky* will feel some of the surprise that the collection's first admirers experienced. Unlike traditional Japanese poetry, these are not snatches of fleeting sensations nor terse evocations of minor events; no white fans remember a lover's presence; not a single syllable tells of butterflies on temple bells. During the first decades of this century, Kōtarō and his poetic contemporaries dedicated themselves to writing poetry in a new way, discarding the subject matter and formal literary language of the past. These poets also strove to liberate themselves from the rigid syllable structure of classical poetry, which to this day rings 5–7–5–7–7 in the ears of many Japanese poets. Kōtarō, like the others, wanted to write in a colloquial style that spoke frankly of what was in his heart. He preferred his emotions full-blown and direct. "Takamura Kōtarō was the first poet," the poet and critic Yoshimoto Takaaki has written, "who took what we now unequivocally consider the internal workings of the modern consciousness and turned that into the stuff of poetry."

Such daring did not come easily to Kōtarō, and in *Chieko's Sky* he perhaps can be excused for leaning heavily on the example of Emile Verhaeren, the Belgian poet who had also written love poems about his wife. In the first poem, Kōtarō seems to have mastered the trick: "I just hate thinking / that you will leave," he announces, very candid and conversational. "How can you so casually— / What's the right word?—Well, shall we say / feel moved to sell yourself / actually sell your own self." In poem after poem, he repeats this success: "That won't do. No, that won't do at all. It won't do to put a hand on these quiet waters"; "It's not just a game, / it's not just a way to pass the time of day / when you come to visit me," he declares in another. Even now, when read aloud in Japanese (preferably by a lovesick Japanese male), the poems convey just the intimate and intense effect Kōtarō sought: "The weight of the snow falling soundlessly / presses upon the ground and the roof and both our hearts. / The world catches its breath gazing with a child's sense of awe." Again, forthrightness does not come easily to anyone—poet or not—and that's why Japanese fans who know little about poetry at least revere Kōtarō for his sincerity.

Chieko is always the object of the poet's adoration, and she joins him in his attempt to "live for the truth." Kōtarō makes no secret of their disdain for social conventions in the poem about how he and his ideal mate will ignore "those smooth-talking cowards" of the world, "as ugly as frogs," who do not share their interest in reaching "a place where our every move and thought do not go against the laws of nature." In contrast to these beasts, Kōtarō and Chieko will live "in nature and freedom . . . like the blowing wind and the floating clouds." Chieko is well qualified to serve as Kōtarō's partner, since she is unfailingly sincere, spontaneous, and attuned to nature. She rejoices at the birds' songs and greets the morning light by stretching out her hands "like a baby." Renowned as love poems, these are also hymns of defiance from a poet who battled Japanese society on many fronts.

Chieko matches Kōtarō's vitality. He declares she is "fire," "reality," "alive within me." She shares his tolerance for Spartan food—radish, pickled ginger, dried mackerel—and when they dine on such modest fare, she has no complaints. On the contrary, a carnality flames up in both of them, and they feel a magical power after their "evening meal in poverty." In another poem, they journey together back to her country birthplace as he seeks to comprehend the "infinite sense of woman" within her. When he writes about them lolling together beneath the trees on a hillside, he brings to mind ancient Japanese poems about the pleasures of nature, mixing this genre up with his newfangled mode of expression. He points out the famous local landmarks ("Over there is Mt. Atatara, / what glimmers over there is the Abukuma River") as did poets of old, and amid the pines of her northern home he declares that her love has purified him and drenched him in "a bracing fountain of youth."

Back in Tokyo, Chieko retains her perfect serenity, undaunted by the poverty they endure in their studio; in fact, her beauty grows as she is forced to "gradually get rid of her accessories." The only real dissatisfaction has to do with Tokyo's heavens—"Chieko says that Tokyo doesn't have a sky"—and she longs for the blue sky of her hometown. Nowadays, Kōtarō's love may seem soppy and overwrought, but this is love as idealized in a traditional world, where loving freely did not come easily. In this ideal world, bliss does indeed warm the lovers' poor but adequate home, and the poet feels a matchless peace as he busily handles clay for his sculptures and Chieko weaves at her loom.

Later, Chieko frolics with the wind on the beach, mute and thoroughly mad. Yet even in a deranged state, she remains the child of nature and makes friends of the blue magpies and plovers. Not a messy business in these poems, insanity heightens Chieko's uncanny perceptiveness, and she can see beyond the ordinary shapes ahead. Her burdens have lightened. She has left suffering and the human world behind. The birds call out her name. These otherworldly communications can fatigue her, though, and at times she wishes to return to the world of the normal. Wretched, she weeps in her husband's arms: "Soon I'll be just useless."

Chieko dies, but on her last day she gets to savor the lemon juice she had been longing for. The taste of the lemon momentarily restores her lucidity and, in a stirring end, she becomes the "Chieko that I first knew." This somber deathbed scene, moving poignantly from a lemon to a final breath to sprigs of cherry blossoms, has wrenched the hearts of many Japanese readers. After Chieko's death, the poet pays homage by placing a "cool and gleaming lemon" before her picture.

In the poetry of *Chieko's Sky*, Kōtarō just about accomplishes the task of manufacturing the ideal modern love where emotions, not social mores, rule. Simple poetic language and conversational rhythms draw us into the love-drenched harmonies of their home. But when Kōtarō tries to repeat this achievement in prose, he seems thwarted by the difficulties of laundry and grocery shopping. He must address too many domestic details in his essays, allowing reality to intrude upon the sunlit, paint-speckled spaces. His mentions of insufficient cash and weak lungs remind us that the artist in the garret experiences not only the well-known ecstasies but also drafty rooms, hunger, and debilitating bouts of influenza.

Usually appended to the poetry of *Chieko's Sky* is "The Latter Half of Chieko's Life," the essay by Kōtarō that describes his years with Chieko. In tone and content similar to the poems, this work continues to depict her as a mysterious, purifying force. Depending on the sex, the politics, and the age of the critic, this document has either been viewed as another of Kōtarō's touching elegies for his departed wife or as evidence of his complete insensitivity to the feelings of everyone except himself. Kōtarō did not live in our present age, when every mental tic receives expert scrutiny, and his inexperience with emotional woe does show. Clearly, he had trouble discerning the clues. He writes that the wife he so affectionately describes in these pages went mad one day without him noticing many preliminary symptoms. Some readers find this hard to forgive.

In this essay, Kōtarō again describes how Chieko "cleansed" him and how her love saved him from decadence. At pains to show that Chieko lived in an uncomplicated way, moved only by pure feelings of love, joy, and artistic passion, he cannot say enough about her simplicity.

As I knew her, Chieko was simple and sincere. Always brimming with an ethereal quality, she was a woman who threw her whole self into love and trust. . . .

I don't know how many times I felt that I had been cleansed by this clean and pure inner life of hers. Compared to her, I felt myself truly sullied and adrift. I only had to look into her eyes and often would receive more than a hundred moral lessons. The soaring sky above Mt. Atatara certainly was reflected in her eyes. When I made a bronze bust of her, I keenly felt her eyes well beyond my reach and was ashamed of my own dirtiness. Now, looking back, I can see that she had within her being a fated inability to live in this world free from harm. That is how much she lived isolated in a world whose atmosphere differed from our own. I remember sometimes feeling that she was a soul only temporarily of this world.

Immediately the problem is apparent. These words describe a bower of roses, a shooting star, a figment of Kōtarō's imagination. His critics now demand a flesh-and-blood woman. The gap is intolerably wide and cannot be bridged. This aspect of Kōtarō's work has, of course, been noted before. Decades ago, Yoshimoto Takaaki wrote about how Kōtarō, when living in Paris, had visions of being able to fly through the sky and of blood flowing down the Seine. Yoshimoto believes that Kōtarō's mystical moments allowed him to veer away from the truth when writing poetry about his marriage. Seeing only magnificence in the bleakest heap of fish, Kōtarō regularly improved upon his domestic life for his art.

While beautifying the dust in rooms brought wonder to Kōtarō's poetry, his adversaries now ask whether such gifts wore well in daily life. At times, they want to say, it is helpful to recognize dust for what it is: a real and disturbing part of the landscape. Yet Kōtarō has a habit of pretty scenes and so he insists, over and over again, on his late wife's childlike and awesomely feminine nature. "One would have to say that she was much like a baby in the force and depth of her love and trust for me." These remarks have generated furious rebuttal, and a certain category of reader seems to bristle and moan, imagining exactly what it was like to live with the man who wrote them. The writer Kanai Mieko, surely Kōtarō's most implacable foe, offers her views:

In Kōtarō's poems, Chieko is the eternal lover rather than a wife; she is womanliness in its entirety; she is the muse who inspires in a divine way. But what if this muse herself is trying to become an artist and is waiting for the arrival of her own muse? Can such a person be satisfied and happy to serve as someone else's muse? . . .

She became Takamura Kōtarō's sacrifice. Bearing down upon her was the madness that came from Kōtarō's inner "animality" and his strong sense of himself as an artist. She could not find liberation in her painting and was pushed into being his "sculpture." Perhaps only madness would give her the liberation she sought.

As if this were not enough, Kōtarō has come under fire for waving his magician's wand over his wife's activities and again trying to turn the weeds into lilacs. "Her life was truly simple, lived from beginning to end in utter privacy, and did not in any way have contact with issues of social significance," he writes, perhaps aiming not exactly for factual accuracy but for a tranquil twilight photograph. It is no surprise that the facts go easily against him. Chieko formed some friendships among the female iconoclasts of her day, drew the first cover for a controversial feminist journal, and fought through her silences to subdue family opposition to her life in Tokyo. These and Chieko's other grown-up ambitions Kōtarō briskly brushes aside, leaving himself open to the ugly charges. According to him, worldly issues—the feminism of the period, say—meant nothing to her, and gossips have vastly exaggerated the extent of her involvement with the most advanced women of that period (the precursors of today's troops who are after his head). Similarly, he contradicts the recollections of others with his memories of a "guileless and unconcerned" Chieko who had no interest in fashion or society. In any case, Kōtarō did not care to dredge up details about her past. For years he did not bother to learn Chieko's age.

When Kōtarō goes on to search for what caused her mental collapse, he brings more rebukes upon himself. In the famous poem ("Chieko says that Tokyo doesn't have a sky"), he had noted that the sky itself lacked crucial qualities; she longs for the flowers and hills of the countryside. In this essay he wonders whether a genetic disorder triggered more problems. Her inept brother caused the ruin of the family's business—maybe all did not function properly inside his head either? Perplexed, Kōtarō brings up the time Chieko was hit in the head by a stone in childhood. The list goes on. Her doctors even asked him whether he had contracted a sexual disease while abroad and transmitted it to her. Since there was no evidence of such a sickness, Kōtarō cannot fathom the sources of his wife's illness. Finally he hints at menopause as a suspect.

In other passages, Kōtarō seeks to find clues in her behavior:

What first struck me about her was the beauty of her unusual character. May I say that everything about her was out of the ordinary. In the poem, "Two People Under a Tree," I wrote:

> This is the place where you were born
> the universe that gave birth to your strange
> and special body.

As he moves closer to the real symptoms of her illness, he keeps to his usual sincere and forlorn tone. Yet he has no habit of psychologizing, and so Kōtarō speaks of Chieko's struggles in the voice that comes most naturally to him, that of an artist coolly and objectively organizing his insights. Too often, it must be said, he takes refuge in the inviolability of art.

At the time, I was not aware of it, but when I look back, I can see that half of her life was spent inching toward the destination of mental illness. In living with me, it seems, she had no other course to take. Before examining why this is so, it is best to think of her living a different kind of life. For example, what if she had not lived in Tokyo, but in her hometown, or in some rural setting, married not to an artist like myself but to a farmer, someone in another profession who had an understanding of art. In particular, I wonder what would have happened if she had a husband involved in farming or the raising of cattle. She may have enjoyed a natural life span. In this regard, Tokyo did not suit her particular physical condition. . . .

She was gentle, but also liked to win. Thus she kept everything stored up in her own heart and went forward, without saying a word. She regularly put her utmost effort into her endeavors. She felt that she had to get herself to understand the very core not only of artistic matters, but of culture in general, and of spiritual matters too. She could not tolerate vagueness and was contemptuous of any kind of compromise. In short, she was like a bow stretched tight without a respite. Her brain cells could not bear this kind of extreme strain and gave way. Exhausted, she collapsed.

Kanai and others review such passages with much dismay. They wish to remove Kōtarō from the sidelines, where he placidly studies Chieko's decline, and drag him onto the field to take some responsibility for her mental collapse. *This is madness idealized for Kōtarō's purposes!* his critics rail at him. *He sees only the purity of madness here in order to protect himself!* Where is the grimness and the sorrow and the beauty of the mad? A livid Kanai does get carried away when she writes in protest:

In short, Takamura Kōtarō did not understand until the day he died that madness is a kind of mirror reflecting two human beings. Didn't he understand that Chieko had sunk into madness because of him? . . .

It is clear that Kōtarō's existence forced Chieko into madness. A person doesn't go mad all alone. The relationship with the person closest brings about a mutual process of osmosis, and the mind that cannot stand this tension—that is, the mind of the weaker person—creates another closed world out of a desperate attempt to survive. That very attempt swells with the seeds of ruin.

Yet it is the housework that gets Kōtarō into the most trouble. Since they had little income, he reports, he sculpted during the day and wrote articles at night to earn money. In a comment whose repercussions one wishes he had foreseen, Kōtarō writes that "when all was said and done, she was a woman and therefore had to take charge of the household chores" and as a result, she had little time left for her painting. He has paid dearly for that remark; had he been tied to a mast in a hurricane as punishment, the winds would have howled that phrase. Trying to make sure that her husband had enough time for his work, Chieko took on still more of the household duties and therefore could spend fewer hours painting. All this, in those far-off days, Kōtarō accepted without blinking an eye. On the night of Chieko's attempted suicide, he discovered a fresh basket of fruit, perhaps intended for a still life, beside a fresh canvas in her studio. At last aware of his wife's blocked and tormented state, Kōtarō confesses, "I felt like wailing."

Kōtarō also gives a brief account of their early romance, describing incidents familiar to his many fans. By now, the trysting spots and the scenery mentioned in his poetry have been commemorated endlessly on picture postcards and in tourist brochures. His admirers warm to the retelling of their "chance" encounter at Cape Inubō where they sketched and he fell under the thrall of her "self-effacing, guileless temperament." Kōtarō works hard to bolster the legend as if he knows that dissident bands will follow in hot pursuit, shouting epithets that have nothing to do with nature poetry. His description of the yellow leaves of the katsura trees in Tokugō Pass does much to recall their idyll in the mountains. "Suppose you were not there for me / Oh, I can't even imagine it / Just trying to imagine it is idiotic / For me, there is you / You are there."

Finally the autumn leaves and Kōtarō's essay fail to create perfect rapture. Instead, grave and banal issues lie scattered on the ground with the beauteous remnants of fall. There are signs that at least some of the questions asked in Chieko and Kōtarō's Tokyo studio were not so different from those often posed in other domestic settings. If there's not enough money, who is going to do all the housecleaning? Who will chop the scallions and take out the trash, if husband and wife both work? If the husband has high principles and doesn't want to toil for the family business, then whose schedule will be wrecked when the only servant has to go?

Chieko's partisans cannot abide Kōtarō's account of his wife's life. They deplore his hedging, since they feel they know where the blame for her decline belongs. Her side proclaims that it would have been better if Kōtarō had presented himself as a husband in the feudal mode, who demanded only tidiness, thrift, and fertility from his wife. Instead, he professed to have an enlightened modern attitude, which, in fact, he could only write poetry about. In practice, he was strictly from the Middle Ages. Supposedly enlightened, he sculpted birds from wood while his wife wore herself out making meals from what they could afford. Enlightened, he composed essays about Rodin while she tried to keep track of the food supplies and shivered through lung ailments during the months when they could not heat the studio. "He's just a typical —" a Japanese woman once muttered to me over the phone, leaving the end of that sentence to my imagination. Chieko not only had to whip up meals from cut-rate fish, the critics say, but she had to assure her husband time and again of his genius. "After a day's work, I used to go over what I had done with her and nothing gave me more pleasure," Kōtarō writes. No wonder— Chieko's sympathizers hiss—the poor woman's nerves gave out.

Kōtarō's supporters will have none of this and view Chieko's decline as an inescapable result of her diffident, sluggish, and unstable mind. Besides, his loyalists note, the doctors diagnosed her condition as schizophrenia, a chemical or genetic disorder that had nothing to do with her marriage. Throughout a number of biographical studies, Kōtarō's side speaks loudly and in a convincing voice. According to these volumes, unsteadiness of mind dogged Chieko from her youth in the country. As the oldest daughter in a large family, Chieko took her responsibilities seriously and from a very early age showed signs of an excessively fastidious, self-flagellating nature. Much has been made of her family origins, the wheeling and dealing of her relatives. Entrepreneurship during the early years of the Meiji period, when the family business was getting established, required quickly seizing opportunity, and this often meant chucking old loyalties and journeying forth to set up shop in a new locale. The haphazardness of her family background—there were a deserted wife, an illegitimate child, and irregular behavior along the way—may have eroded Chieko's sense of security.

Those speaking up for Kōtarō also make much of the gap between Chieko's family, who were, after all, merely parvenu sake makers, and the Takamuras' loftier social position—Kōtarō's father was a highly respected sculptor with commissions from the imperial court. Although the Takamuras had only recently risen to this position of eminence, the perceived difference in status was vast. This surely fueled Chieko's sense of inferiority, Kōtarō's side declares. It is said that Chieko's mother humbly remained in the entranceway when visiting Kōtarō's family home and refused to come farther in, as acknowledgment of her lower station. With only good country sake behind her, they say, Chieko was doomed to shrink and wither once she joined Kōtarō's family.

Biographers from both camps have searched elsewhere for the reasons why Chieko became mentally ill. In the main, these researchers have been frustrated and unable to hide it. They have labored long, mined a wide field, but only come up with trivial examples of childhood diligence, bizarre speech patterns, and mild mischief. From these shards of a life the chroniclers work hard to frame significance, and the strain often shows. It is difficult to blame anyone for trying to embellish Chieko's life story, since she passed her youth during a stirring period for Japanese women and came in close contact with leaders of the unrest. Magazines proudly promoted improvement of the contemporary woman's lot, and in general the old morality was under strenuous assault.

The times called for formidable figures to join in the great debate over woman's place, and some proved worthy of the challenge. There were women like Hiratsuka Raichō who, in 1911, founded Seitōsha (Bluestocking Society) and published the women's journal *Seitō*. In her very famous opening declaration in *Seitō*, she wrote,

In the beginning women were truly the sun. They were true human beings. Now women are the moon. They live dependent on others and shine with another's light. They have the pale, sickly face of the moon.

While these sentences express regret at the state of women in Japanese society, the aims of *Seitō* stressed literature more than revolution. Yet an all-women's journal, even one with a literary flavor, was sure to cause a stir.

Inevitably, the media focused not only on the writings but also on the private lives of *Seitō*'s contributors, and their researches did not go unrewarded. Hiratsuka Raichō herself had inspired a media frenzy when she attempted suicide with her lover in 1908. She also caused a scandal when she and two cohorts went on a visit to the Yoshiwara, the pleasure quarter of Tokyo, to view conditions there at first hand. In the press, which took such delight in excoriating them, Hiratsuka Raichō and other women of "advanced" ideas came to represent Japan's "New Women." There was disagreement about exactly what the so-called "New Woman" represented. As Sharon L. Sievers writes in *Flowers in Salt*,

To the public and the press, the term meant an indulgent and irresponsible young Japanese woman, who used her overdeveloped sexuality to undermine the family and to manipulate others for her own selfish ends. The literary establishment had its own definitions, based on a reading of Ibsen, which emphasized the uniqueness and heroic proportions of the New Woman. For many feminists, neither definition was useful; they preferred to emphasize the New Woman's legitimate struggle for autonomy and equality, and linked her emergence to international feminism, particularly to suffrage movements and social reform.

Chieko does not cooperate with the attempts to resurrect her as one of these female icons, decked in outrage and acting according to that mood. She often seems at the threshold of so much, beguiled by the heady atmosphere of those days and getting ready to hobnob with the "New Women" collected down the hall. But then, on the verge of walking in to take her place beside the others, Chieko begs off, murmuring about how the air inside is too rough for her delicate lungs.

Searching for telltale stains that will make sense of what happened later, biographers have scanned the footpaths, the walls, the greenery from Chieko's childhood home in Nihonmatsu to Tokyo, but they end tentative about almost everything except the tastiness of the persimmons harvested from her family's garden. Commercial forces have not assisted these biographical researches, since in recent years Takamura Chieko's childhood home has been turned into a tourist attraction. For the benefit of sightseers, workers have scrubbed off the black mildew of mental disease, sanitizing the house where the revered poet Takamura Kōtarō's wife grew up, as Naganuma Chieko. After the scouring, no one can find a madwoman's beginnings, neither the source of her gibberish nor the reason why she later made those berserk climbs to liberty up the back fence of her married home.

The advertising billboard for Hana-gasumi (Flowers in the Mist), the sake brand once manufactured by Chieko's family, now hangs in front of her restored and rambling old home. An ancient wooden wheelbarrow waits just beside the front door, seemingly ready to lug casks of sake off to customers at a moment's notice. Visitors to the house will find Chieko's own tatami-mat bedroom and pass by the sitting room where her prosperous family gathered by the brazier on cold winter nights or prayed before the Buddhist altar. Outside the house, the garden flowered throughout the year, and fall brought many persimmons from the backyard.

Close by this house is the newly built Chieko Memorial Museum, a sleek, state-of-the-art structure that enshrines her meager memorabilia. Letters dating back to Chieko's adolescence are expertly displayed in glass cases, as well as drawings, paintings, and the cut-out collages from her later years. Again, the walls do not memorialize that mental patient who writhed and spewed curses in imaginary languages at her husband. This is insanity as conceived by tourist boards, and it comes equipped with glorious spring sunsets and the fruits of autumn. "Here is the world of a pure, quietly smoldering love," the tourist advertisements proclaim. "You will hear the sound of the wind blowing through the greenery and breathe the fresh tree-scented air. Here is where those two, lost in true love, joined hands and climbed Mt. Kuraishi."

Despite these efforts, credible accounts of Chieko's youth make clear that her early years were not all nature walks and girlish dreams of seedy poets. Commentators emphasize that her family expected much of Chieko, perhaps causing her permanent damage. At the time of Chieko's birth in 1886, the sake business was entering its second generation. In its heyday, the family had a sizable house, sake shop, and storage facilities, and "Hana-gasumi," as their advertising slogan went, was a brand "whose fame sparkled from sea to sea." Chieko's father married into this sake-producing family, took over the business, and improved profits. But the enterprise had originated on the mother's side, and this perhaps explains that matriarch's arrogant and eccentric nature. Neighbors remember Chieko's father as a saintly person, always warm and soft-spoken, while the mother struck many as hard-driving and strong-willed. Her unmistakable voice, bawling out members of the household, sometimes carried to nearby homes. In particular, daughters-in-law felt her wrath, and one son had to divorce two wives in succession when his mother found them lacking.

Biographers like to dwell upon the psychological implications of this cast of characters, but just so much can be garnered from the fact that Chieko was the oldest child of a demanding mother in a family that included five more daughters and two sons.

Born into this newly rich, turbulent family, Chieko excelled. In analyzing her early years, all stress this point. Chieko's report cards preserve her superb scores, and even her primary school classmates noted her competitive nature and her talent for drawing. In high school she continued to show much promise, but even then she had an strange way of talking. Classmates recall that Chieko would look down, her neck bent and with her right hand held just below her mouth as she spoke. She was competitive, accounts stress with foreboding, but also—as befits a legend—extremely considerate of others.

This paragon's achievements did not end indoors, for she gave no quarter on the tennis court either. They say that her classmates, perhaps weary of her relentless superiority, once disposed of her tennis racket. At high school graduation too she did not yield. The student with the best speaking voice usually read the valedictory address, but throughout Chieko's life, her oral abilities earned only alarmed comment. Because of her outstanding record, she won the honor anyway and delivered her speech to the audience in 1903. No descriptions remain of this, her first, and perhaps her last, public speaking engagement.

Then we learn that Chieko decided to go to college in Tokyo. Where did that girl whose sentences melted away like ice cream find the courage to set out on her own? Solitude, after all, did not suit Chieko, who had written morose letters when living away from home during high school:

There may be people who think that Fukushima is nice, but it doesn't suit me. There is the old saying, "Wherever you live, it is the capital," but I have lived amidst the mountains and rivers of home, where there are hardly any people, and remember the sky. Now that the May rain is falling hard, I feel homesick. . . . I don't go out much and so I haven't seen the old ruins.

Perhaps being alone scared her less than taking up a conventional life in the country. If she did not make a move quickly, she would soon be eaten alive by custom and routine. In this mood, perhaps, she steeled herself to dash toward the risks of a life in Tokyo.

In 1903, Chieko became a student at the recently established Japan Women's University, the first liberal arts college for women in Japan. The college's founder had declared that he hoped to produce individuals "able to harmonize their roles as people, as wives, and as citizens of our nation." This soothing proclamation did not adequately describe the total atmosphere of the college where a number of forward-thinking students assembled. Just by providing a place for progressive women to meet and think together, the college became a breeding ground for "New Women" in the making. Chieko did not storm any barricades at the time, and she played no leadership role in that scandal about boys spotted playing New Year's card games in the alumnae dormitory. In her rebellions Chieko did not bluster, but was a small gust of wind across a snowy landscape. Only a subtle brush could capture the effect.

Hiratsuka Raichō, a classmate and that future leader of Japan's feminist movement, offers a vivid view of Chieko in those days:

I started to play tennis at my women's college. I always played with Naganuma Chieko, who was a year behind me. . . . She spoke in a low voice that you could hardly understand. She was so shy that she didn't seem to be able to utter a single sentence clearly. . . . On the whole, she seemed like a very mild person, but when she talked to you, she would look down and avert her gaze. Even on the tennis court, she seemed to be always looking down as she ran around. Her strong serve and powerful net shot always gave me trouble.

Although we welcome the news that she played close to the net, hitting smashes at Raichō, other reports about Chieko do not approach this vigor. From a wan, hard-won vignette we learn that as a college student Chieko concealed a box of persimmons in her room, violating the rules against keeping food in the dormitory. When a teacher discovered her eating one of these forbidden fruits, Chieko did not quaver and die. "Sensei, what can I do for you?" she asked in a most collected tone. Disarmed, the teacher replied, "Could you lend me a pen?" We hear about how Chieko couldn't stand the tedious job of folding her *hakama* skirt into neat pleats and so started a fashion in the *hakama* that featured gathers at the waist. "I'll call this the convenient, lazy *hakama*," she announced. The style soon swept the dormitory. Lest these mild proofs of spirit and naughtiness get our hopes up, another classmate begs to differ: "Chieko had a gay side, but she was also taciturn and a solitary kind of person. She often was off by herself, apart from her friends, and lost in thought."

It was after Chieko graduated from college in 1907 that she made her most significant statement about her future plans. Presumably, she spoke to her parents about her intentions in a clear and audible voice. Instead of dutifully returning home to marry properly at last, she decided to stay in Tokyo and continue her study of oil painting. This was a sensational career choice for a young woman with legions of relatives back home eager to arrange her life along more traditional lines. Quelling opposition from her family did not daunt Chieko in those days, and she began attending classes at the Pacific Painting Research Institute, where she immersed herself in Western oil-painting techniques and calmly drew the human figure from live nude models. In these painting classes, she adopted a zealously realistic style and did not even flinch at reproducing the models' private parts, which many other students left blurred. "There were some students who thought Chieko-san's peculiar embrace of total realism very odd," a contemporary reports, "but I found nothing objectionable there, only a complete honesty." From this we are either to conclude that she possessed the audacity required of a budding artist or that she demonstrated the weird intensity of the soon-to-be insane.

Women painting students were rare then, and so her every move caused comment. As usual, few could get her to utter many conversational or comprehensible words, since she kept silent when drawing and headed out the door quickly at the end of the day. But in her style of dress she did not hesitate to act the part of the bohemian painter. Chieko showed off a liberated-woman panache in her stunning cobalt blue cape, which announced her arrival and departure. Her way of walking disturbed the onlookers following her every move, since she didn't stride about like the other women students but maintained the slow and stately pace of a Nō actor.

In fits and starts, the pensive young woman in the photographs with the plump face and big pile of hair on top of her head struggles to come alive. Never a big talker, she walks deliberately, the collar of her cape upright and her head tilted to one side. When trying to fathom the character of this young woman, no biographer can bear to overlook the hubbub over green. Once a painting teacher criticized Chieko's work and told her to avoid the "unhealthy" emerald green color in her painting. As soon as the teacher departed, Chieko kept adding more emerald green to her canvas. The single episode from her early years that shows signs of life, this fight for green has been seized by hungry biographers and analyzed to death. Did her green revolt stem from Takamura Kōtarō's iconoclastic ideas ("Even if someone paints a green sun, I do not intend to find fault with this," he wrote around this time in an important essay. "That is because there are perhaps times when it looks that way to me as well")? Or did Chieko's own rebellious nature get her splashing green paint across her canvas in this moment of silent but unmistakable fury?

Others move from this green paint tantrum to her deeper anxieties about her color sense, a source of anguish throughout her brief painting career. "She really suffered about color," Kōtarō wrote after her death. "And because she would not settle for a half-baked success, she would berate herself mercilessly, almost to the point of self-torture." Apparently, Chieko once confessed to acquaintances from her high school days that she feared herself color-blind. She never shared these suspicions with her husband (who wrote elated poems about the perfect understanding between them). No one knows whether Chieko truly suffered from color blindness, but she must have suspected a problem. If so, only stubbornness—some might say masochism—could have got Chieko to embark upon a painting career when she worried that she couldn't tell green from blue.

Another source of much hand-wringing is a newspaper interview with Chieko—part seventeen in a series on leading "New Women" of the day—that was published in 1912. Chieko could not have asked for more illustrious company, since other articles had focused on such female stars as the poet Yosano Akiko and the actress Matsui Sumako. Like any proof of early promise unfulfilled, the interview with Chieko makes for gloomy reading. "In Japan, Western painting continues to develop in new directions every day," the article declares. "Only our Naganuma Chieko possesses a freshness that surpasses even a man. We look forward to the blossoming of her future." The interview suggests much about Chieko's later weaknesses, and reviewing it now with knowledge of what happened later, the reader wants to bolster her confidence, and definitely urge her to speak up in public. It's one thing to be meek and mild in class or with friends, quite another to speak in a voice that can't be heard by the reporter seeking to publicize your work.

While the article proclaims the arrival of a fearless new talent, the accompanying photograph tells another story. Posing for the camera, Naganuma Chieko does not look capable of defying anyone, much less established schools of painting. She has collected all her strength to face the camera and seems to gaze out, scared, resolute, and shyly awaiting permission to run back to her room. The wide-eyed look reveals that she is not quite up to the job. At this time of her life more than any other, Chieko appears almost capable of sounding the gong of insurrection, spreading the good word far and wide, but at the last minute she again balks and flees from the podium.

During this, her most revolutionary period, Chieko became involved with *Seitō*, the new journal for women that had been started by her former college classmate and tennis partner, Hiratsuka Raichō. For *Seitō*'s first cover, Chieko's drawing of a "New Woman" with long hair and an adventurous look in her eye captured the saucy spirit of those days. It was an attitude that Chieko reproduced best on paper, since in real life her involvement with *Seitō* did not last long. Chieko also mustered stamina enough to form a fast friendship with the feisty woman writer and *Seitō* stalwart, Tamura Toshiko. Tamura, whose love life would later take her to adventures in Vancouver and China, had been another "New Woman" featured in the newspaper series. In a short story that is supposedly based on their friendship, Tamura seems to be inviting Chieko to join her in a flight from the entire male sex:

When I think of us separating ourselves from men and sharing a relaxed life by ourselves, just we two women together, my whole being fills with the sweet sense of bobbing to and fro on the wide sea.

The anarchic promise of this bond effectively vanished when—according to the same short story—Chieko went to the seaside with the man who would later become her husband and wrote Tamura a bland postcard about the scenery.

Yet with a paintbrush in her hand and Cézanne's apples on her mind, Chieko could have been getting started on her way to opportunity, chalices of light, and independence. Actually the end had come. Here is Hiratsuka Raichō writing about what happened next:

Just as I, almost unconsciously and instinctively, searched for freedom and personal liberation in philosophy and religion, Chieko looked for the same things in art and beauty. After graduation, Chieko became more earnest about her study of Western painting. Then suddenly she married Takamura Kōtarō. I don't know anything about how this love came about, but I thought this marriage would be not be bad for her artistic pursuits. Yet once she married, Chieko distanced herself completely from me and from the world.

At this juncture, Kōtarō once again dominates considerations of Chieko's life. After the marriage the couple secluded themselves in his studio, and aside from his writings about her, virtually no other accounts of their daily life exist. When Chieko next makes a memorable appearance, years later, she is clearly not in her right mind, hurling herself through locked doors and delivering lectures to passing children from the second-floor window.

Takamura Kōtarō never seems within his biographers' embrace; he inspires too many powerful emotions, and finally eludes their reach. At times Kōtarō gains our sympathy as a hero from the earliest of modernist myths. Outfit him in a beret, set him in a Paris café, and he becomes another artistic exile seeking to shed nationality and convention in his quest for the new. At other times, though, Kōtarō moves into shadow and seems too fussy about personal hygiene and too prone to long discourses about himself for our tastes. He then takes on the less pleasing aspect of a man capable of ignoring his wife's hopes and promise.

It was on a quiet spring day in 1912 that the romance between Chieko and Kōtarō got under way, on a Tokyo street lined with cherry trees. They had already been introduced by mutual friends, and their relationship quickly deepened after she came to visit him in his new studio, bearing a potted gloxinia as a house-warming gift. Chieko was under pressure to marry a man selected by her family back home; after all, she was already twenty-six, past the proper age for a traditional marriage. Kōtarō soon imagined a more glittering future and could not bear the thought of her settling down to an ordinary existence. In a poem, he wrote: "It's just like / a painting by Titian / being put up for sale in Tsurumaki-chō / I'm lonely and sad / I can't quite put my finger on how I feel / But it's like watching that big gloxinia you gave me / go to rot."

The tall and mustachioed Kōtarō, who after a sojourn in Paris could sprinkle his conversations with French phrases and informed views about the Impressionists, was probably hard for Chieko to resist. Any sensible parents of a daughter, however, would have put up a mighty struggle before accepting this imposing and opinionated man as a son-in-law. There was first of all the supremely arty and erratic nature of Kōtarō's background, which says much about the unsettled state of Japanese culture in those days. Kōtarō's forebears had not submitted to the disciplines of the professional classes, but had been shaped by the rollicking, raw life of the old part of Tokyo. Though his father, a noted sculptor, eventually occupied a place of esteem in the art world, social wrecks and gang bosses figured in the not-too-distant annals of the family's history. The lore included gadabouts like Kōtarō's great-grandfather, who was famed for his storytelling talents but lost his voice when a jealous rival poisoned his drink. In order to survive, his son (Kōtarō's grandfather) became a street peddler and attained a position of authority among local gangsters.

Kōtarō's father Kōun called upon this inherited quick-wittedness in establishing himself as a sculptor, but he had not chosen his career for the kind of sober, aesthetic reasons that placate average citizens. In his early youth, just before he was about to enter into priestly service at a Buddhist temple, Kōun stopped off at the barber. Feeling that such a career would be a waste of Kōun's talents, the barber told him about a sculptor of Buddhist images who needed an apprentice. Thus, in the nick of time, Kōun's future was determined. After the Meiji Restoration, when Buddhism lost favor in official circles, Kōun scrambled to earn a living by carving the wooden models for casting the trinkets admired by foreigners—pen stands in the shape of crabs' claws or elaborate mirror stands. He was particularly good at wood sculptures of a miniature Japanese fowl called a *chabo*, and decades later, his son wrote in praise of his father's realistic cockscombs. When funds were tight, Kōun enthusiastically participated in money-making schemes like the replica of Nara's giant Buddha that he made for the amusement of Tokyo citizens. Customers roamed through the hollowed-out Buddha's insides via a staircase, and on a clear day, visitors could get a good view of the ships off Shinagawa Bay when looking out the Buddha's eyes and nostrils.

Although Kōun carved countless knickknacks to earn a living, finally his abilities received very serious attention. The emperor commissioned him to make a sculpture for the palace, and he became a professor at what is now the Tokyo University of Fine Arts and Music. At this time the Japanese arts were making yet another turnabout, and interest in traditional techniques was reviving. Kōun is best known for his bronze statues of a fourteenth-century loyalist on his horse, which can be found in front of the Imperial Palace, and of Saigō Takamori, a hero of the Meiji Restoration, in Tokyo's Ueno Park.

That was Kōun, the father of the groom. As far as Chieko's parents were concerned, Kōtarō must have posed the bigger problem. Kōun's oldest son and presumed heir to the family sculpture business, Kōtarō studied at the Tokyo University of Fine Arts and Music where he, like many artists of his generation, turned to Western-style painting. He next went abroad to study in New York and London. When he finally reached Paris in 1908, Kōtarō thrilled to be in the same city where his revered Rodin still worked.

Once settled down in Paris, Kōtarō tried to play his part among the other twentieth-century artists, jubilantly surging ahead with his achievements. In the end, though, art's transcendent power did not suffice to propel him forward; Kōtarō got snagged by obstacles as ordinary as a thumbtack and remained behind. He had longed to join life in the French capital, savoring *la vie* in all its flavors, but he always needed money and went for days without food. Gradually the strain of living abroad, combined with the lack of nourishment, told on him. Visiting friends were sometimes unnerved by Kōtarō's eccentric behavior and worried about whether he had a gun hidden somewhere. Kōtarō has confessed that he never had a steady French girlfriend, even though his models were willing to do more than just pose. His fastidiousness more crucial than his sexual needs, Kōtarō kept these women at bay because he thought them "full of germs."

In addition, he writes that he could not fathom his European models, who seemed as distant as "animals in the zoo." Incomprehension of his subjects did not improve the quality of his artwork. Exhausted by 1909, Kōtarō returned home to Japan much earlier than planned. A frequently quoted essay by Kōtarō describes the sense of inferiority he felt as a Japanese in Paris. In this essay, he tells of spending a fine night with a Frenchwoman, but looking with disgust at his face in the mirror the next morning: "I am Japanese after all. I'm *Japonais. Mongol. Le Jaune!*" It is said that these difficult experiences abroad fueled Kōtarō's nationalistic spirit; during World War II he would become notorious for his virulent anti-Western poems.

Once home, Kōtarō fared little better. After a reunion at the pier in July 1909, his father described plans for a new bronze

sculpture business. He hoped Kōtarō would head this enterprise, which would churn out statues to order for paying customers. Fresh from Paris, where he felt artists like Rodin sculpted nothing but the truth itself from nothing but their own inspiration, Kōtarō was appalled at the prospect of creating on demand. He drew a distinction between the craftsman, who made commerce of art, and the artist, whose goals were beyond money or words. He knew which category described his own intentions. At the time, Kōtarō would have called himself a selfless advocate of modern art and modern attitudes, principled and heroic. "I had no use for the whole established art world," he wrote later, "and I was disgusted by the awful toadying and the mean-spirited factionalism that permeated it. All they appreciated was fame and money. Those who were foolishly earnest in their approach to art were seen only rarely and at the bottom of the heap."

Not only did Kōtarō let his friends and family know about his disdain for the old order, he also took the trouble to air his ideas in magazine articles. Undaunted by the effects of such honesty, he did not hesitate to say a few scornful words about his father's close associates in print. Soon Kōun started to hear complaints when he went out in public ("Your son seems to be making quite a name for himself, isn't he?"). Finally the sorely tried father felt moved to caution his son about his writing. Rather than compromise his ideals, Kōtarō gave up his reviewing career.

As time passed, Kōtarō discovered that he could not feed and clothe himself merely on essays that urged artists to paint as their individual natures moved them—a green sun if they so wished. He worked part-time as his father's assistant, making the models for the sculptures and receiving a daily wage just like any other hired hand. This was a compromise Kōtarō would often have to make—advocating the loftiest artistic values while at the same time accepting a salary and gifts from his father.

Once employed at his father's studio, Kōtarō still would not give Kōun any peace. Little things plagued interactions between father and son in the sculpture trade. For example, there were faces Kōtarō took to and those that he could not abide. Gentle, upbeat models did nothing for his artistic sensibility. Ears, in addition, caused a lot of trouble. If a subject had ears with a slight curve, Kōtarō would improve on them, giving them points as sharp as the devil's. Plump ears that exuded auspiciousness and cheer, he would endow with more depressing overtones. His father, who had a business to run, would regularly make Kōtarō's ears softer and more aristocratic in order to please clients. This pandering to a customer's whims infuriated Kōtarō, who had more profound goals in mind than a flattering replica of what he saw before him.

In his reminiscences, Kōtarō's brother writes of these conflicts:

The commissions for portraits that we received had to please the customer. We didn't have the freedom to do as we wished. Even in France it's the same. The style Rodin employed in his Balzac would not do for commissioned work. But my brother wanted to follow the example of Rodin. If he didn't want to do something, he would refuse to do it. But that wouldn't earn any money, and he wouldn't be able to make a living. So my father would fix up the model to please his customers. My brother wouldn't like this. He'd declare that it was false and slipshod. He'd get angry and say that you couldn't call this sculpture. When I assessed both their positions objectively, I saw that my father really didn't have much of a choice. He wanted to establish a way for his son to earn a living. My father wanted to get as much money as possible and then give it to his son. He put all his energies into this. But a child doesn't really understand a parent's heart, as the saying goes. My brother would say that if he had to work under such conditions, he'd quit, that he didn't want such a life. He wouldn't make lies of his art. He argued like an impractical student with his head in the clouds.

Adrift in his native land, Kōtarō drank heavily and caroused with libertines. In 1911 he left Tokyo for Hokkaidō, where he tried to support himself by making butter. This didn't last long, and Kōtarō soon returned to Tokyo, a failed and frustrated entrepreneur. Again he lost himself in hedonism, drinking, and passing his time with women from the pleasure quarters. "His various problems piled up during this period," his brother comments. "Nowadays they would call him neurotic." It was around this time that Kōtarō informed his father that, though he was the oldest son, he had no wish to inherit the family business. Turning his back on tradition, Kōtarō decided to give up the responsibilities and the financial security in order to pursue his own art.

Kōtarō embarked on his lonely artist's life, but as befit a son of an imperial sculptor, he did it in style. Unashamed then to advertise his admiration of the West, Kōtarō designed a steeply roofed, two-story studio that looked vaguely like an English cottage from the outside. His father paid for everything. It was to this studio that Naganuma Chieko brought her gloxinia that day in June. Kōtarō gave her credit for saving his life: "With your childlike honesty / You discovered what is precious in me," he wrote in a poem, and forever after thanked her for cleansing him of his impure ways.

The real nature of Chieko and Kōtarō's courtship remains obscured by the legend, and no one will ever know her true motives, for example, on that day in 1913 when she hiked up to Iwanadome to rendezvous with him. A newspaper, learning of the meeting, showed no hesitation in identifying Chieko's impulses and published a scandal-mongering article called, "A Woman

Artist," which included surprising hints about her other romantic attachments. While little independent evidence verifies the facts in this article, there is no question about the journalist's desire to believe the worst. In those days, newspapers often resorted to this tabloid tone when reporting about the activities of "New Women."

She's a woman who talks in a high and mighty manner about how she will live as her pride moves her, a woman who argues about liberation from the bonds of chastity—this is Naganuma Chieko, that New Woman who has caught the attention of our present society. . . . At first glance, she looks the type who speaks in a quiet and serene way, but if you rub her the wrong way, she will argue vigorously and won't give you any special treatment just because you're a man. . . . She and a certain Mr. Nakamura had a lively romance going, and we hear that a number of love letters went back and forth. There was much talk about the time he was very sick and Chieko went to visit him in the hospital . . . No one knows which side got tired of the other, but now the relationship is over and they act like perfect strangers. Apparently Mr. Nakamura said, "I got tired of such a loose woman." . . . Recently, Chieko and Takamura Kōtarō have come to some kind of understanding, and there are rumors about them getting married, though she denies it and says they're just friends. . . . They have even taken a trip together.

This press coverage left the principals' families aghast, and propriety—Kōtarō's lifelong foe—required decisive action on his part. The couple was officially engaged soon after.

Kōtarō and Chieko married in December 1914, although they did not officially register their marriage in the family register until years later. All commentators remark on the heavy rain that day. They held the wedding banquet at a fashionable Western-style restaurant, but had to provide a special menu of Japanese dishes since some wary guests refused to touch the foreign food. No one has written a credible account of the bride and groom's expectations, and so we are free to imagine their moods as they gazed out at the downpour. Like so many women before and after, Chieko must have had rescue on her mind. In this case, she may have dreamed of being saved once and from all from ordinariness and from the muffled world of the shy. Kōtarō, for his part, had not been able to achieve grand success as a modern artist independent of his father's influence. More modest than she in his ambitions just this once, he perhaps sought only the standard consolations of love.

What happened next? How did the young couple fare? Did they hum through days consecrated to art, as Kōtarō's poetry claims? Or did they quarrel frequently over not having money to heat the studio and the steady diet of mackerel? Neither Chieko nor Kōtarō had any regular employment, and his myriad noble beliefs—glorifying art, scorning bourgeois society, refusing compromise—ruled out most potential sources of income. At odds with conventional Japanese life day after day, did the young couple ever weary of the struggle? On some wintry evening, just as the chill set in over the studio, did they ever come close to relenting? Did they discuss taking up work at the family sculpture factory full-time and leaving pure art for the summer season?

No one can say for sure. Nor does anyone know whether she objected to reading the poems he published about their sublime, frugal life while she was recovering from her latest attack of pleurisy. Kōtarō reports that Chieko worked hard at her oil painting while he toiled at his own projects. He concedes that she suffered an enormous setback when her works were refused at an exhibition. She never recovered from this blow to her confidence. "She would not submit her paintings to any exhibition after that," Kōtarō writes, "no matter how many times I urged her." Thereafter we learn only that Chieko, the formerly passionate art student, has given up oils for weaving.

Those who wait for a dramatic turn of events will be disappointed. There should rightly be reports about alcoholic disarray or a night on the town when the wife jumped into the fountain and finally exposed her unhinged mind. Instead, the door closed on that studio with the steep roof, and from the outside only indistinct figures moved where full-blooded life should have been. The poet Murō Saisei lived in their neighborhood, and he is one of the many people who tried to give a shape to that darkness. He often took walks by their studio, en route to the pawn shop or to sell books for much-needed cash. His imagination could ramble freely as he strolled by since he had very little information about the house's inhabitants.

There was a red curtain hanging from the second-floor window. They put up a white curtain whenever they placed a potted hollyhock there. The flowers faced the street. Clearly, this window decoration was calculated to get the attention of passersby and gave off an aura of pride and beauty. During the years before and after 1910, I was so poor that I couldn't even look up at that window and come up with the cold and supercilious words to express my scornful contempt of their frivolous ostentation. I even wished I could live in a studio like that. Here I lived in a four-and-a-half-mat room, and it was infuriating to think that they had the nerve to write poems about only having enough money to buy radishes and a quart of rice when they were ensconced in a large studio.

Kōtarō's brother saw their lives at closer range:

I would go over to visit my brother in the morning and he would say, "Have you had your breakfast yet? We're having ours now." When I looked over at what they were eating, I saw wonderful fresh items on their plates — bread with tomatoes, asparagus, cabbage. It was a European-style breakfast. They put mayonnaise on top. For breakfast at our house, I had eaten only miso soup, pickles, and two or three pieces of seaweed. Of course, that was not the only time we ate such things. At our house, we ate the same thing year round, but at my brother's, they would splurge when they had money. . . .

They were a little different from the usual couple. In the old days, married life meant that the wife did all the work in the house, but my brother and his wife understood each other well. For example, if Kōtarō had a visitor, he would tell Chieko not to go to great lengths to come out. He felt it was all right if she didn't greet the visitor. I don't know whether

you would call this a liberated style, but they did just what they wanted. . . . In my brother's house, it was the wife who was free to do as she wished, and my brother who had to worry about every little thing. This was the opposite of ordinary households.

Hollyhocks in flower pots, fresh vegetables for breakfast—out of these fragments, no sturdy outline of their life can be formed. From within those walls, Kōtarō wrote a poem about their bliss and harmony ("Without saying a word, I work the clay / The room hums with Chieko working at her loom / A mouse scampers after a peanut dropped on the floor / that a sparrow grabs away"). Kanai Mieko, unpersuaded by Kōtarō's poetry, speculates about another kind of routine. She suspects that Chieko found Kōtarō's talents daunting:

She wanted to be an artist, but perhaps she did not succeed due to a lack of talent. The most painful times for people trying to become artists are when they cannot get the painting to look as they wish and realize they have no artistic talent. How much more Chieko must have felt this living with a gifted artist like Kōtarō. She must have developed an inferiority complex, always comparing her talent and competence to his.

Another woman writer, Tsumura Setsuko, also imagines what Chieko endured during this period:

Chieko did not care much about money and knew nothing of the horrors of poverty. It is not likely that she enjoyed a life where there was no food or coal. In addition, after she graduated from college, she suffered from pleurisy and from that time was so weak that she had to spend half the year in the countryside where the air was clean. Even after she married, her health demanded that she spend three or four months a year back home. The fifth year of her marriage, she was hospitalized with a serious case of pleurisy.

The Chieko of "Tokyo doesn't have a sky," the Chieko of "The blue sky that each day appears over Mt. Atatara is Chieko's real sky"—that Chieko gradually could not bear to live in the stifling city with the dirty sky of Tokyo above.

During these years, Chieko herself wrote a few magazine essays about her life, and one of these catches her in a pensive mood:

These days my husband is busy day and night with the orchestration of his sculpture, writing, reading, receiving guests, various other chores, and taking walks. Apparently, at 5:30 this morning there was snow collected upon the third-floor bed. In the afternoon my father-in-law, who lives at 155 Banchi, came to visit. We listened to him talk about the old days— the old-style currency, satirical poems, the dramas of eastern and western Japan, the ballad-dramas. His talk was logical, interesting, and moreover, valuable.

Today we received our year-end gifts from him. Last year I gave him a handmade cushion, but this year I didn't have anything ready. I just don't seem to be able to get myself to find the time to do any embroidery or weaving. I thought I might get him something warm to wear, but my father-in-law has enough of such things. I'll think about this some other time.

At night I read Charles Blanchard [sic] and took a bath. There is no particular theme that I can assign to the day, but perhaps there is something that cuts through everything and continues into eternity. . . .

There is only one form of heroism in this world. That is to look at the world as it is and to love it. This is from Romain Rolland.

In 1918, Chieko's father died and her incompetent brother took over the family sake business. Eventually the concern went bankrupt, leaving her family destitute. Their home lost, some members of the family moved to Tokyo to be closer to Chieko. She kept their presence secret from Kōtarō for a long time—once again betraying the perfect trust they supposedly shared.

A few letters that Chieko wrote to her mother during the period after her family's bankruptcy have been allowed to see the light of day. These precious letters gleam like the sun itself beside the other dreary biographical data. For just a moment Chieko forms the words herself, gets to unravel some of the puzzle. Without the letters we would not be able to fathom her suffering. We would not know that she berated herself for her weak nature and for her lack of resources and resourcefulness. While downstairs Kōtarō turned his back on commerce in the hopes of creating cheeky sculptures like Rodin's Balzac, upstairs his wife was cursing her failure to make any money. It is a shock to hear Chieko's voice speaking from these letters about grief and spare change:

Please everyone, be strong, don't become despondent. Take good care of your health. Stay well. Fretting won't make things any better. As much as possible, let's be courageous. Six months will pass all too soon. I quickly made inquiries about the nursery school. I'll let you know as soon as I find out. I'll inquire around for you, but you also have to do some looking for work on your own. Let's try to do this and that. Let's not tell Takamura anything. If you leave quickly, there will be no need to say anything. If Takamura has to go on a business trip, I'll let you know right away and so please come here then. When he's around, let's all not say a word about it. Let's just say that you're in Fukushima. I also want to work to earn some money.

I'm sending you five yen for July. (This is the money that Takamura's father gave me for the Obon season.) . . . You three or four people are probably trying to live on thirty or thirty-five yen a month. I don't know what will happen tomorrow (no one does). I'm trying to cut down on my expenses, even a little bit, for my daily needs and as many other ways as possible. I'm not just spending money to buy you things. I'm dividing the food in the house little by little and giving some to you. I'm just not eating what people gave me and sending part to you. From now on, I will also be sending you some portion of my daily supplies. None of us has any money and so all I can offer is what I can do for you from the bottom of my heart.

In her most pathetic letter to her mother, written in July 1931, Chieko makes a brave stand against inadequacy and failure:

We both were so very disappointed yesterday, weren't we? But we must not, absolutely must not allow the world to beat us down. We must not die. If we must live, let us do our very utmost to stay alive. Let's put our strengths together and make this one great effort. Let's work without worrying until we drop. Let's each of us take up our work to go on living. This summer, I will do the same. I will. I will work hard every day so that I won't regret it if I die. And I will see a way to make money. Mother, please, please, don't be sad. My courage has increased a hundredfold. I'll keep at my work until the sweat comes pouring out of me and finish it this summer and exhibit it to the world. I'm not at all sad. I will do this for myself and also for you all. Once I have found a way to earn money with my own hands, you won't be in such difficulty. Then how happy I will be! Of course, I will do it. Of course I will. With good cheer and pleasure, I will do my very best. . . . I will work. Mother, please don't worry. Don't even try to do any work. It will be bad for you. Take care of yourself. If you worry, you must take care not to get wrinkles. . . . Let's all be strong. For the sake of you my poor mother I will work.

In 1931 Kōtarō went on a month-long trip, leaving Chieko for the longest period since their marriage. When he returned home, he was taken aback by her family's reports about the first signs of her mental illness. The next year she attempted suicide, leaving an apologetic note in her studio. Madness followed.

After this there is no more direct word from Chieko, and we must look for clues in Satō Haruo's novel about the marriage, *Chieko's Sky: A Novel*, which was published in 1957, about a year after Kōtarō's death. While he knew Kōtarō well, Satō did not have much contact with Chieko, and so he relied on the poems and his imagination in creating her fictional character. He must have also drawn upon anecdotes that Kōtarō had related to him, since many episodes sound as if they have been reproduced verbatim from such accounts. A movie was based on this novel about a madwoman and her beleaguered husband.

Kōtarō could not have hoped for a more flattering view of himself. Here is a case where the subject, if he had been alive to read the novel, would certainly have congratulated the author, not summoned his lawyer. This thoughtful and vigorous hero stands up for his ideals, serves as mentor to his diffident wife, and even helps around the house to give her additional time to paint. A more talented and liberal Japanese husband, according to Satō, could not have been found in Tokyo at that time. In trying to nurture his wife's gifts, the Kōtarō character shows great gentleness and tact. When he discovers that she is imitating his painting style as they work side by side on the ground floor of the studio, he urges her to paint alone in an upstairs room: "They say that a married couple starts to hold their pipes in the same way," he knowingly advises,

and that really doesn't matter. But it's cause for worry when the couple's art starts to look alike. . . . You must verify Nature in the flowers and fruits that you see before you, not with Cézanne's eyes nor my eyes, but with your own.

He also could not be sweeter when teasing about her difficulties in keeping their expenses down: "Still can't do it even though you took all those courses on home economics?" Kōtarō asks, ever the indulgent spouse.

Satō sees Kōtarō as the principled and hapless son of a famous father, craving recognition in his own right yet at the same time remaining on the family payroll. As this Kōtarō fights these battles, his mental health and his energies never flag. He may face dire financial woes, his wife may be cracking up, but his powers of concentration remain miraculous. Kōtarō works ceaselessly to see his many projects to completion.

Chieko fares far worse in Satō's novel. That such a limp, dependent, and silent creature harbored grave mental disorders comes as no surprise. In an early scene, she meets Kōtarō for the first time in the company of a mutual friend (as actually did happen in real life), and Chieko's manner during this initial encounter does not seem the auspicious beginning of a divine romance. "Her friend, trying to get Chieko to express agreement with what she had just said, looked over at her," the novel reports, "but Chieko, as usual, didn't say a word. Her black eyes just opened wide and bright as she gazed at the large and reliable-looking man in front her as if he had come from another planet." When Chieko does manage to talk, wit and brilliance do not punctuate her conversation. Even if they did, her sparkling observations would be lost since no one can make out exactly what she is saying. Like many other biographers, Satō delights in finding ways to describe Chieko's curious way of talking: "Her words seemed to get caught up in her mouth for a while, and when something finally did come tumbling out, the ends of the words were swallowed in a corner of her throat and became barely audible."

After the marriage, Chieko should have flourished and matured, turning out canvas after canvas in the warm glow of Kōtarō's encouragement. If only the novel's heroine absorbs her husband's many rousing lectures on art and life, surely stellar achievement will follow. Instead, she despairs of continuing to paint with oils after her submissions are refused at one exhibition.

She tells Kōtarō that she will never again expose her work to the scrutiny of strangers. "If you alone praise me," the wounded Chieko declares, "that's enough for me. I don't have any desire to have my work assessed by anyone else." She turns away from painting and starts to weave incessantly on her loom.

Once Chieko's mental state deteriorates, Satō abandons any attempt to understand her. A heroine who suddenly becomes a complete mystery to the writer trying to bring her to life cannot expect much, and Chieko is no exception. Satō's Chieko becomes a ghost who wanders through the studio, dressed in worn trousers and a sweater, driven to spend many intense hours at her loom.

To our modern eye, of course, this woman is no ghost at all. We instantly recognize her desperation, her unkempt hair, her insomnia. Before us is a solid and familiar figure we have seen more times than we care to count: the melancholy, sleepless housewife who works feverishly at all hours of the day and night in order to find a reason to live. The puzzlement of the men around Chieko perhaps can be excused since they had not been bombarded, as have men of our time, with information about such female emergencies. Sympathy for the males, however, soon shifts to the woman who must live amid this lack of understanding. Here is Satō Haruo trying to explain why an extremely timid woman who has devoted her life to becoming an artist suddenly abandons that work to weave winter clothes:

She could not possibly have lost her confidence just because she had been refused at one exhibition. It is more likely that she had visited her hometown after a long absence and there was struck by the beautiful hand-woven clothes that were unavailable in the city. She admired these so much that she decided to make the same beautiful clothes for her husband and herself. In addition, since her youth, she had possessed an intellectual curiosity regarding the dyes that were made from grasses and leaves of trees. This is what attracted her to weaving.

In the novel, as in real life, Chieko's father dies and her family's business suffers great reverses under her brother's management. Her painting all but abandoned, Chieko is left behind in the studio when Kōtarō leaves on the longest trip since their marriage. While he is away, she attempts suicide. Her doting husband responds to the news with much surprise. "But what made her do such a thing?" the stunned Kōtarō character mutters to himself.

In actuality, Chieko's decline continued for seven more years after her suicide attempt and ended only with her death. Hoping for a cure, Kōtarō went off with her on bracing trips to hot springs in various parts of Japan. He next sent Chieko to the countryside to live with family members; later he brought her back home again to live with him. Finally Kōtarō found his wife's fits too much to manage. As his letters show, the problem involved more than the sighs and moods that we associate with the artistic temperament.

Chieko's condition gets worse with every passing day. . . . I'm completely exhausted from taking care of her and seeing to her treatments. For whole days and nights, she just goes off into her crazy fits and I don't sleep for days at a time. I am of course at my wit's end and must do something about this situation. . . . While I am writing this, Chieko is lying in her bed shouting nonsense. She won't have any nurses around and so I virtually have not a moment to spare throughout the day. . . . When the patient is in a crazy state, she'll go on talking to herself or sing in a loud voice for six or seven hours at a time. Sometimes she gets hoarse and out of breath. I've had to nail the doors to the house shut, since twice recently she went rushing out to the street and bothered the neighbors. She breaks the utensils, she won't eat, she curses me and the doctor. She won't take any medicine saying we're trying to poison her. . . . When she has a convulsion, it is as if she is possessed. She behaves like someone possessed and makes movements that she herself cannot control. She wiggles her hands and shakes her neck. . . . When she talks to herself, she seems to be addressing some figment of her imagination and talks in a very low man's voice. Sometimes she lapses into a country dialect, sometimes she uses the old literary style or English, or words that I can't make head or tail of.

He committed her to James-zaka Hospital in 1935.

Madness and her hospitalization transformed Chieko—in ways guaranteed to stimulate discussion in our contemporary society. The woman who had always spoken faintly and with female modesty overcame all those inhibitions when she was ill and hollered in a deep, incongruous man's voice. Also, Chieko's creative powers reawakened once she departed from the home she had shared with her husband and from the world of the sane. In the hospital, Chieko made art from scraps of paper—pictures of flowers, fruits, vegetables, fish. The pinks and yellows and blues and reds dazzle. No art teacher could complain now about her color sense.

Takamura Chieko never returned home; she died in the hospital, of tuberculosis, in 1938. She was fifty-two years old. Kōtarō wrote:

You were so waiting for a lemon
On that sad, white shining bed of death
you took one lemon from my hand
and firmly bit it with your fine teeth . . .
Chieko became the Chieko that I first knew
and in an instant an entire lifetime of love poured out
then a moment later
you took one deep breath as you did on a mountaintop long ago
then your organ stopped.
Beside the cherry blossoms in front of your picture
I shall place a cool and gleaming lemon again today

After her death, the turmoil continued for Kōtarō. He was vehement in supporting Japan's role in World War II and wrote numerous poems that extolled the war effort and attacked the

West. He later acknowledged that he had behaved like an "imbe-cile," but he had cheered the militarists on too enthusiastically, too persuasively, and done serious damage. Shortly after the defeat, the literary critic Odagiri Hideo wrote a scathing critique of Kōtarō's jingoistic activities: "Not only does Takamura Kōtarō, among many poets, bear the largest responsibility for what he per-sonally did to the people of this country during the war, but he bears the greatest responsibility for the moral ruin of our poets as a group. This is the reason why he is a 'Class A' war criminal." As a public act of penance, Kōtarō exiled himself for seven years to a cabin in Japan's snowy north.

Until he died, Kōtarō continued to grapple with the mystery of Chieko's mental illness, and in his private letters—some opti-mistic, some annoyed, some guilt-ridden—he sought the causes of his wife's unreason. At times he tried to convince himself that hereditary factors had caused her deterioration, but in a contem-plative letter (written while she was still alive), he reviewed the evidence once more:

When I think about it, I believe that Chieko's competitive nature caused her the most trouble. In my opinion, the imbalance between one's desire to succeed and one's talent causes anguish. I blame myself for not having been able to get Chieko to realize this.

Later on, in a poem written after Chieko's death, he involved him-self further: "The husband drove his honest and sweet wife crazy."

The fashionable young woman art student, once glowing with the freshness of the countryside but reduced to tattered sweaters and insanity, does not only unsettle her surviving husband. She is a fearsome sight to anyone who has sought to go beyond the every-day and find the magic in words on paper or dabs of paint on can-vas. By way of a reaction, Kanai declares:

Takamura Kōtarō wrote, "I took as truth only what I saw with my own eyes." There is no doubt about it. For this reason, he beautified everything. He beautified madness, he beautified war. He sincerely believed that he had sanctified all Chieko's suffering and hardships by placing a lemon at her deathbed pillow. Precisely because of this belief, he "drove her crazy," and *Chieko's Sky* wrested a life for itself as a poetry collection about pure love.

The scholar Kitagawa Taichi takes another view:

Chieko and Kōtarō ignored all forms of sham power. When they set their sights on discovering the true path that human beings should take, poverty became a normal part of their everyday existence. The voices of ordinary, uncomprehending people rose around them, while they persevered in their insatiable attachment to beauty. They yearned for the heavens where they would fly free, but the weight of mundane life on earth bound them firmly to the earth. Such were the complex causes. Furthermore, Chieko did not evade the life they had chosen. The string had been stretched tight, and one day, it snapped.

In the saga of Takamura Chieko and Kōtarō, many of our cherished beliefs collide. Afterward, it is difficult to make sense of the mess. Those of us who would be sympathetic to others will feel the pathos of Chieko's fate. She had the ambitions, but not the strength, to find her own place in the world of oil painting. Although she tried to be a modern woman, she cut herself off from those who could assist her and spent her days tending to the house. Finally there was only the drifting and the madness.

But those of us who would be artists or art lovers may balk at condemning Kōtarō too roundly for his flaws. He was a man whose self-absorption was apparently monumental, and with a cold eye he drew upon his wife's sufferings to give focus to his work. Yet Kōtarō possessed talent enough to help change the course of modern Japanese poetry. Whether he should also have possessed perfect virtue is a matter of opinion.

Chieko and Kōtarō don't only make us ruminate once again about men versus women, they also force us to think further about the prosaic nature of sanity and the insights of the mad. In their lives are romantic notions to consider too, the wickedness of cities contrasted with the purity of nature in the countryside. Their story also allows us to imagine the turmoil that faced a Japanese, out of place in Paris, who then tried to become a twentieth-century artist in Tokyo. Along the way, Chieko and Kōtarō make us ask grave questions about how a creative spirit can maintain any integrity without any money.

After reading about this couple, we also muse over whether art in our present, tell-all age can survive the revelations of biographical sketches like this one. There was a time when we could have spent a peaceful moment appreciating the tender poetry Kōtarō wrote in memory of Chieko's demise. "She was so longing for a lemon. . . ." Now the poem feels less sincere, since we know that in real life this husband hadn't visited his wife for five months prior to her death. The true story, vivid and compelling, intrudes more and more upon our poetry, fiction, and painting these days. Chieko and Kōtarō's tale makes us watch with worry as the facts once again encroach too closely upon the beauty of art.

YANAGIWARA BYAKUREN'S NOTORI-
ous letter underwent major revisions
before publication. Her advisers felt
that she had not stuck to the point in
her original draft, but had merely
dilated upon trivial domestic woes.
The final version, shaped by an experienced male hand, sought to move
beyond her petty gripes to a more
general female misery. In so doing,
her handlers hoped to throw her husband and all of Japan into turmoil.
Only the irate opening sentences
remain essentially as Byakuren composed them. All agreed that no one
could improve on this dramatic start.
"This is the last letter I write to you as
your wife," Byakuren informed her
husband in a refined calligraphic
hand. "This letter may come as a
total surprise to you, but for me it is a
natural consequence of our marriage." After this, her editor took over,
and the combination of his remarkable skill with a polemical essay and
her remarkable outrage did manage

to make an impression on Japanese society. "As you know," the communication went on,

our marriage has lacked love and understanding from the very first day. I only submitted to this traditional kind of marriage because of misunderstandings within my family and because of my own youthful naiveté. . . . Filled with hopes that proved so fleeting, I journeyed from Tokyo to your home in Kyūshū ten years ago and since then, my life has been nothing but a vale of tears. All of my hopes were betrayed. My efforts turned to dust. Life in your home was complicated beyond my wildest expectations. I don't intend to go on and on, but may I say that among the many maids who served you, there is one person who did not have an ordinary master-servant relationship with you. There were even times when my authority as the wife in your home was stolen by another woman, and this was of course done with your consent. I was utterly shocked by the goings-on in your household. In such a situation, there is no chance for us to nurture any real love or understanding. You surely recall that when I protested and told you about my discontent and opposition, you responded in a very cold way, threatening to divorce me or to send me back to my family. . . . My only consolation in coping with this unhappy fate was poetry.

I had resigned myself to living out my life in the darkness born from the sorrow of my loveless marriage and from the wounds I had sustained as a result. But to my great good fortune, I have been given someone to love. That love is bringing me back to life. If I continue like this, I fear I will commit a sin against you that is truly not a sin.

Thus, today, following the demands of my conscience, I must make a basic change in my life. Now the time has come for me to stop living a lie and to embrace the truth.

Through this letter, I forever break my ties with you who have used your financial power to ignore a woman's personal dignity. In order to protect and foster the freedom and preciousness of my individuality, I hereby leave you.

I want to sincerely acknowledge the consideration you have shown in seeing to my development over this long period.

Such an epistle would surely catch the eye of any husband going through his morning mail, but Byakuren aimed for a wider readership. A well-known poet with influential friends in publishing, she made sure that the Osaka *Asahi* newspaper also received the ultimatum. On October 22, 1921—before her husband had even received his copy—the letter appeared prominently in the newspaper's evening edition.

Reporters soon caught up with Itō Den'emon, Byakuren's husband, in Kyoto where he had stopped off for a rest en route home. Itō had made a coal-mining fortune for himself in Kyūshū, Japan's southernmost island, a place as distant and unappealing to urban Japanese of those days as the South Pole. Until then, he had been known as an extremely savvy entrepreneur who had started out peddling fish door to door. After the nationwide airing of his domestic troubles, Itō would take his place in the history of Japanese males as a far more ambiguous figure.

Although he might have preferred a more dignified locale for his first interview on this breaking story, Itō received reporters at Isato, an inn run by one of his mistresses. Itō looks bad in many accounts of this marriage—particularly those written by his talented and aristocratic ex-wife—but he sometimes behaves like an affable bumpkin who has unknowingly bought his way into an arcane royal rite. It is as if he is enjoying the superb tuna sashimi at a regal banquet, when guards appear demanding his head because he has used the wrong chopsticks. Itō's encounter with the reporters after his wife's revelations has that quality of stunned and naive apprehension.

By then aware that he was about to be divorced, Itō described his last trip with his wife to Tokyo. She had seen him off on his journey home and, not giving the slightest hint of her intentions, had promised to leave soon for Kyūshū herself. In his first comments about his wife (whom he called by her real name, Akiko), Itō managed to keep his emotions hidden, and when he bantered with the journalists he gained a number of sympathizers:

> The first I heard about this was what I read in the newspaper so I still can't believe that this kind of thing really goes on. . . . As I look back on our married life, I see no reason for her pain and woe. I gave her all the financial support necessary so that she could make her mark in the world as a poet or whatever. I gave her fifty yen a month spending money, sometimes as much as a hundred. There was even gossip about how only the Itō family would take care of such a selfish woman. I'm just an uneducated man from the countryside, and since I don't know the first thing about Akiko's literary circles, I never once complained. . . . Likewise, Akiko also knows nothing about what I do. Aren't married people supposed to show some humility in the way they treat each other even if they live in different worlds?
>
> But you do see that a man like me, who has just received a notice of divorce from a woman, can't just stand by twiddling his thumbs and doing nothing.

In Tokyo, Byakuren resurfaced at the home of her lover's friend. For her first public appearance, she did not look like a woman who had just launched one of the century's most ingenious assaults on Japan's feudalistic morals and mores. Byakuren had little to say on the day she agreed to meet reporters, and the photographs show her solemn and thin to the point of gauntness. Conservatively attired in a black crepe kimono jacket, she admitted that she was confused and had no idea what would happen.

According to their later writings, Byakuren and her lover Miyazaki Ryūsuke had not at all anticipated the hullabaloo that followed the public announcement of her separation from Itō. At the time, Miyazaki was involved in various left-wing activities dedicated to reforming Japan's entire social system. In light of how disastrously he underestimated the aftereffects of the "Byakuren Incident," Japan was lucky that Miyazaki began his career as a revolutionary on a small scale, by concentrating on the reformation of this one marriage. Under Japanese law, a married woman and her lover could be imprisoned for adultery, and in 1912 a prominent male poet and his companion had been jailed for such an offense. By publishing the letter in the newspaper, Byakuren and Miyazaki hoped to gain public support that would keep her husband from filing charges. The crusading Miyazaki also hoped to promote the cause of justice for all women.

Even the imperial court took an interest in these events, since Byakuren was a first cousin of the emperor (to be precise, her aunt had been an imperial concubine of the Emperor Meiji and had given birth to the reigning Taishō emperor). According to some people, a royal relative who left her husband and furthermore openly confessed to an illicit love sullied the morality of the imperial house. The recent Russian Revolution also played a part in the public outcry, since critics believed that Byakuren was a pawn of communist advisers who sought to topple the establishment.

Ultra-right wing groups soon took to the streets and to the media protesting against such immorality. There was also a flurry of death threats. Some brutish right-wingers did turn up at Miyazaki's house, and his mother made him protect himself in the old samurai fashion by wearing a padded jacket under his kimono. To be on the safe side, his brother hid in the room next to the parlor with a wooden sword, but the visitors settled for just a vigorous denunciation of Miyazaki's treachery before departing.

Byakuren's brother, a reprehensible character who thoroughly deserved everything he would get, was a harsh, deceitful family head and an ambitious member of the House of Peers. His sister's love life terminated his career plans, especially after ultranationalists held him accountable for her actions and started stoning his house. Driven to nervous collapse by these attacks (and again, it couldn't have happened to a better person), he eventually had to resign from his post in acknowledgment of responsibility for his sister's behavior.

Liberal forces in the country also had a field day, since no more promising vehicle for educating citizens about the need for social change was likely to come around soon. Here were the evils of the old family system, the hypocrisies of emperor worship, the glories of romantic love, women's rights, the abuses of capitalism, the fight for individuality—all gathered together in one complex crisis. Besides, Byakuren was a poet and also beautiful. "As a matter of high moral principle," one of her partisans wrote, "flinging a notice of divorce at her husband and leaving his house were inevitable acts. . . . This is the kind of action that must be taken to end marriages that are nothing but a form of prostitution or slavery, to forge an identity as a human being, and to remain true to one's character."

•

Nagahata Michiko, a writer from Kyūshū, remembers:

My mother was born in Hakata and grew up in what is now the Higashi Park section in Fukuoka City. Her family ran a catering business and frequently serviced the Ippōtei Restaurant. In her bedtime stories, she wove detailed tales that drew from life on Hakata's streets. She sometimes told stories about people from nearby China who came to town and, in baskets hanging from poles on their shoulders, abducted little children; about the fort; and about the peninsula jutting out into Hakata Bay. She also told us about the boy Ishidōmaru who left Kyūshū to search for his father at Kōyasan monastery. She told us these bedtime stories over and over again every night. Propping herself on one elbow to the side of where we slept, she would lie down still dressed in her work clothes.

A bright sparkle would come to her eyes in the darkness of night when she told us about the flight of "Byakuren-san."

"One night," she would say, "Byakuren-san fled from the mining king Itō Den'emon. Her face covered with a purple scarf, she wore a long black silk coat and straw sandals with red thongs. . . ."

This was the perfect attire for a tale of lovers' flight. At the time of the Byakuren Incident, my mother had already married my father and was living in Kumamoto, in the neighboring prefecture. She had one child by then. I imagine that my mother, now distant from her birthplace, had been moved by reports she'd heard of Byakuren. She would set her mind to imagining Byakuren's appearance in the dead of night and create the stories she told me when I was a child. . . .

To my mother, her birthplace was an incomparable dreamlike place that filled her with longing. The Byakuren my mother described to her children had become an idealized creature in her mind. The whole incident had perhaps grown into almost an imaginary tale for her, and this helped her create a one-act play about a glamorous, fantasy love.

•

Once news of the elopement spread, Japanese started calling Byakuren "Reverse Cinderella" and "Japan's Nora," among other, much less pleasant nicknames, as they debated whether she deserved ostracism or a place among the twentieth century's heroines. Before this, some Japanese had known Yanagiwara Akiko (Byakuren was her pen name) only as "Akiko, the Queen of Tsukushi," after the region in Kyūshū where she had lived for ten years amid the excesses of her husband's newly minted fortune. Three years previously, in April 1918, a graphic newspaper series with that title had devoted ten installments to an examination of Byakuren's life, past and present. The image of Byakuren as the imperious and idle wife of a rich man twenty-five years her senior stuck in the public's mind long after, and perhaps accounted for the mixed response to her divorce announcement. Complete with much titillating speculation, the articles described the ups and downs of Byakuren's very moneyed exis-

tence to the not-so-moneyed readers who eagerly awaited every
new detail.

Byakuren had first come to the notice of feature writers looking for gossip in the course of a bribery scandal involving a government official and leaders of Kyūshū coal-mining operations. It
was just the sort of sleazy, under-the-table operation, smeared further by the grime of the mines, that showed off her regal appear-

ance and elegant manners to best advantage. In fact, Itō
Den'emon would complain later—and many agree with his
assessment—that she had chosen her pen name Byakuren, which
means "White Lotus," to draw a distinction between her own
matchless purity and his filthy coal-mining origins. During her
testimony at the trial, she denied all allegations that a gift she had
given to the accused official's wife was intended as a bribe. As she
spoke, the journalists saw newsworthy potential in Byakuren's wil-
lowy figure and the silk handkerchief she always carried with her.
Proving her grand success as a witness, the first part of the series
"The Queen of Tsukushi" appeared on the newsstands just a few
days later.

The articles were accompanied by photographs of Byakuren,
whose long, "melon-shaped" face epitomized aristocratic loveli-
ness for Japanese. The newspaper also included shots of the pudgy
dolt who had been her first husband and of Itō, the grizzled, much
older man she married next. Byakuren had a distinguished pedi-
gree, but blemishes here and there kept her a few steps behind the
purest bluebloods. Her noble-born father was a diplomat who had
been an active participant in the Meiji Restoration. Her mother,
however, had been a geisha. Byakuren was taken soon after her
birth to live in her father's home. Her father entered her name
into his family registry, and his official wife brought the new baby
up as her daughter. At the time, the offspring of concubines were
frequently accepted like this in such families (both her father and
his wife were children of mistresses) and suffered no discrimina-

tion. Yet some commentators suspect that the wife may have had ambivalent feelings about the child of another woman and that this accounted for the treatment Byakuren received after her father's death.

The newspaper series next went on to examine Byakuren's first marriage, which her family had forced upon her when she was about sixteen. Some questions arise about the connection between this experience and her somber poem:

It won't turn!
The key to the riddle made by
the gods is corroded with rust
and my life will end
with that unchanged[*]

Though a son was born the year after the marriage, it ended in divorce. When a reporter inquired about the reason, Byakuren's brother merely said that the marriage had failed due to a lack of common interests. But if the absence of common interests doomed this first alliance (her desire to get out of her first husband's home had been so intense that Byakuren left her son behind), then why, knowing of this young woman's devotion to poetry, did her family select an unschooled man who called himself a coal miner as her next spouse? In answer to its own question, the newspaper quickly revealed rumors about the money Itō gave Byakuren's brother in order to acquire this noblewoman as his bride. For a significant sum, the article stated, "they made a pitiful sacrifice of Akiko."

Once the series was published, Byakuren's fame extended beyond the small coterie of poetry lovers who had admired her work. Forever after, many Japanese citizens remembered her for reports of how she locked the bedroom door against her wealthy

*The poetry in this chapter has been translated by Janine Beichman.

husband when he sought her favors and for other such personal details. "It seemed like flattery, but actually, the articles just made me look foolish," Byakuren said of the series later, echoing the feelings of many a disappointed media subject. "I was just grist for the gossip mill."

"People say that she openly displays her aristocratic ways to her husband Den'emon," reads one passage in the newspaper text, "avoiding him like the plague, but toward everyone else, she behaves like a regular person and is kind and warm." The series tries to placate readers who might think that Byakuren found true happiness living in a fortress of ostentation complete with a gleaming copper roof. (This house, known as *Akagane goten*, "The Copper Palace," was actually not finished until a few years later and sheltered, among other treasures, precious Kanō-school screen paintings fitted into the sliding doors.) To the relief of those who could not furnish their homes with such costly doors, the articles emphasize that great wealth had merely inspired Byakuren to write poetry about her misery. Gloom, in fact, became her hallmark as a poet. "She is a woman of many passions and sorrows and has written hundreds of love poems," one article states. "Tell her that you're going to show her works to a staunch Confucianist and she'll tell you not to waste the effort. As one of her poems says, 'Lies like / cold dead trees: / Should we call / them the Way of Humanity / even now?' "

One article enthusiastically conveys the gossip about a certain scholar who had lately been paying her far more attention than was properly given to a married woman. He was one of the many literary and intellectual leaders of Kyūshū who regularly gathered in her sumptuous home. And could people blame Byakuren for such dalliances, the waggish articles imply, for what on earth would a stunning and high-born thirty-two-year-old woman with literary gifts have in common with a husband who is an uneducated former coal miner old enough to be her father? "He always fails her when it comes to learning and feeling," the text observes.

"She always fails him in tolerance and warmth. This is a very strange couple indeed."

Throughout her life, Byakuren wrote tanka, a thirty-one-syllable poetic form. Yet the newspaper series only ventures close to literary analysis when pondering the exact sources of her many passionate poems. Clearly, one did not have to look any further than her own domestic situation to find the origins of certain poems:

"Even devils may dwell
in a wife's soft bosom"
   I picked up
   those words somewhere
   and now they've stuck

And personal experience surely informs other grim moods:

Grown used to
loneliness, amusement
is to dance
   a dance of madness
   alone in a cold room

It doesn't go
it doesn't come, it doesn't
stay in place
   Is it alive, this self
   of mine? Or is it dead?

The images of western seas and volcanic islands in her poems were obviously inspired by the many years she spent in Kyūshū. Was it safe then to assume that she also drew from life in her love poems? Does she—the articles ask—describe her own romances in these works? Does she address an actual lover when she writes:

The joy of someone
there awaiting me
    I cross the mountain
    eager for you, I hurry
    over the twilit road

Surely her crude, aging husband (who munches noisily on rice crackers when she takes him to classical music concerts) is not the object of her ardor and longing:

If I did not exist,
my world would not exist,
he would not exist and
    then there would be no
    passion to burn my soul

The question of whether she writes of true love or not is pertinent since Itō—the husband who certainly did not inspire this fervent poetry—supplied all the money needed to publish her collected works as a book.

Apart from you now
I belong to Tsukushi
and gaze on
    plum blossoms
    in a village empty of you

This was another poem subsidized by her husband, perhaps confirming for certain nothing but the rumor that Itō Den'emon had never learned to read.

•

From the poet and scholar Sasaki Nobutsuna's introduction to Trodden Images, *Byakuren's first poetry collection (1915):*

Byakuren is a woman who can trace her lineage back to the ancient and noble Fujiwara line. She was born in the eastern capital, the eighteenth

autumn after imperial rule was restored. She now lives far away, in a cor-
ner of Tsukushi. Fated to live like a beautiful bird in a cage, she applies her
face powder on a May morning and feels nostalgic for the blue light of
Kyoto; overwhelmed by her own feelings, she curses the days her blundering
self must face. Sometimes, she wonders about where her soul will take its
final rest; on a lonely night, when the stars sparkle above, her thoughts turn
to God. Other times, she prostrates herself before a voice reading the sutras
by the flickering candles of the Kannon Temple. Or her mood saddens on
a boat trip around Shikoku when she hears the local legends. . . .

With half her life all but gone, she looks back on the flowers of feeling
blooming on the white road of existence—flowers that she now thinks of as
enemies. . . .

There have been many women poets in the past. . . . In sentiment,
Byakuren's poems resemble those of the gifted women of the court, but their
poetry has none of her intensity and emotive power. In this respect, she is
more like the women poets of the Man'yōshū. . . . Yet Byakuren is uniquely
herself in the yearning, anguish, deep melancholy, and meditative quality
found in the three hundred or so poems in this collection, and in the grav-
ity and pain of her poetic style. And thus one must say that she is a woman
poet of the modern Meiji and Taishō eras, but also a poet who is completely
herself.

For these reasons we can take pleasure in looking at Byakuren, the poet
of our Trodden Images, a woman of the Fujiwara who comes trailing regal
purple and makes her home in the western provinces. I hope that this vol-
ume will be known widely, making the poet a source of pleasure to us and
living on through eternity.

•

Only a reporter writing a newspaper series like "The Queen of
Tsukushi" could read Byakuren's poems and come away thinking
foremost about the exact identity of her male admirers. Only a
reporter searching for a story could seize on passion as the principal point of these thirty-one-syllable outpourings. For the reader

untouched by deadline pressures, Byakuren's early tanka do not qualify as stirring hymns to love and romance. They give a stronger impression of bleakness, and this has little to do with trysts in Kyūshū mansions. Certainly the joys of lust do not fill these corridors. A grave loneliness clings to Byakuren's carefully chosen syllables, since she walks within rooms so quiet that you can hear a blossom drop. Even the birds do not converse with her; nor, in a famous poem, do the gods explain the reason for her suffering.

I am here
and where is God?
On this lonely
night of
shining stars

Certain members of the older generation must have felt that Byakuren's ego had caused all the difficulties. Some surely disapproved of the "I" she brings up so often in her poetry, an "I" with an extensive list of troubles.

The high seas
blaze with flame
I live
in a land on fire
Who is my true love?

My own soul
turns its back on me, I cannot
see its face
Yesterday, today
o lonely days!

One whole year I spent
wandering along

the western seas and now
   the lights of the capital
   welcome me home
If I broke
a hundred men's hearts
would I efface
   all trace
   of this grief?

A more docile woman would perhaps have blended more easily into her husband's family and settled for the small diversions of
daily life. Low expectations and adaptability are, after all, the
virtues that keep traditional family systems working. A docile
paragon of forbearance might have tolerated the breakfast conversation of Byakuren's dim-witted first husband (who had not
managed to graduate from middle school at age twenty-four) and
the sexual intrigues that marked life with her second spouse. A
docile woman perhaps would not have refused food for days when
outmaneuvered in domestic tussles, or given in to crying fits after
repeated humiliations.

Yet Byakuren, instead of hiding her dissatisfactions, examined
them repeatedly in sorrowful poems. She is best known for her
audacity and her quest for freedom, but in fact her works more
often dwell upon the anguish facing those who turn their backs on
tradition. Byakuren yearned for open spaces and the right to love,
but she understood the loneliness, isolation, and despair waiting
in those grassy meadows. Her words, written in another time,
describe a very contemporary kind of suffering.

If there were someone
somewhere in this world
to cry for me
   I would gladly die
   at this very moment, now

Byakuren started to write poetry as a schoolgirl, when she went to live with a family of authentic but impoverished nobles. She later wrote that no one had told her beforehand that she would be moving in with these people. As her father was confined to his bed for a long time, she was abruptly taken away to live with the aristocratic couple whom she would come to look upon as her second parents. (She did not know until much later that her true

mother had been a geisha and had died long before. The murkiness of her origins only increased Byakuren's desolation.) For a number of years Byakuren thought this move temporary, devised so that she could live closer to her school. The permanence of the situation would gradually dawn on her; it was the beginning of a series of changes in Byakuren's life that her family instituted without affection and without consulting her. To ease the adjustment they bought her many gifts, and in her reminiscence, "The Road I Have Taken," Byakuren has written: "From that day, I became a pitiful young girl who had exchanged the freedom of her soul for a doll."

Her new father maintained courtly traditions in the household even though his dire financial condition could not support his exquisite sensibilities. He referred to his humble residence as *goten*, "the palace," because, as he said, "No matter how ramshackle it may be, the house that nobles live in is always called a palace." Byakuren remembers that he posed as a family servant when writing to the carpenter since he could not bring himself to communicate directly with the working classes. Although never quite prosperous enough to buy Byakuren decent clothes, this adoptive father at least introduced her to the intricacies of the tea ceremony and also made sure she could play court music on the koto.

More important, when she was about ten, he insisted that she start studying poetry. "It wouldn't do if a daughter of the nobility couldn't compose poetry well," he declared. In the Japanese classics, nobles often take up their writing brushes in magnificent domiciles or amid the glories of nature, fashioning poetry for all occasions. In the old tales, they can write of the sea grass hidden among the rocks or of aching for companionship at the Suma seaside. Soon Byakuren too, in less impressive settings, was making tanka from her school songs and anything else that came to her mind.

In ancient days, literary women gained much prominence in Japan, as is always noted when anyone comments about the abysmal status of females in the Japanese arts. *The Tale of Genji* and *The Pillow Book of Sei Shōnagon*, immortal works by women, are always proudly cited in any list of feminine achievements, even though the writers lived a thousand years ago and few women have matched them since. Still, a handful of women, particularly poets, have made their mark over the centuries, and the anthologists never fail to include them in collections. As far back as the eighth century *Man'yōshū*, some women poets brought much deep emotion to their works, one declaring that she would surely perish from loneliness like the bright dew on the evening grasses. The torments inflicted by imperfect men left them disheveled at times; their tangled hair was a giveaway of nights of love. Sleep could elude these women while the bells struck the lateness of the hour. In an unquiet moment, one woman poet hurried away to pick sedge buds from a spring meadow.

Though Byakuren follows in this line of fervent women, her hair never gets mussed up and despondency does not drive her to hectic activity. Perfectly coiffed and unmoving, she still has no difficulty conveying her desperation. In prose writings she explains that her sadness developed from mistreatment in childhood, compounded by her appalling marriages. Yet unlike those ancient poets, whose mental states frequently improved with the arrival of long-absent lovers, Byakuren required more than a suitor to soothe her spirit. She was the type to wake at dawn, pale and shattered by the meaninglessness of everything around her.

I've made a poem cursing
all the bottomless anguish
of my heart
    The name of that poem is
    myself

In Byakuren's day, traditional poetry, along with other Japanese institutions, was being overhauled for the modern age. Thirty-one-syllable poems had lost much verve since their first flowering in the eighth century. Some poets abandoned the usual 5–7–5–7–7–syllable line lengths and other arcane rules for the liberation of free verse. Others stuck by the tanka, determined to bring it up to date. These reformers vowed to go beyond such standard poetic subjects as descriptions of the moon or the plum flowers in early spring. At first, some men tried to adapt the tanka to the modern spirit; instead of decorous spring breezes, one poet set tigers roaring through the hills for the required line lengths. But blood and tigers proved too much of a shock for the tanka; wild animals did not survive this transitional period. At last Yosano Akiko, a woman poet, called upon her own immense human passions and her genius for startling imagery to revive this poetic form.

This hot tide of blood
beneath soft skin and you don't
even brush it with a fingertip
    Aren't you lonely then
    you who preach the Way?

Pressing my breasts,
I softly kick aside
the curtain of mystery

How deep the crimson
of the flower here

Byakuren could not hope to equal such frankness about the raptures of love. Afraid to even walk out on the streets alone, she was too constrained in circumstances and character to sing of rashness and abandon. Byakuren made her most noteworthy contribution to the poetic rebellion when she took her tanka indoors and into her own psyche. "The garden in Byakuren's home was fantastic," one contemporary poet has observed with some surprise, "in the formal Chinese style. But there's not a word about how that garden looked in her poetry. By temperament, she must have been completely wrapped up in her own emotions." Byakuren could pack a lot of depression into thirty-one syllables.

With a life lived for
no one I've passed the years
How many times
have I parted
from spring?

As she grew older, Byakuren turned more often to poetry for comfort. She could not turn to any family members, since they repeatedly conspired in setting up her foul domestic arrangements. Her first husband was a dreadful, moronic creature forced upon her by her odious older brother. This mentally defective groom was the son of that noble couple she had moved in with at age ten. Though Byakuren had lived together with the son in the same house for years, she had no idea that she had been betrothed to him. Again, her family had not revealed a crucial bit of information. She thoroughly despised this adoptive brother/fiancé from the start, and in a harrowing essay, "I Never Had a Childhood," she has written about how he stalked her during their childhood:

He was like a terrifying wolf trying to eat my flesh, a terrifying eagle only looking for a way to tear open my breast. Always weak and quivering, I had to go a long long distance to school and would reach home exhausted. Night would have hardly fallen before I had to fight off his poisonous claws. . . .

Men see something they need in a woman's body. Men and women fight a strange and frightening battle with each other. To my sadness, I had a vague inkling of this as a young girl. My friends at school laughed and cried in an innocent way, but when I laughed and cried, I could not show what I was truly feeling.

Nowadays legions of therapists, social workers, and police try to prevent such goings-on, but child welfare issues did not loom large in the minds of Byakuren's family. They could tolerate the hazards of marrying one of their daughters off to her molester.

As if they were merely throwing away a piece of garbage, the inconsiderate people in my circle had absolutely no qualms about offering me up to the very man who was slurping his tongue at the prospect of getting at my flesh. . . . My flesh, which had been born from the body of a young and beautiful woman, was gnawed at and harshly violated. . . . It was the case of many women in those days. There were just too many men burning with hellfire from their numerous sins.

Her older brother had become the head of the family upon her father's death, and he summoned vast powers as family patriarch when he insisted upon the alliance. Although the teenaged Byakuren protested fiercely, the family triumphed, and she embarked on a monstrous marriage that lasted five years.

At sixteen I carefully pinned
a black flower
in my hair
    and stained my diary
    with tears

In the end, when she could endure no more, Byakuren returned to her original family's home. A disgrace to her relatives as a divorcée, Byakuren was made a kind of prisoner there. Forbidden communication with the outside world, she was not even allowed to see her sister, who lived next door, and could visit her brother only once a year. Under virtual house arrest for four years, Byakuren read the Japanese classics to fill up her days (these were smuggled in by her sister). In later years she still raged about the damage done to her:

The living breath of my girlhood, as cherished as a treasure or a jewel, was stolen from me. The seeds of my whole lifetime of sadness were sown at this time.

Byakuren did manage to fight back more successfully when her family presented their next woeful candidate for marriage. To emphasize her objections, she fled from the house on foot, even though she had been so protected growing up that she had never ventured out on the city streets alone. Once they persuaded Byakuren to return home, her family abandoned this particular marriage prospect and allowed her to attend school. The pleasures of student life lasted for four years. Soon after graduation, her family came up with Itō Den'emon, a mining magnate from Kyūshū twenty-five years her senior, as her next, wildly inappropriate husband.

Byakuren married this man amid rumors that her family had sold her off for a large sum of money. (Her brother needed funds to stand for an election, and also his house required expensive renovations.) She traveled next to a new life in Kyūshū where some Japanese thought of her as "The Queen of Tsukushi." After ten years of this marriage, Byakuren went on a visit to Tokyo. There she managed to take a taxi and flee from her husband forever. She also published that infamous letter to Itō in the newspapers, outlining her precise grievances.

From *"Love Is Best," part of* Modern Love, *an essay series by Kuriyagawa Hakuson that extolled romantic love and happened to be running in the* Asahi *newspaper around the time of the Byakuren Incident. "Love Is Best" was published on September 30, 1921, a month before Byakuren left Itō.*

One summer evening, on the outskirts of a field in Compagna in the sub-urbs of Rome, the meadow and the hills at twilight were enveloped in gloom, and all was lonely and quiet. A flock of sheep seemed almost in a trance, chewing at the grass. I realized that this was the remains of a capi-tal of the great Roman empire. Wasn't this the site of the royal capital where, long ago, the great ruler had lashed out at his large army, wielded the power of life and death, and lorded it over the entire world? Now there was not even a tree to boast about, only thickly growing weeds.

What do the great achievements of the Emperor Augustus amount to? What has happened to the marble palace with its cupolas rising to the heavens? Now the visitor must make a path through dense creepers and grasses to find only the remains of the foundation.

But over there is a small jar, a relic from a small tower that is now cov-ered with dense weeds. Isn't this the last trace of the great stadium where, in ancient days, royal princes would assemble their favorite retainers and concubines and watch the chariot races?

Hidden in that tower was a fair blonde young woman who waited impa-tiently for her evening rendezvous with her lover. Her heart beat loudly as she worried about why he had not yet come. She stood there with bated breath, and her eyes watched intently for his approach. When her lover arrived, she must have immediately walked over to him, and the two of them silently embraced.

There are no vestiges now of the golden chariots and the large armies. What remains is only this ruin. But the love between a man and a woman possesses a permanency and immortality now as well as in ancient days. The love between a man and a woman does not decay even though a thousand years may have passed. After so many centuries of foolish activity and useless effort, let victory, glory, and gold be buried in the ground.

Love is best.

•

Miyazaki Akiko (pen name Byakuren) wrote her very disturbing autobiographical novel *Fruit of Thorns*, about her childhood and her first two marriages, after she was finally able to marry Miyazaki Ryūsuke and live with him as his wife. By then she had run away from her ten-year marriage to Itō, published her notice of divorce in the newspaper, withstood many public outcries against her behavior, and given birth to a son under these very difficult conditions.

Miyazaki Ryūsuke's family home still stands as it was then and seems a stubborn, seedy relic of old Tokyo. All around are the cement high rises of the modern metropolis, but the traditional wooden gates of the Miyazaki residence, the manicured garden, the narrow corridors, and the large, drafty tatami-matted rooms remember long-gone rhythms of the city. In 1923, Byakuren and Miyazaki came to live there as man and wife, but they could enjoy only the sort of domestic tranquility his family could cobble together. It did not amount to much. Miyazaki had become seriously ill with a lung ailment and would spend the first years of their marriage recuperating in bed. His family had long been known for its dedication to social reform at home and abroad (handwritten scrolls by Chinese revolutionaries still adorn the sitting room). Money, never plenteous in that very engagé household, now caused more disruptions.

Byakuren must have taken some time to settle down with her sick husband, his family, and her new baby son. "My mother never cooked," Byakuren's daughter told me recently in Tokyo. "I don't remember ever seeing her in front of a stove." Besides being helpless in the kitchen, Byakuren still could not overcome her childhood fear of going out into the streets alone. Throughout her life, she required an escort even for a walk down to the corner. To this day, her daughter excuses this weakness as the natural result of a coddled and aristocratic girlhood, when servants had accompanied her everywhere. Less tenderhearted observers, impatient with the idiosyncrasies of the noble class, roll their eyes and mutter that Byakuren could have overcome these trepidations with a little effort. Certainly, she did not have an easy time adjusting to the life of an ordinary citizen who was asked to tend babies and support the family.

Almost as soon as she arrived at the Miyazakis', Byakuren sat down and started to write for money. With Ryūsuke ill and a child, mother-in-law, and hangers-on to feed, she was suddenly expected to serve as breadwinner. "My mother never thought she could earn her own living," her daughter told me. "But my father helped her become more confident about her talents as a writer. This was his gift to her." Miyazaki also presented her with a dire financial situation that could keep her sense of purpose sharp if her confidence flagged. Byakuren turned out *Fruit of Thorns*, her best-selling novel, under these trying circumstances, and though it focuses on the past, the book says much about her new situation. (She also took full advantage of her switch from poetry to prose, letting herself go with whole sentences and paragraphs that tear her family members and former husbands to pieces.) While *Fruit of Thorns* dwells at first on her privileged upbringing, the novel holds greatest interest for us as the product of a woman in the throes of *jikaku*—awakening to a comprehension of what has been happening to her.

Byakuren calls upon the wondrous power of literature to tell all about those (mostly males) who connived to shatter her spirit. Men conspired against her. Men used their power to manipulate her like a puppet. Men took advantage of her innocence. Men treated her without compassion. Men lied. She tries to go beyond mere descriptions of her experiences—though these chilling passages would be enough—to write with new political awareness about the social forces oppressing a helpless woman. "Is this world so irrational?" Sumiko, the heroine of the novel wonders, her consciousness rising before our very eyes. "Do men have such absolute power over women?" Such passages must echo the discussions that took place in the early years of her marriage to Miyazaki—when Byakuren received a crash course in radical thought.

Looking back on her first marriage, Sumiko understands that authority figures do not have her good in mind when they make decisions. In the course of the novel, they force her to marry the dopey son of her adopted parents, who has been harassing her sexually for years.

"Why don't you want to marry him?" her brother asked.

The total lack of concern in her brother's question saddened and angered Sumiko. Before he had married, this brother had often been very kind to her. Now she found it painful to realize that he treated her like a stranger.

Her brother threatens to expel her from the family and reduce her to the status of a "commoner" if she refuses to marry the idiot. In her ignorance, Sumiko believes that as a commoner, she will have to sell radishes by the roadside or starve. Here Establishment Power shows its wicked and exploitative nature:

"Minoto-san, thank you for coming. Excuse me for asking you over on such short notice, but there's a problem with Sumiko. To tell you the truth, she doesn't want to marry the Ōta's son Masaharu. Since you specialize in law, I must ask you. Isn't it true that a woman can be removed from the family if she doesn't obey her elders? If she doesn't obey, she can be married off to a commoner, right?"

"Yes, that's true." Viscount Minoto had a troubled look on his face as he confirmed what her brother had said. Sumiko began to feel desperate and totally trapped.

The words uttered that day reverberated within Sumiko's heart until her adulthood. Much later, she secretly checked in a law book and discovered a passage about how even family members couldn't force a person into an unwanted marriage. As she read this, Sumiko burned with helpless resentment to discover that she had been deceived by her relatives. Viscount Minoto had gone on to become a powerful official, and she felt particularly sad to remember his words of confirmation that day.

She marries the despised man when still in her teens, and suddenly they move with his family to Kyoto. This unexpected departure from everything familiar makes Sumiko even lonelier. At twenty-four, her fool of a husband hasn't graduated from middle school, and she attends sewing classes to avoid being at home with him and his teenage classmates. A year after she reaches puberty, she notices a change in her physical condition. Frank talk about the facts of life did not interrupt the rhythms of that household, since only her mother-in-law realizes that she is pregnant. ("Are you telling me the truth?" the heroine cries when she hears the news. "Mother, that can't be true!") With the new baby comes greater despondency because her mother-in-law assumes control of the infant. Sumiko feels even more used and abandoned.

It must be repeated that Byakuren wrote this novel years after the actual incidents occurred, after she had married a left-wing activist and overhauled her ideas about equality and social change. Retrospectively, she tries to shore up her liberal positions. Some of the comments in the novel have more of an altruistic attitude than she probably possessed in her youth. For example, later on, when describing her second marriage, Sumiko claims that she agreed to marry a rich, far older man from Kyūshū only because he had built a school for girls in his hometown. "He's certainly not the type of person who just hoards his money," a relative tells her. "Your brother was satisfied once he heard about this." (Presumably, her real-life brother was also satisfied to find out that in exchange for giving his sister in marriage to this man, he would receive enough money to finance that upcoming election and redecorate his shabby house.)

Sumiko insists that she only agreed to marry into wealth in order to teach the unfortunate at this school. The claims to such idealism are not immediately convincing. Though uplift of the villagers could have impelled her into this marriage, an equally plausible explanation is that Sumiko/Byakuren faced a miserable situation in her family home and had resigned herself to unhappiness. She may have decided to be unhappy, far away from her family, and rich. Once they are married, Sumiko discovers that her new husband's school, which she had dreamed of running, has already been given to the prefecture as a gift. Therefore, public officials have taken it over and she cannot hope for any role in the administration.

Then there is the confusion about the inhabitants of her husband's household. More of a crowd greets her upon arrival at his home than she had expected. It was Sumiko's understanding that her groom had no children, but upon reaching Kyūshū she discovers a brood of real and adopted offspring with assorted origins. One of these is the child of her husband and a mistress; another is his half-sister; two others are his sister's sons, both adopted into the family. Sumiko also hears about other maids and mistresses who have become official members of his family; she never figures out the exact status of everyone in the group.

In recounting these first impressions of her heroine's new home, Byakuren pays respect to egalitarianism and scoffs at any notion that Sumiko craves copper roofs or luxurious living. Though she tries hard to establish these down-to-earth credentials, she needs greater imagination to conceal her heroine's snobbishness. In particular, the vulgar taste of Sumiko's newly rich husband causes her endless amusement. Whenever she gets a chance, Sumiko needles him about not keeping up with others.

"Even the garden back at my home in Hanazono has as much as three thousand tsubo," Sumiko said. "And that's in Tokyo where land is expensive. You're a rich man, and you live in the country. You can buy as much land as you want. When I imagined how you lived, I thought you would have a palace like the ones in the old novels and stories, with a huge garden, ponds, mountains, fields of flowers, wooded groves, and forests. After all, I had heard that you lived in a grand house."

"But don't you agree," he replied, "that this house has been built with only the finest materials? Why, the wood for the ceiling of this room is straight-grained cedar without a single knot. And the whole of that long corridor is made from a single tree. Your house in Hanazono is dirty and old, built way back sometime in Meiji. The bugs have ruined the wooden verandas."

"Well, of course the house in Hanazono couldn't begin to compare to this one. It's old and dirty. I was talking about the garden."

At once the husband sets to work expanding his garden into an elaborate pleasure park, suitable to her high standards. Witnessing this, Sumiko professes to regret hurting his feelings. In other passages she says that she is willing to educate her husband, but he resists reformation, preferring clothes shopping for his mistresses and geisha parties to her poetry clubs. Indeed, the husband behaves abominably whenever he makes an appearance in the novel, displaying temper, coarseness, and an overly robust sexual appetite. Yet here and there a reader can feel some sympathy for the man, since he had surely not prepared himself for the ordeal of this marriage.

Byakuren can afford a few nods to the husband's hardships in this novel because she has correctly gauged that his tribulations will not be noticed much. The preponderance of heartache is unquestionably on the wife's side. In fact, the reader feels a physical agitation as Byakuren examines her doleful life. It does not help when Japanese try to be soothing and declare that many other novels by women tell more gruesome life stories. For anyone with little experience of the genre, this work suffices to get a ghastly point across. Byakuren labors under a handicap since, unlike other authors of autobiographical novels, she cannot rely on poverty to gain sympathy. Her heroine certainly does not have to work in Tokyo's sake bars to earn a living, nor get deloused in seedy flophouses. In spite of this, Byakuren convinces readers that even a wealthy woman, who is a snob and also flawed in other ways, doesn't deserve to live like this.

Beneath the large chandelier, a number of women guests were thoroughly enjoying the banquet, which was in full swing. They were fascinated by the dance being performed by a geisha from a nearby establishment. Sumiko was seated at the table beside Yamamoto.

"Stand up and walk to the center of the room," he said to her.

She assumed that Yamamoto worried about her getting bored from sitting for so long. "It's all right. My feet don't hurt at all."

"No, that's not what I mean. You go and show everyone your kimono."

"My kimono? How should I do that?." Sumiko was having trouble comprehending what Yamamoto meant and tilted her head a bit.

"All you have to do is get up and walk over to the tokonoma."

"To the tokonoma?"

"If you just keep sitting here, no one will be able to see the design at the hem of your kimono."

The narrow corridors of Japanese houses suit Byakuren's sensibility, since she writes best about being nervous in a confined space. Above all, Byakuren shines in her meticulous dissection of trivial and intolerable incidents. Life's true horror, she confirms, is not in large matters but in petty things. Soon after her arrival at her new home, Sumiko realizes that her husband and his head maidservant are on intimate terms. Sumiko could have tolerated this arrangement if the maid had not usurped all her wifely powers. Repeatedly, Sumiko describes how the conniving of the maid blights her life. The inconsequential but constant indignities erode her equanimity like the slow drip of the Chinese water torture (which does in fact slowly eat away at the victim's skull). The maid arranges the cleaning of the rooms and the washing of the clothes, and even selects what the husband wears. Her responsibilities range so widely that she leaves the wife with no domestic tasks. In one galling episode, this maid asks the wife for permission to visit her family, and when told to leave in the afternoon, talks the husband into giving her a ride in the morning. Later on, the maid takes out a photograph of the wife and stomps on it in front of the other servants. The wife hears about this insult from a manservant and informs her husband. He dismisses the second servant for tattling on his favorite. "Sumiko was silent and didn't say anything in reply. In fact, her husband terrified her. A husband who could humiliate her further by making such a distorted judgment was indeed terrifying."

These are not colossal events and perhaps fall flat in the retelling, but cumulatively, such scenes create an atmosphere of unbearable oppressiveness. Sumiko remains inside day and night. Even going out alone is beyond her. She wants to live a high-minded life dedicated to writing poetry. Instead, she constantly finds herself sunk by picayune and demeaning encounters. Anyone who has been similarly thwarted en route to the sublime will hear the sighs floating above the tatami and feel the heaviness in the heart when the hydrangeas come into bloom.

The new day dawned, but still Sumiko did not have the strength to get up. The resentment she felt from the previous night's events had settled into a bleak sadness. Everything she saw and heard brought on more of Sumiko's tears. She remained in bed like an invalid and at least found solace in crying her eyes out.

Yamamoto, her husband, has little patience for the constant bickering in the house (he complains that she's giving him headaches). One day, in a fierce demonstration of male power, he asks Sumiko to prepare for a visit back to her family home in Tokyo.

Soon after that she was to go with Yamamoto to Tokyo. Sumiko looked forward to Tokyo where her brother and sister-in-law lived, beloved Tokyo where her friends lived. One day when Sumiko was busy preparing for her trip, Yamamoto came in.

"Take as many kimonos as possible," he said.

"It's October and so I'm only planning to take fall things."

"No, you should take your heavier things, so that you will have clothes for the cold weather too."

He walked out after he said this. With her hand still on the bureau drawer, Sumiko reflected deeply upon what Yamamoto had said. I wonder if he plans to divorce me, she thought, and her heart suddenly filled with an unbearable fear. Just because I can't get along with the maid, I'm going to be kicked out? She then imagined her life after being forced out of Yamamoto's house. It would be a repeat of those miserable years she had spent as a divorced woman! Wasn't it better to die than to go through that again?

During the visit to Tokyo, her brother takes a moment to comment on her situation. Just in case she has any plans about returning to her family, he sets her straight:

"I don't have any sons and so I will have to adopt someone as my heir. What do you think would happen if you decided to return to this house after that? It's high time you started to think of this house as if you were an outsider, even though you were born here. You do see what I'm saying, don't you? Why just today, that poor student Ōmura had to take a vacation from school because we had a guest. You don't seem to realize how much trouble you cause."

Eventually, the heroine has no choice but to return to Kyūshū and her husband's home. Once back there, she broods over the opportunities that would have been available to her, had she been another person—not so withdrawn, so unsuited to an active life, so impractical: "I have no other place to go but here. When I was living at home I should have studied to become a teacher. Then I would have been able to support myself."

As she lambastes her tormentors in this novel, Byakuren spares no effort. She demonstrates less resourcefulness when she tries to extricate herself from difficulties. This novel does not make any bones about the rich Kyūshū husband's indefatigable sex drive. In effect, the maids comprise his stable, and if one dies young he switches effortlessly over to her close relation. An adopted daughter was or was not once his mistress, but that messy matter belongs to the distant past. Geishas serve on the off days, and he's got other women who are now or were once his steady companions in Kyūshū, Kyoto, and beyond. The wife in this novel has no wish to join this brigade of giddy handmaidens, and so she cannot rejoice for long when the maid she has detested finally leaves the house. Instead, she starts to worry that her husband may pester her with new demands, physical and otherwise. Soon after, the wife hires a young woman as live-in help to service his needs.

In real life, Byakuren hired a young woman to serve as her husband Itō's sexual partner under the same circumstances. At the time of their public separation, Itō Den'emon made sure to inform all of Japan (and would have sent flyers to galaxies beyond if possible) about his wife's personal selection of his mistress. He realized that the presence of such an employee in the house seriously undercut the lofty pronouncements that Byakuren had been making to all and sundry about promoting women's rights. "You say I trample on women with my money," Itō gleefully declared in his public response to her. "Didn't you yourself sacrifice a woman and reduce her to tears?" Many Japanese abandoned Byakuren's cause once they learned that she had procured another woman for her husband's bed.

Byakuren attempts to defend herself against the attacks in this novel, but her excuses waft up feebly from the pages:

Since her husband would never love her as much as he had loved the maid Oseki, Sumiko felt she had no other choice but to get him to love another woman. And if her husband loved that woman more than Oseki, Sumiko would gain a measure of peace.

Some time later, she talked to her husband about this. She had a big smile on her face but it wasn't clear whether she spoke sincerely or was just joking: "I'm thinking of getting you a mistress."

Yamamoto also smiled. "What made you think of that?"

"I haven't been able to have any children. Maybe if you had a healthier woman, you'd be able to have a child with her. If you were able to have a child of your own, then you would probably want it to be your heir. . . ."

Yamamoto's mood immediately improved. He had always thought of Sumiko as overly jealous, high-strung, and difficult. Her suggestion, though tentative, took him completely by surprise.

Nor is she more convincing on the night the new mistress Yū sleeps next door to them:

Yamamoto and Sumiko slept in the same room. Sumiko couldn't sleep at all. She thought she would get to bed early, but couldn't sleep. Yamamoto also seemed to be having trouble sleeping. He had brought his tobacco tray close to the bedside and she could hear him banging the pipe he had smoked against his ashtray. This disturbed Sumiko's peace, making sleep even more difficult.

After a while Yamamoto turned to Sumiko and asked, "What if I went to see Yū for a while?"

Hesitation in his voice, he seemed to be seeking her advice.

"Go right ahead," she answered casually.

Yamamoto immediately got up, opened the sliding door, closed it quietly behind him, and strode off to the other room.

Sumiko, her eyes wide open, stared at the ceiling. "You cruel monster! She's a nineteen-year-old virgin!"

It was so sad. Men were such beasts. But worse, how wicked she was to commit this terrible sin. Could she be excused for doing such a thing to another woman, a member of the same sex? She could hardly bear to think of herself as the moving force behind such an unforgivable act.

At the end of *Fruit of Thorns*, we leave Sumiko to sort out her contradictions. Her home spinning with shifting sexual shenanigans, her ethics compromised, and her humiliations continuing, Sumiko welcomes the attentions of a new young admirer with leftist political ideas. He writes to tell her that he's been ostracized by his friends for falling in love with a rich, upper-class woman. Moved by the sacrifices he has made on her behalf, she writes back to him immediately: "Let's meet in Kyoto."

•

From the Asahi *newspaper, October 31, 1921:*

Akiko's flight from her marriage has caused an unusual stir throughout society and as of today, we have received 412 letters from our readers. We selected 123 representative letters and came up with the following results:

55 against Akiko's actions

43 in favor

25 neutral

We further investigated and discovered the following objections to her behavior:

(1) she left only after she had found a lover;

(2) she made her divorce announcement public;

(3) she abandoned a marriage that had lasted for ten years. . . .

Only ten percent of the respondents were women, and it is significant to note that eighty percent of these were opposed to her behavior.

From the letters:

No matter how you look at it, it was wrong of her to behave just like a common fishwife. Why didn't she wait until after she was officially divorced to go off with her lover? If the divorce was refused and she had been forced to continue to live like a slave, then that was the time to behave as she has now. It was also unforgivable that such an action to destroy the very basis of our society was taken by Byakuren, who was seen by young people as a greatly gifted poet with an intellectual bent.

When Itō became involved with other women after his marriage to Akiko, the rules that bound the two of them together as man and wife were nullified. Akiko had already become free to do as she liked. If there was any wrongdoing on Akiko's part, it was at the very outset. Marrying Itō, for whom she had no love, was a sin against heaven. You can say that the misery she endured in the ten years of her marriage to Itō was divine retribution.

While I approve of the route you have taken in these recent events, there is one thing that I cannot remain silent about. With your help, a twenty-year-old girl who resisted with all her might and tried to flee was thrown under the poisonous hooves of Den'emon. You bought another human being in your own name. You assisted in forcing another human being into the muddy pit of immorality that you yourself, with all the great prestige afforded a wife in our society, could not endure. In my opinion, this behavior contradicts all your present talk about your total commitment to love.

The worst person in this affair is Count Yanagiwara, her elder brother, who sold off another human being. I can easily imagine that when the two of them talked, he told her, "Look, think of yourself as the savior of the Yanagiwara family. You just do me a favor and live there temporarily." Isn't it too bad that she couldn't have just left? . . . To say that at age twenty-

seven she didn't know a thing about what kind of marriage she was embarking upon sounds unbelievable.

•

Miyazaki Ryūsuke, Byakuren's lover (and later her third husband), showed much daring in defying Japanese society to liberate the woman he loved. But in matters of daring, Ryūsuke seems a pale firefly in the dim light of evening when compared to the swarm of hotheaded bees that buzzed around his father. Ryūsuke was the oldest son of Miyazaki Tōten, a crusader for Chinese liberation and comrade of Sun Yat-sen. Tōten did not limit himself to individual acts of charity—saving a woman trapped in a loveless marriage would not have satisfied his vast ambitions. Whole provinces and continents better suited his ideas on social change, and so he devoted much of his life to freeing China from domination by the Manchu dynasty. If he had any time left over, he planned to liberate downtrodden Asian peoples throughout the world.

Flexibility in the face of catastrophe marked Tōten's approach to revolution. He could quickly consider alternative ways to effect a Chinese uprising after his guns and his comrades sank in a cargo boat off Shanghai. He could lift himself from despair over stubborn bill collectors with the cups of sake that flowed as interminably as the Yellow River at the social-political gatherings he attended. He asked for public understanding of his weakness for drink and women; Tōten also asked his wife, back at home, to meet the challenge of raising two children alone on no money. And when his career as a revolutionary came to an impasse, Tōten swiftly set about finding a new profession. At the end of his rollicking autobiography we leave Tōten, his prospects for triumph in China temporarily thwarted, preparing to apprentice himself to a professional storyteller. "When we pursue a dream in a world of dreams," he writes, in his new balladeer's vein, "we enter yet another dream."

So let me sing of fallen flowers.
Let me act out a play of fallen flowers
Let me gather the flowers of Musashino
How can they console me?
Ah, how can they console me?[*]

Compared to such derring-do in the Middle Kingdom, Tōten's
son Ryūsuke adopted a tamer brand of activism. Though slower
and less rambunctious, Ryūsuke still has earned mention in the
history of social disruption. He received an elite education, entering the Law Department of Tokyo Imperial University in 1917, but
Ryūsuke never considered shaming his father's principles by join-
ing the government bureaucracy, as did many of his peers. Uplift
of the oppressed was a family cause, and Ryūsuke promoted this
principle in the debating halls of Japan's most prestigious university. He and his friends regularly reviewed just how they were
going to restructure Japanese society. During their discussions,
they debated Lenin's precepts and discussed how to link the labor
movement with the student movement. Ryūsuke joined the
Shinjinkai (New People's Group), a left-wing student organiza-
tion formed at the University of Tokyo in 1918. The Shinjinkai
went on to become a major force in left-wing student politics. The
early members were from the debating society, and later they
organized themselves into an activist group, advocating democracy, universal suffrage, and other reforms. "Now when I look
back on it," Ryūsuke has written in his 1967 reminiscence, "Half
a Century with Yanagiwara Byakuren," "I can see that we were all
just starry-eyed socialists. We had all heard about the Russian
Revolution and thought that any day there would be a revolution
in Japan." Though still a student, Ryūsuke became an editor of

[*]Miyazaki Tōten, *My Thirty-three Years' Dream*, trans. Etō Shinkichi and
Marius B. Jansen (Princeton University Press, 1982), 279.

the group's magazine, *Kaihō* (Liberation), which aimed at "firing up the people's discontent that was rampant in the city streets."

Here Ryūsuke shows his father's flexibility in revolutionary outlook. He worked for a radical magazine, yet took time off in January 1920 to visit Yanagiwara Byakuren, a woman poet married to a wealthy mining entrepreneur in faraway Kyūshū. Their collaboration does not seem natural since at the time, her style of life did not prompt left-wing gatherings in the sitting room. Ryūsuke knew her by reputation and could not have missed hearing about the lavish standard of living. In fact, the copper roof of the estate that her husband began building at the time of their marriage was a perfect symbol of bourgeois excess and, had Ryūsuke's comrades been successful, could have appeared on postage stamps commemorating the outrages eliminated by the Japanese Revolution.

The romance that would be immortalized in bedtime stories and denounced in public places began when Ryūsuke went out to Kyūshū to discuss some business regarding Byakuren's play, *The Heresy of the Finger Wreath*, which his magazine had published in 1919. This play was based on a Buddhist tale of lust and enthrallment, murder and redemption. Byakuren's version introduced a new female perspective on a journey down the Path of Enlightenment. "Does this hopeless misfortune derive from karma in this world or from some curse in my past life?" a love-starved wife complains, bringing Byakuren's lonely poetic persona to the stage. "I wait for the light of love that I anguish over day and night, but it does not come. Although the peace of midday arrives, I cannot see the light of the day."

The plot heats up when a female character complains bitterly about her wanton husband and his attachment to another woman. Take away the Buddhist icons and the incense and you have Byakuren, sitting under a copper roof in a Kyūshū mansion, expressing her low opinion of her highly sexed husband:

He loses himself in carnal pleasure and has got his fill of many women's kisses, thinking nothing of stomping on the soul of a pure, soft woman who abides by the commands of heaven. Indeed, he is not even aware that he destroys her. And the younger, the more beautiful, and the prouder the woman is, the more inflated becomes the man's ignorant vanity. He inflicts more pain, becomes meaner, trifles with me like someone proud to be rough and casual with a precious treasure in public.

One commentator links that passage to the pleasure Itō took in showing off his control of his noble-born wife. It seems he enjoyed having Byakuren massage his feet in the presence of guests.

The origins of *The Heresy of the Finger Wreath* hardly get a mention in biographical accounts, since the meeting between "The Queen of Tsukushi" and Tōten's rebellious son that winter day in Beppu offers far more fascinating possibilities. Byakuren says that she wanted to clarify some publishing details and so, in an act of noblesse oblige, she sent Miyazaki Ryūsuke the train fare from Tokyo to Kyūshū. With some female family members serving as chaperones, she met him for the first time at one of her homes, in Beppu.

I expected a bookstore clerk or something and was surprised when my guest turned out to be a student in a college cap. After we finished our business, we spoke of other matters, and I realized that he was a member of the Shinjinkai of Tokyo Imperial University. Miyazaki talked to us of a world we knew nothing about, of sincere students who devoted themselves to social reform with the zeal of those students in the old Russian novels.

Byakuren cannot herself do justice to the drama of this first meeting, since she is at pains to prove to her readers that she entered into the adulterous relationship reluctantly. While her writings avoid rehashing the event, other Japanese writers have not hesitated to expand upon the superb material. And who can blame them? The scene offers the brilliance of Kyūshū's very best cuisine, her aristocratic, tragic beauty, and a student speaking of revolution on a volcano-specked island.

The story of Byakuren in Love cries out for a Russian writer who will not flinch at her vanity, coquetry, or pessimism. At the start of this Russian novel, she should appear picking at her breakfast (lifelong, she was a bad eater) in Itō's Kyūshū estate, no thought in her mind about the suffering masses as she coldly chastises the servants for tardiness. She needs a scene with the members of the country women's auxiliary, who come around to seek her participation in their social circle. Byakuren must sit upon a floor pillow with the perfect posture of a royal, venturing to say nothing more in her elegant Japanese than that the azaleas have bloomed late this year, while the women from the village—in horrific dialect—gab about the postmaster's chronic dyspepsia and slurp their tea. At the initial meeting with Ryūsuke, the Russian writer must take care that Byakuren not lose an iota of dignity when she joins him for dinner and describes her hopelessness. It should be absolutely clear that Byakuren reels between the pride and the unsteadiness of a woman whose fortune is her lineage and her face.

In the absence of a Russian master, the Japanese novelist Hayashi Mariko has done her utmost with the love story in her recent novel *The Yearnings of Byakuren*. Born almost seventy years after Byakuren, Hayashi does not fly to imaginative heights worthy of the Russians in trying to inhabit her heroine's thought processes. Rather, like a canary caught in an oil slick, she gets bogged down and never recovers. Hayashi has chosen to reduce the range of Byakuren's thoughts to very few, very obvious emotions. Most prominent among those selected is her heroine's constant self-consciousness at being older than Ryūsuke. (Byakuren was thirty-four when she met the twenty-seven-year-old Ryūsuke.) Byakuren no doubt worried about the age difference—Japanese society still does not take lightly a romance between an older woman and a younger man—but perhaps, in contrast to Hayashi's view, she thought of more than her wrinkles and her seniority when she met him, wrote to him, or corrected her posture (to emphasize her dignity as an older woman). "I'm no longer young," Byakuren mutters to herself at a critical moment in Hayashi's novel.

Her own voice reverberated quite naturally and clearly within her. She was beautiful, yes, but she also was no longer young. She could wear a kimono of impeccable taste and attract the ardent attentions of the young man she briefly met. That was all. But she had not stirred up his desires or got him to ask her to undress. Nor did she have the courage to untie her own sashes.

The deficiencies in *The Yearnings of Byakuren* would be of little importance if Hayashi Mariko were not the only writer to whom the Miyazaki family has shown Byakuren and Ryūsuke's letters. Perhaps rightly sensing that a horde of female writers soon would swoop down to laud, demolish, deconstruct, renovate, and otherwise fiddle with Byakuren's life, the family wanted to get its own version of her story into the bookstores quickly. Already some skeptical authors have come forth with writings that diminish Byakuren's heroism. Giving Hayashi access to the letters has proven a wise preemptive strike, since she expresses so much gratitude for the family's help in the afterword that she cannot take anything but an adoring look at Byakuren.

This said, one must bemoan the fact that only a tiny selection from the many letters has been inserted into Hayashi's novel. The excerpts are diamonds gleaming with the hesitations, brazenness, and sorrow of reality. Scattered (sparsely) throughout the dull tin of Hayashi's sentences, the correspondence between the lovers shines with even more luster. Since biographical information about these events remains scarce, it is some consolation that the Miyazaki family at least confirms the accuracy of Hayashi's quotations.

According to this novel, Byakuren embarked upon her grand romance with some caution. The fictional Byakuren sends Ryūsuke a telegram before he has even returned to his office in Tokyo, but tries to stick to business, writing that she wants to correct more mistakes in her manuscript before publication. Meanwhile, he has stopped in Osaka and quickly sends her a letter, thanking her first for her hospitality. The intimate tone of his next sentences shows that they had discussed more than her royalties over the dinner table:

I have been haunted by a number of visions ever since I left Ogura. The wounds upon your soul and your lonely appearance. The murmurings of your heart as it anguishes over human suffering. The listless movements of your body. These thoughts flickered through my mind as I crossed the Shimonoseki Straits.

Miyazaki Ryūsuke also requires a shrewd writer to take over his character development just about here. In Hayashi's novel, he gets neither credible dialogue nor the kind of complicated thought suitable to a committed leftist suddenly consorting with the enemy class. In other accounts too he always behaves like the blandest of revolutionaries, rising to every occasion with offers of solace and sage strategies. The portraits of Ryūsuke have too much of the peerless samurai whose swordplay saves the woman in distress and not enough of his father's very believable, very drunken idealism.

In his 1967 reminiscence, Ryūsuke wrote of how Byakuren spoke to him when they first met. "This is my life," she said. "I write and that is all. I have no other pleasures." Later, as their intimacy developed, she urged him to save her, confessing her frequent thoughts of suicide. It would be churlish to condemn him for capitulating to such a frontal assault on his humane instincts.

In this essay, Ryūsuke explains that aside from everything else, his social conscience accelerated the progress of his love life:

The more I thought about it, the more I found myself at a turning point. What did my political activity and my devotion to the socialist revolution mean? Wasn't this a commitment to save people from oppression? Even if I came across just a single suffering, oppressed individual, surely each and every one of them must be helped. Wasn't Akiko oppressed and suffering? Do it! Do it! These audacious emotions gradually filled my entire being.

The publication of the letters in *The Yearnings of Byakuren* proves beyond a doubt that Byakuren brought some expertise to bear upon effecting their elopement. These letters also show more than the striking contrasts between reformer and poet, socialist and aristocrat, student and older woman. Ryūsuke writes from a world warmed by office chitchat and dreams of the coming uprising, while Byakuren forms her words in a less congenial environment:

I am delighted to hear that you are so well and so busy day after day. Knowing there is nothing I can do about my situation, I was crying just now. Please please tell me, what exactly do you plan to do? I know I shouldn't be so impatient. After all, if I wait long enough, all will be settled naturally. Time will answer all my questions. And so I sit here waiting for that time—the time that will bring the answers. At the most, perhaps in fifty years, I'll get all the answers to my questions. At that time, I will without a doubt be in my grave. When I go to my grave, the answers to the questions I am asking day and night now will finally be horribly clear. Ah—at that time, where will you be buried? I suppose it doesn't matter because you will be so famous and honored by then that you probably won't know where I have been put to rest.

And in a hundred years, there will be a beautiful name unknown to me inscribed next to your glorious grave.

To which Ryūsuke can give only the most pained reply:

You can't imagine with what bitterness I read through your letter. I felt the sarcasm and nastiness in your words. You are being more unreasonable than I wished. Haven't I told you over and over—*my whole body belongs to you*. There is not a bit of falsity in these honest words of mine. I carry this thought with me when I am sleeping and when I am awake, and you alone know this. . . . I am not working hard each day to gain personal glory. Fame and prestige mean nothing to me. If you asked me to throw away everything, I would do it. That is my greatest desire.

The romance proceeds through letters and clandestine meetings (in a tantalizing twist, the fictional lovers meet at the inn owned by Itō's erstwhile mistress, as Byakuren and Miyazaki did in real life). Japanese society had placed many obstacles before the lovers. Greatest of all was the threat of jail for an adulterous married woman and her lover. Divorce laws still overwhelmingly favored men; husbands usually initiated divorces and got custody of the children. A man could flaunt any number of mistresses, but a wife who took a lover was subject to punishment by legal authorities. During the first decades of this century, progressive trends had begun to whittle away at male rights somewhat, and in one ruling a prominent judge had gone so far as to declare, "Men also have a responsibility to behave chastely." Still, in 1921 imprisonment remained a real enough possibility for Miyazaki to warn her: "If Itō files a complaint, we'll go to jail. I've already steeled myself for this. Are you prepared to do the same?"

Ryūsuke not only had to contend with the criminal justice system and Byakuren's moods; he also endured his left-wing political colleagues' serious objections to his consorting with a woman of such an unacceptable class background. At last, in the summer of 1921, he had to give up his editorial position at *Kaihō* and membership in Shinjinkai because of his relationship with "the wife of a mining king and the epitome of petit bourgeois power." Gossip about them started to circulate more widely. Then she became pregnant and the need for action intensified.

In October 1921, Byakuren traveled with Itō to Tokyo, where she was scheduled to attend a royal function. Later, after Itō set off on his return trip to Kyūshū, Byakuren remained behind in Tokyo. She had told her husband that she was going to visit her family, but instead took a taxi to her hideaway and vanished. Although there were rumors about her disappearance, the *Asahi* newspaper waited a day before publishing her notice of divorce in order to guarantee her safe getaway. In exchange, Byakuren and Ryūsuke granted the paper exclusive rights to her last communication with Itō. The letter had been drastically revised by one of Ryūsuke's Shinjinkai colleagues, who sought to inform the Japanese public about the sufferings not only of this lone woman but of Japanese women in general. He and the couple hoped that the publicity would keep Itō from suing and set citizens thinking about the country's social ills. Although the possibility of an extended upheaval did not occur to anyone, the bedlam that resulted went on for a few years. "When we flee, everyone is going to be surprised," Byakuren had written to Ryūsuke in a staggering burst of understatement. "It amuses me to think about that."

•

From "The Sad Love of the Upstart Mining King":

*Byakuren's husband was the coal-mining king Itō Den'emon (1860–1947).
. . . He was the son of a fish peddler and came from a poor family. As a child, he sold fish door to door from a shoulder pole. He did not even have the means to attend a village school and so all his life he certainly seemed to lack culture and education. There's a humorous episode, called "The Coal Has Arrived" that earned him a reputation as a real country hick. In 1903, Den'emon was elected the first representative of the Seiyūkai political party and went to Tokyo. As soon as he arrived there, he sent a telegram*

home to report his safe arrival. He wrote: "The coal has arrived," employing the same phrase that coal miners used for telling each other that shipments of coal had arrived. But in this case, Den'emon used the same words to announce the safe arrival of a human being.

As a result of this incident, Den'emon was stuck with the image of an illiterate, lecherous coal-mining king. This image plagued him during the Byakuren Incident, when people would deride him as "That lustful old man who bought a beautiful woman with his money."

. . . In 1907, Den'emon married his high-born bride Byakuren and set about renovating his main home in Kōbukuro to suit her tastes. He began this project in the hope that these changes might please her, even if only slightly. . . . Byakuren's quarters were on the second floor. She had two connecting rooms of her own, which were designed like formal tea-ceremony rooms. There was a corridor with glass doors that overlooked the huge and magnificent Japanese garden. Byakuren probably spent her days in this room, looking out on the garden and writing poems. . . .

I listened to the guide talk about their house, and he said that Itō Den'emon had pampered Byakuren like a daughter and treated her with much kindness. He gave her whatever she wanted. All he asked in return was that she manage the household efficiently and fulfill her role as a proper wife. That's all. . . .

However! On February 20 [sic], 1921, Byakuren, or more precisely, Itō Akiko, put a full stop to her ten-year marriage to Den'emon. She ran off with Ryūsuke, the son of that adventurer in China, Miyazaki Tōten.

This was immoral!

Unchaste!

An adulterous act! . . .

Itō's friends went wild with anger saying that the selfish and willful Byakuren must have lost her mind to chuck away not only the copper palace, but also the money and the prestige and then send a notice of divorce off to her master. Some rough boys had extreme measures on their minds when they threatened to kill her and throw her into the Onga River. . . .

Itō Den'emon had spent ten hard years unable to rid himself of the trou-
blesome Byakuren. Byakuren was, as he said, an alien element in his
house, a strange species of wife. As it turned out, she was a woman who did-
n't give a second thought to throwing away everything.

When we toured Itō's home and read his little-known reply to her, we
understood that this was a magnanimous, daring man. He was a "good
guy." It was a tragedy that Byakuren intruded upon his life.

•

Until here, the story has proceeded smoothly enough. A beautiful
and talented Japanese princess, clutching only a small suitcase,
dashes off one day in 1921 to join her left-wing lover. She leaves
behind a public letter to the Japanese nation, denouncing the
oversexed old goat who has been her husband and a rotten social
system that enslaves women. The old man seems to deserve every
bit of the condemnation heaped upon him. Has he not spent ten
years exulting in his acquisition of an aristocratic woman? Has he
not enjoyed ordering her to massage his feet in public? Has he not
strutted and preened about his female chattel? Has he not
brought Byakuren to her knees with his threats of divorce? Who
would not sympathize with the downtrodden victim? We prepare
to pay honor to Byakuren as we consider rustling silks, claustral
rooms, and her grievances.

The sludge still on her cloak, Byakuren walks into the spot-
light. In a somber voice she introduces herself as a person just
escaped from purgatory. Yet the catcalls of dissent start to sound
from the upper galleries almost immediately. It is apparent that
certain visitors will not permit us an untainted heroine. As they
rattle off their list of charges, suspicion grows yet again about
another way of looking at the evidence. White turns to black in an
instant; gray grins naughtily in the interstices. She was not bold
but selfish, they tell us. She had no reason to complain about anything, what with her poetry circle, her sumptuous residences, her

jewels, and her fawning, ever-present young men. This was no pioneer, no symbol of female courage and resolve, just an aloof, self-centered, and spoiled brat of a noblewoman.

Many women rise to register protests. She was unkind, they say, a conniver, too promiscuous. In particular, certain critics resent that Byakuren adopted the vocabulary of the liberated woman to justify her elopement. Byakuren claimed to have experienced *jikaku*, self-awakening, and said that this realization propelled her out of her marriage. Why, one cynic asks, did Byakuren start to burn with *jikaku* only when she met a young and attractive lover? A smart woman like that must have felt the stirrings of *jikaku* during all those years before when she was writing poetry and plays about her life. Why did she not see fit to pack her bags and walk out earlier? Byakuren may have attributed her abandonment of Itō Den'emon to a very modern, very correct, very chaste case of *jikaku*, but some doubters see the motivating factor as nothing but old-fashioned lust. And furthermore, even Ibsen's heroine Nora, that personification of *jikaku* worldwide, had goodness enough to inform her husband about her enlightenment before walking out. Nora did not take cruel revenge on him by exposing their private life in banner newspaper headlines.

The woman writer Nagahata Michiko makes the most of this blurred impression. In her element among these dissenters, she refuses to light candles to Byakuren as a sacrifice to masculine power. Nagahata has written a biography, *Flower of Love: The Byakuren Incident*, and throughout it she exhausts herself in dispelling the notion of Byakuren's valor. Nagahata belongs to the breathless school of nonfiction writing and, true to form, spends much of her book gasping over evidence of Byakuren's defects. In relating many snippets about Byakuren's luxury-loving ways, Nagahata smacks her lips over the rumors of assorted love affairs, even tracking down some scorched, possibly intimate correspondence between Byakuren and her friend's husband, salvaged from the ruins of a burned-down house. Unable to resist mentioning a tale about how Itō, his wife, and his mistress slept side by side in the family manor, Nagahata then goes on to blame the arrangement entirely on Byakuren. It is in this biography that we find the bitter testimony of the son Byakuren deserted when she divorced her first husband. Decades later, Nagahata trots out this forsaken offspring, and he gives vent to the resentment he has felt toward a mother who never paid him any attention:

When she became a mother, she was little more than a child herself and so could not be expected to bring me up. Akiko was a self-centered woman with literary pretensions and didn't like her husband. So when I was five, she just left me at my father's house and quickly returned to her own family. . . . When I attended middle school at Gakushū-in, I used to go to class from her family home. Yanagiwara Yoshimitsu and his wife tried their best to arrange a meeting between this long-separated mother and son. Akiko had married into the Itō family by then and finally preparations were made. Did we have an emotional meeting? Not at all. All the warmth seeped away. It was completely cold.

In particular, Nagahata cannot forgive Byakuren for hiring that very young woman to service Itō's sexual needs. ("Byakuren had no sense that she was doing anything wrong," Nagahata has said.) She writes dourly of Byakuren's sex life and at times leaves the bother of documentation behind for the exhilarations of fiction. In reconstructing Byakuren's thought processes, Nagahata supplies the kind of specific detail that is known only to the long-dead.

Yet in the end, Nagahata's approach, though faulty, does inflict real damage on her subject. A splash of petulance now spoils Byakuren's portrait, and nothing can excuse her procurement of another woman for her husband. As a result, others have come forward to espouse Nagahata's positions in a more credible fashion that leaves out the novelistic embroiderings and the back-alley tone. In a recent issue of the poetry magazine *Tanka*, a Japanese woman poet gets the irritated mood just right:

> Itō told everyone in his family to keep silent no matter what was said. I really admire him for that. A true Kyūshū man. . . . I have the impression that Itō was a wonderful person. After all, Akiko had spent his money like water, then one day announced that she had awakened to her plight and wasn't going to be a puppet to the wishes of others anymore. She just suddenly issued her public declaration of divorce. . . . Up to now, the women's histories have viewed this as the story of the barbaric, uneducated Den'emon and the woman who gave up a glamorous life to live in the truth of love. But I'm not convinced. . . . To be absolutely clear about it, this is the story of a woman who betrays her husband and runs off with her young lover. . . . After the fact, she spoke disparagingly of Den'emon, thinking that this would not cause him any pain. I find such arrogance inexcusable.

Itō Den'emon, Byakuren's spurned second husband, would seem the principal beneficiary of these developments. Some, in fact, now seek to rehabilitate him, pointing out that he behaved no worse than many Japanese men of his generation. Now Itō comes to us from where he has languished all these years, protesting that his only mistake was marrying a woman with enough literary firepower and physical beauty to demolish him in the media. In this he echoes the complaints of the scholar whose pet theories get overlooked because other, lesser colleagues write flashier research reports; the novelist from an obscure foreign country who insists that only the lack of a good translator has precluded international acclaim; the prince whose wife gets better press than he. Like them, Itō feels that he has substance behind him and has failed only in presentation. Itō's complaints are not without foundation; he and his cohorts, with cogent points to make, simply cannot match Byakuren in the battle for public opinion. On every front she arrives fully prepared with sad and graceful responses to all queries. Beside this impressive witness, Itō can only gesture clownishly to get any attention.

A few days after the publication of Byakuren's divorce announcement in the newspapers, a reporter in Osaka persuaded Itō Den'emon to sit down for an interview. Published in the form of a reply to his wife, this letter to her constituted his final, official word on the subject. By then he had considered the effects of his wife's departure, and although he did not know that his name would figure in a parody of a popular song ("I am like the dead grass on the river bank / Rejected by Byakuren, Den'emon also is like the dead grass"), his comments show that he had an inkling of ignominies to come:

My home became darker with you there. After your arrival, I had to put up with your hysteria and selfishness, but I never said a word of complaint about you. In spite of that, didn't you tell the world that I was your great enemy? . . . You think of yourself as a daughter of the nobility and feel that respect is due to you as a matter of course. I'm just an ordinary person and have got to where I am today by my own blood and sweat.

Fury rising, he reviews the slights he has suffered:

When you wanted to publish your first book of poetry, *Trodden Images*, you asked me to foot the bill. I handed over 600 yen to pay the publication costs. At this point, I don't want to say anything about the contents of this book you finally published after coming begging to me. Your reputation gradually grew. Here I was, a husband constantly scolded and cursed, but since you were doing something you enjoyed I put up with it, and there were several times when I kept silent and did not say what was on my mind. . . . I am not saying that I am any paragon of virtue. I'm at least ready to admit my own immorality, but you constantly amused yourself with young men and sometimes shocked society with your behavior. I just kept my mouth shut and watched.

Itō lists her acts of duplicity, committed even as she claimed to embark on a life of "truth": the child from her first marriage, whom she never told him about and to whom she sent tuition money every month; and again, that woman she recruited as his sexual partner. Still, he did his duty to her without complaint. His parting shot adequately expresses his position:

Just think—if you really hated it, you could have left after a month. Why was it necessary to endure these past ten years? You sound high and mighty when you say that you fear committing a sin that is not really a sin, but I wonder if you really had the kind of sincere feelings that really fear sin. I regretted this marriage, but as the old saying goes, a husband and a wife have been brought together by a karmic tie, and so I decided to make you see how warped your character is and to make you into a lively, spontaneous person. I tried hard to accomplish this, but all my efforts ended in failure.

Well, why don't you have this man you call your lover figure out if you really are qualified to be a wife or not?

Itō Den'emon's adopted son Hachirō adds more domestic details in *A Short History of Our Family*, the most guileless—and comical—of hatchet jobs. Hachirō, who wrote this account as an act of filial piety to his late father, knew that enemy forces had a head start in the campaign to vilify the Itō family. In spite of this, he believes that the truth will triumph. Humble throughout, but with a stiletto up his kimono sleeve, Hachirō says that he has attempted to be objective ("I have no wish to criticize my stepmother and should not forget the debt I owe her for bringing me up for ten years"). Nonetheless, he finds a way to overcome his gratitude and express his contempt.

In Hachirō's view, Byakuren cast an unrelenting pall on the household from the moment of her arrival. It was the darkness of decorum and female instability for a decade. The warm bustle of a country home teeming with servants, relatives, and business

associates soon gave way to lessons about how to hold the chopsticks correctly. Once she moved in, he couldn't even eat in
peace, and she gave his father ulcers with her fancy ways. Hachirō
sees nothing wrong with marrying a beautiful woman to show off.
After all, he notes, men of great ambition throughout history have
sought to raise their social standing through marriage. "It is a
desire for some kind of distinction, but many people use this as a
stepping stone to huge material gain. My guess is that my father
merely wanted to get some kind of distinction for himself." In the
abstract, Hachirō can excuse the social climbing, but he definitely
had difficulties when the family's very own princess turned up in
person. They met for the first time at a train station in Kyūshū,
and their relationship proceeded from there:

Inside the train, my father said, "This is Hachirō," and my stepmother
only mumbled, "I see." Her face was expressionless and she didn't even
say so much as a word to me.

While Hachirō tried to be a good sport at home, he wishes that
Byakuren had shown more consideration for his feelings. Once
he was standing in their crowded kitchen after a memorial service
and snacking exuberantly on a leftover rice ball. His stepmother
rebuked him for this breach of etiquette:

What on earth are you doing, Hachirō, eating rice standing up like some
beggar? If you do things like that, I won't let you call me "Mother." I'll
make you address me more formally.

This not only mortified Hachirō in front of many servants, but dis-
tressed his real, biological mother, who happened to be present.
As she told him years later, she rushed crying to the bathroom and
even contemplated taking her maltreated son back home with
her. But for Hachirō the pain was greater:

At that time I didn't really think of my biological mother as my real parent, and so I had a strong need to consider whatever mother I found at

the Itōs'—even a stepmother—as my mother. That's why I was so deeply shocked when she told me not to call her "Mother."

Byakuren also told him not to eat the pieces of food that accidentally fell off his dish and onto his tray. The dropped-food rule caused a crisis of conscience because a teacher from a farm family had taught him about the sanctity of every grain of rice. "He told me that even if the rice that the farmers had toiled to produce fell on the floor, it should be picked up and eaten." Furthermore, Byakuren instructed him to eat everything that was put in front of him, and when as a little joke he started to eat his chopsticks, she was not amused. "Although she didn't say anything, I won't forget the expression on her face that was full of her disgust for me. That was the one and only time I opposed her wishes, I believe."

The language-improvement regimes galled Hachirō particularly, and here we see Byakuren at her snootiest. She had come to live in the countryside, which, according to her, had not yet absorbed the benefits of civilization. She insisted on everyone saying "Good morning!" and "Good evening!" each day even though they had survived until then without any such formal greetings. She didn't appreciate the country words they used to address each other and these too had to go. She made the maids practically touch their foreheads to the ground when they bid their master and mistress good night. Hachirō gets his own back when he writes:

These were the customs of the old aristocratic families, and she must have felt that it was her duty as a housewife to educate the Itō household in these customs. Or perhaps she just couldn't stand living among the boorish old customs of the countryside. Or perhaps it was a little of both.

•

From "The Miyazaki-Byakuren Incident: Looking Back" by Asō Hisashi. Kaihō, December 1921:

There is no disputing that this incident, with its enormous impact, was intimately connected to the whole issue of contemporary Japanese social life and exerted much influence. In the history of our world, there have been many examples of incidents essentially similar in significance to this one. There are countless people who may not have taken such a bold step, but who have felt the dangerous stirrings of such actions in their hearts. For a moment let us put the rights and wrongs of the case aside and consider the influence the incident has exerted on our world. Parents who thought of ignoring their daughters' objections and forcing marriages to aristocrats or rich men must be looking at each other red-faced. Men and women who have been inattentive and oblivious to their situation must be thinking seriously about their own marital problems. Husbands who would have been mortified if their wives walked out but who anyway arrogantly ignored their wives' thoughts and emotional needs will probably be circumspect for quite some time. Such then were the effects on society. . . .

There have been furious criticisms regarding this problem. Some people are irate, saying that society's moral code has been ignored. Such people should not criticize Akiko, but should instead turn their rage toward contemporary Japanese society. Those who go on about morality should not be so critical. Why? Because this incident did not start with Akiko, but instead Akiko came to represent the many defects in Japanese society that invited such a breakdown. Akiko's actions were caused by society itself and by a lack of awareness. Rather than railing against Akiko, men and women should reflect upon the many traces of Akiko in their own hearts and try to extricate themselves from trouble at an early stage. To inveigh against Akiko in a high and mighty fashion is infantile and unthinking. Also, it is vital that people who are like Itō and the Yanagiwaras reflect deeply about their own characters and rid themselves of such tendencies.

In summary, this incident has shown us many different problems in present-day society. We have been compelled to think deeply about the institution of marriage. As part of this, we must consider the great number of defects in the family system. The incident has also exposed the lack of awareness among modern women. Their weakness has also been entirely exposed. But this incident has also made contemporary wives wish to live meaningful lives, and they have gradually begun to awaken from the ignorance of the past. Indeed, society is progressing even now, and there will be no stopping this onward movement, whether one agrees with the process or not. Women are born to live out their lives and it is natural that they should wish to live life to its fullest. There is no reason why they must be the slaves of men. There is no law that says that one must continue in an unsatisfactory marriage until death just because one was not fully awakened in the past. Having once recognized a lack of awareness, one should embark on future activities in a state of awareness. . . .

To move beyond this incident—even if we get rid of such notions as marrying for money or for high social position, we still have the unsolved problem of how to deal with love and the institution of marriage. I have no objection to making love the basic condition of marriage, but once we do this we will confront certain difficulties. If human beings fall in love once and once only and the first love continues for a long time, then all will be well. But human beings have the capacity to fall in love any number of times in their lives, and on top of that they tend to tire easily of their partners.

Talk of free love is very common nowadays, but if the man says that he is abandoning his home because he has become tired of his wife and fallen in love with someone else, the women in our present society will become pitiful creatures. To begin with, women of today cannot support themselves and so they will not be able to buy the next day's food and clothing. Let us suppose that the economic system changes and women can be economically independent. In such a case, no one will be concerned if both members of the couple tire of each other at the same time and find themselves new loves, but tragedy will result if one side still loves the other.

How will those who publicly promote the primacy of love and free love deal with such a situation?

•

Yanagiwara Byakuren lived for forty-six more years after her notice of divorce appeared in the newspapers. While most accounts trail off after she leaves Itō, the next few years brought her any number of astonishing predicaments. She would endure a second lengthy period of house arrest because her family refused to permit her marriage to Miyazaki, give birth to their son in seclusion, and go into hiding at a religious retreat. She would also be kept on her toes by rightist thugs constantly ordering her to become a nun or kill herself.

Sadly for the biographer, reliable evidence about these doings is in short supply. To this day, the Miyazaki family chooses to release little information about their most famous female relative. She was courageous, she wrote poetry, she brought them celebrity, but she had offended the morality of the nation with her illicit romance. Perhaps the less said about such kin, the better.

In December 1921, Itō divorced Byakuren without pressing charges against her and forever after forbade mention of her name in his house. Yet there were legal procedures still to be completed that prevented her immediate marriage to Miyazaki. Right-wing ruffians threatened to track her down if she ever tried to set up housekeeping with her lover, drag her out onto the street, and burn her living quarters to the ground. Against a background of daily demands for her ritual suicide, Byakuren began to live— pregnant and not legally married—with Miyazaki. Soon her family stepped in and put an end to this arrangement.

More basic facts would do much to transform what is now a stormy, enigmatic landscape into a recognizable scene with familiar landmarks. It would be helpful to know, for example, exactly how Byakuren's family broke up the lovers' household. What precise words were exchanged on that winter day when the Yanagiwaras stepped in to end the idyll? How did her relatives spirit Byakuren out of the house she shared with Miyazaki? What arguments persuaded her that violence could be averted only if she went to talk with her brother back at the family residence? Hayashi Mariko sets this scene on a snowy night. "Your living like this will cause the Miyazakis a lot of trouble too," her sister and sister-in-law tell Byakuren in Hayashi's novel. "So it's best that you come home to talk about what to do next." Because their car has broken down along the way, these fictional characters have to walk through the snow to the station. This provides Hayashi with opportunity for a tense evening scene. Actually, snow seems too mild a backdrop to illustrate this episode; it would not be too much for all the stars in the heavens to turn magenta at this moment or for the willows to speak. Such extraordinary portents would not be out of place, since Byakuren's walk away from her lover and her return to her family meant capitulation not only to thugs, but also to blood ties, custom, and centuries of culture.

There is some dispute about whether Byakuren's enraged brother actually cut her hair off as soon as she reached the family home, or some time passed before Byakuren herself performed this act of contrition. Others doubt that such an old-fashioned punishment was ever exacted. There is no question that once Byakuren reached home, her family refused to allow her to leave again or to communicate with Miyazaki. Her brother reportedly promised her that if she killed herself to expiate the family's shame, he would follow suit. Is it true that she managed to communicate with Ryūsuke by writing on paper from the shoji screens? Again, these tidbits come from the novelist Hayashi Mariko. "Save me," Byakuren supposedly wrote on the shoji paper, "Help me," and later, "I want to die." After she gave birth to her baby boy, still held prisoner in the family home, did nasty servants in fact tell her that Itō would claim the child as his own? In her reminiscences, Byakuren recalls a more stoical state of mind during these travails: "I had confidence in the future and so I didn't lose heart or put up a fruitless struggle against my fate."

Fearing more demonstrations after the birth of Byakuren's baby, the Yanagiwaras trundled her and the child off to the retreat of the Ōmoto sect in Ayabe, Kyoto Prefecture. Accounts of her stay there describe her attempts to learn aikido for self-defense, her walks through the countryside disguised as a farmer, and her musings about whether there could be anything worse than life with a disagreeable companion. Finally Miyazaki did manage to locate her, and they were at last able to marry. Once informed of this visit, her family ordered Byakuren—without Ryūsuke—to the home of wealthy Tokyo friends.

In the end, heaven and earth, combining forces on the couple's behalf, moved, and this got her family and other citizens of Tokyo to let the lovers live together. In September 1923, the Great Kantō Earthquake devastated much of the city. After this catastrophe, most people had enough on their hands with fires, starvation, and the murderous rage of some survivors. No longer could people take time off to menace the two most famous lovers in Japan for their immorality. Since the Miyazakis' home had survived the earthquake, they could send emergency supplies over to where Byakuren was living. Her hosts, grateful for this thoughtfulness and angry at the Yanagiwaras for not sending over even a single inquiry about their situation, finally released Byakuren in the care of the Miyazakis' messenger.

Over the more than four decades of marriage that followed, Miyazaki Ryūsuke campaigned for the betterment of the underclass and Byakuren performed her duties as the wife of an activist. She sold her poetry on street corners to bring in money for his elections, and when her consumptive husband was too ill to attend political gatherings, she read her works aloud to appreciative crowds. She wrote and earned money, bore another child, and edited her own poetry magazine. As the years passed, Byakuren absorbed the Chinese influences in her husband's family. Photographs show her at home, straight-backed in a Chinese dress, and later, posed in China with government dignitaries like Zhou En-lai.

It is said that Byakuren never recovered from her son Kaori's death during World War II. He perished in a bombing raid just four days before the surrender.

That knocking on my wooden door
all the long night through
is only you, wind
    Wake me up to say my
    child's come back home!

In your memory
Mother still the man's
kimono you left behind
    Only now I do not
        cry

When she read her poems of grief over the radio, many other mourning mothers responded with their own tragic stories. Byakuren joined with these women to launch a crusade, and until the end of her life the former "Lover of the Century" campaigned throughout Japan for an end to the wars that robbed mothers of their children.

UNO CHIYO LIKES TO SAY THAT SHE GOT THE
idea for *Confessions of Love* in 1929,
after meeting with Tōgō Seiji. She
had been writing a novel and had
decided to include a lovers' suicide.
Since she felt that she could not
quite convey the emotional pressures
of such a moment without further
research, she telephoned Tōgō, an
artist who had just emerged from a
highly publicized double-suicide
attempt, and asked if he would please
give her some insight into the man's
side of the experience. According to
Uno, Tōgō agreed to meet her at the
White Night, a Tokyo bar. When he
arrived, he was the image of post-sui-
cide-pact chic, for his neck, which
he had slashed in the attempt, was
swathed in a white bandage. Tōgō
did not immediately tell his story.
"Can't talk here," he said. "Too many
of my friends around." He invited
Uno back to his home in the Tokyo
suburbs. There, she reports, they
spent the night together on the
bloodstained futon that had been

used for the failed suicides. Even now, nearly sixty years later, Uno savors the dazzlement of that evening. "We fell upon each other like animals," she recalled in a recent conversation. "You see, it was the bandage on his neck that got to me."

The invitation to sleep on the celebrated futon also won her reckless heart, and although she had arrived with only her handbag as luggage, intending the briefest of social visits, she remained with Tōgō for five years. Uno came away from this union with a vermilion-lacquered bureau that had once belonged to the novelist Tanizaki Junichirō and a new flair for color. (Tōgō had a way with white.) She also made a detailed record of Tōgō's reminiscences, which she eventually shaped into *Confessions of Love*, her most popular work.

At the time Uno Chiyo began to live with Tōgō Seiji, she had already made a name for herself in the Japanese literary world. Her fiction had been well received by the critics, and she was noted for the immense dash of her private life. She had always been a beauty: her skin was perfect; her eyes glistened like dew on plums. She demonstrated other important gifts as well—in matters of prose style and romantic catastrophe.

Uno Chiyo is one of the very few Japanese women with an established literary reputation, having made her mark early by publishing stormy love stories based on her own entanglements. While other women writers of her generation wrote of social issues (the excesses of the militarists, hunger on city streets), she stuck to the smaller world of personal heartbreak. She became famous, even notorious, for her passionate descriptions of torment beside a flickering Tokyo brazier and of frail, frail shoulders trembling beneath a loose kimono. Beginning in her early twenties, she married more times than any nice Japanese girl would ever care to admit. Along the way, there were other companions—real, or cooked up by the scandalmongers. "You have to see Uno's life in the context of Japanese literature," a Japanese writer friend told me, with a smile. "Our fiction since *The Tale of Genji*, a thousand years ago, always has the hero flitting from one woman to the next. Uno-san was different. She took the man's role. She was a female Genji, and she went from man to man. You sense also that she didn't choose the men out of respect for their minds but because their faces were pretty—just as men choose women in our books. And remember, it wasn't simply lust that drove her on but *kōkotsu*—a kind of rapturous enchantment that for us Japanese is always a very kind, very gentle emotion."

Uno was not content merely to drop demure hints from behind her fan about a new lover's arrival. She went on to describe his every idiosyncrasy in racy Japanese for her reading public. As if this were not enough, she started a side business designing kimonos; her unconventional fabrics, splashed with cherry blossoms, further decorated a flamboyant public image. Now ninety years old,[*] she looks with a wry eye upon the Japanese media as they still try to decide whether she is a literary eccentric, too sex-crazy for serious consideration, or Uno Chiyo, writer, designer, femme fatale—a sturdy and independent modern woman. In the past few years, there has been a new burst of celebrity because her autobiography, a best-seller published in 1983, has been made into a television series starring a popular actress. And last spring Tokyo's Teikoku Theater staged a new production of her 1957 novella, *Ohan*, with an extraordinary rainstorm and a cast composed in part of surrealistic dolls from Bunraku, Japan's puppet theater.

I had recently completed an English translation of *Confessions of Love*, and on a trip to Japan I went to pay my respects to the author. *Ohan* had just opened, and she was busy with the attendant festivities. Uno lives in Aoyama, one of Tokyo's most expensive neighborhoods, and owns her apartment house. Her kimono

---

[*]Uno Chiyo died in 1996, eight years after this was written.

shop takes up the first floor. Now that the price of land has sky-rocketed in Japan's big cities, mention of her address invariably incites envy in younger Japanese writers ("Let's write! To live in Aoyama!"). The cherry trees were not yet in bloom in Tokyo the afternoon of my visit, but an arrangement of early-flowering wild mountain-cherry branches had been brought into her living room, as if to promise that spring was on the way. A Bunraku puppet, handmade by a master in Shikoku, brooded wonderfully beside a collection of scrolls and ceramic bowls.

As I sat down to tea on the tatami floor, she apologized for wearing an everyday kimono. Uno's hair is reddish-orange and rises in a pile of curly locks. Her complexion, beneath layers of face powder, remains relatively unwrinkled. Small (just under five feet), she has complained in print about her thinness, yet she wears a kimono majestically and sits with unwavering posture on the floor pillow. The peppy red hair and fastidious makeup do little to distract attention from signs of old age—her thick eyeglasses and failing hearing. Having cultivated the appearance of an ageless romantic, she is said to be fussy about photographs.

That day she was not pleased with the production of *Ohan*, and seemed especially glum about the actor playing the hero. The weak-willed and vacillating lover Kanōya—a stock Uno male—had been portrayed with what she considered excessive vigor. "He's too good an actor for the part," she explained, in a shaky falsetto. "If you go to see it, be sure to go late in the run. The acting troupes don't rehearse much these days, and it shows."

Uno is modest enough about her literary efforts to find a meeting with her translator an excruciatingly embarrassing experience. Having one of her books published in English invites too much direct, non-Japanese-style praise for comfort. At first it was easier for us to pretend that she had never written *Confessions of Love* and that I had never translated it. Given more time, and more vague remarks about how cold the Tokyo winter had been, we might even have been persuaded that neither of us was actually present. Since she chose to stick to earthier subjects, we discussed the foods that would ensure long life (she believes in spinach) and the importance of a proper attitude ("I have no interest in dying, because I always think that tomorrow might bring something exciting"). She almost never appears now without a female assistant, who vehemently guards her boss's literary reputation and in general keeps the rabble out. This assistant was clearly concerned about a recent rash of foreign women showing an interest in Uno. As she looked at me, she seemed to contemplate the alarming possibility that these foreigners—a conspicuously unfashionable lot—might write essays transforming the life-loving, glamorous Uno Chiyo into a bookish, carelessly turned-out woman not unlike themselves.

In her tenth decade, Uno would like to forget her hardships and the long years she spent on some of her literary projects, and glory instead in the romantic wars she fought across various Japanese cities. And who can blame her for taking to the idea that her writings were spontaneously dashed off while she was on the fast train to Izu, en route to yet another hot-springs rendezvous? "Whenever people start to talk about literary theories," the assistant informed me darkly, "our sensei always tells them to go out and do some real work." Uno herself seemed more worried about an issue less important to sober members of the literary establishment: "This playbill says that I married only famous men, but the truth is that I married them and then they became famous."

Uno Chiyo's lack of interest in literary exegesis is not surprising, since throughout her long career she never insisted upon links to high art. A lovely face, after all, helped her escape from a lifetime of preparing tea in provincial Iwakuni, where she was born in 1897. She started out as a country girl, accustomed to walking barefoot through the winter snows, and became one of those

Japanese women who somehow find the courage to stride off as they like, leaving a rigid social structure behind them.

The situation of women is not an item that Japanese patriots usually include in their lists of the nation's greatest achievements. Sweeping generalizations about the female plight are dangerous and always subject to clarification, but perhaps it is safe to state that feudal Japanese codes of ethics, whose influences are still felt today, do not show much enthusiasm for the liberation of women. Nevertheless, there have always been Japanese women who have defied social conventions. These women have been strong, very strong indeed, and even the fiercest female warriors of the West have cause to envy their daring.

In the 1920s, Uno's heyday, a Japanese woman was expected to enter into a marriage arranged by her family. She would subsequently spend several decades under the hearty supervision of her mother-in-law, no doubt dreaming only of the moment when she would become an impossible mother-in-law herself. From the start, Uno ignored the Confucian teaching that a female was to live in successive submission to her father, her husband, and finally her sons. Uno's appearance caused problems in Iwakuni, since she could never bring herself to blend quietly into the population. She had little tolerance for boredom and never begrudged the extra effort required to entertain or shock. In the opinion of the principal of a primary school where she taught as a very young woman, Uno-san dressed in kimonos too flashy for a country schoolteacher. To make matters worse, she had become convinced that her dark complexion was magically, beautifully transformed by face powder, and she would not go anywhere without her makeup. When she arrived at the school yard wearing makeup for the first time, her spectacular glow caused a sensation among teachers and students alike. She received the compliment of a love letter written in blood, and then a marriage proposal that ended in a sexual assault. Finally she was forced to resign from her teaching job after becoming involved in a forbidden romance with another teacher. In "Tales of My Youth," one of her numerous memoirs, she recalls,

The cherry trees were in full bloom when I at last had to resign from the school. They didn't want to tell the children or the people of the village the embarrassing truth about why I was leaving, and they decided to make up a pleasanter story, to keep the school from looking bad. So the principal of the school suggested that I say I was leaving to study in Tokyo. One morning, the schoolchildren were assembled in the playground so that I could say my farewells. I know that you'll find this strange, but although I should have been embarrassed to say good-bye to the children under those circumstances, instead I decked myself out in quite a costume for the occasion and went off to school. I completely forgot that many teachers and children would be there looking at me, since all I wanted was to see my boyfriend. I was dying to have him think, Isn't she cute! Isn't she pretty! I did my hair up like a geisha and wound a dotted pink ribbon around it. Now, where on earth could you find a woman teacher in a purple formal skirt, her hair decorated with a dotted pink ribbon? I had no sooner gone through the school gate than I was called to the principal's office. He told me that I could not possibly appear in front of the children dressed like that. He sternly instructed me to hide in the janitor's small office, at the side of the back gate, until the sun went down. I sat despondently in the janitor's room. From the high window I could peep at the school playground, where the cherry trees were all in bloom. Many children had come, and since the principal's words were carried by the breeze I could hear him saying, "I would like to tell you that the teacher you like so much has suddenly become ill and cannot be with us today to say farewell. When she gets better, she will be leaving us for Tokyo."

Uno went to Korea to escape from this scandal, but soon realized that the beloved colleague she had left behind correctly feared that his future would be wrecked by the ferocity of her passions. "I waited for a letter," her memoir continues.

I lived only for the day I would receive something from him. I didn't hear from him for a long time, and then, one day, I received a letter of farewell. He said he was afraid of love. He was afraid of me, who was so blinded by love. He wanted us to part! He said that maybe someday, if we had the chance, we might meet again. It was full of the overwrought, vague promises that everyone writes in such letters.

Never one to avoid a messy scene, she rushed back from Seoul to confront the cowardly gentleman. Coincidentally—on a whim, she now declares—she bought a knife on her way to his home. "I hadn't brought any souvenirs from Seoul for my family. . . . And we really needed a good kitchen knife. I thought it would make my mother happy." Her boyfriend's discovery of this weapon tucked into the obi of her kimono added considerably to the complexity of the moment.

This kind of hot confrontation is at the heart of Uno's fiction, and once her writing career was launched she would waste no time after each experience in getting every breathless moment down on paper. Her intense tales of love lost, revived, then lost again can be romantic fluff, but at her best she captures a very human craziness, as her lovers try to settle matters between them once and for all. Her prose style has also brought her much praise: "rich, supple, sensual," according to one enchanted Japanese critic, and "overflowing with womanly feelings." Uno's characters tend to be impulsive, and the men—more often than not utterly despicable—are memorable. The women bear a remarkable resemblance to the author. They often love unwisely, gaining our sympathy with the vastness of their affections. These fervent women throw themselves at one undeserving man after another, but at least have the canniness and resilience to pick themselves up after things have calmed down somewhat. They are a rarity among fictional Japanese females even today, for they have boundless confidence and occasionally gloat over their own exploits.

In recent years, however, Uno has turned away from these energetic heroines, choosing to interpret her passionate females' doings in a cooler light. When we met in Tokyo, she was reluctant to dwell upon her heroines' madder escapades—especially those that suggested a mild form of erotic derangement. Times have changed, of course, and what was forbidden decades ago can, with a little fiddling, become a mark of modern assertiveness or self-reliance. Uno has lately become a kind of literary family counselor for her fans (she has even written an advice column for the newspapers), and family counselors don't always like to remember moments of lunacy when they turned up at their boyfriend's home with a knife or took too many sleeping pills to drown their sorrows. "I believe that cheerfulness is a virtue and melancholy a sin," she told me, going to the trouble of inscribing the calligraphy for this sentence in my notebook. "That's really how I would sum up my view of life."

This gloss is perhaps permitted a grande dame of Japanese letters looking back on the past from a magnificent sitting room; indeed, the record shows that Uno remained relatively cheerful through it all, but that she was also willful, fickle, ambitious, shrewd, and, frequently, hysterical. There are, for example, her early days in Tokyo, where she arrived in 1917, not long after the heartbreaking episode with the teacher. According to her present version, she was the simplest of farm girls let loose in the big city. She arrived there, at the very center of the universe, in the company of her cousin Fujimura Tadashi, who turned out to be the most luckless of her husbands. Her family had been hard at work trying to get her respectably married off, and her cousin, excellent husband material, was the prize they sought. As for Fujimura, he thought he had found for a lifetime companion a beauty, a seamstress, a cook. He would soon know better.

They took an apartment on the second floor of a beautician's house, on a lane near Tokyo Imperial University (the present

University of Tokyo), and Fujimura matriculated there. "But we couldn't depend on funds from home, and so he just registered at the university and never attended classes," Uno recalls in her autobiography. "He worked at one of the government offices, while I also worked—at times as a clerk for a magazine publisher, at times as a private tutor—but these jobs did not bring us enough money. . . . Finally I became a waitress at the Enrakuken, a Western-style restaurant on a corner in Hongō-sanchōme."

The restaurant was just across the street from Chūō Kōron, a noted publishing house. In the brief period that Uno waited on tables at this establishment—she stayed only eighteen days—she managed to meet some of Japan's leading editors and writers, who often stopped off for beer and snacks on their way to Chūō Kōron. While Uno's recollections of those days insist upon her provincial innocence, one can make out the crasser notes of a determined country girl hustling for a place in the wide world:

Because I worked at Enrakuken, my fate took an unexpected turn. There was a guest who always arrived for lunch. . . . He had a healthy, ruddy face, and wore fashionable Western-style clothes over his muscular body. He never said a word, always sat himself down at one of my tables, ate with raging speed, emptied a glass of beer in one gulp, then, after paying for the meal, plunked down a big silver fifty-sen coin for a tip and quickly left. I never in my wildest dreams would have believed that this was Takita Choin, famous editor-in-chief at Chūō Kōron, just across the street from us. . . . While I worked there, Akutagawa Ryūnosuke, Kume Masao—literary people so famous that even I recognized them—came into the restaurant with Takita Choin. Kon Tōkō, who wasn't exactly what you could call a writer or an artist then, would also come around, and immediately look over at me. He'd wait outside every night until the restaurant closed and see me home.

Fiction based on actual events has long been a staple of Japanese literature. For generations, Japanese authors have fought with their fathers, eloped with geishas, joined communist cells, recanted, attempted to hang themselves, and then rushed back to their studies to transcribe reliable accounts for their novels, short stories, and poems. Akutagawa Ryūnosuke—the creator of *Rashōmon*—served as witness to Uno Chiyo's first days in Tokyo. Although better known for his imaginary tales, even Akutagawa depended on the facts occasionally. He took an interest in Uno, and she is said to be the model for the waitress in his story "Scallions." He immediately discerned that here was a young woman who would not be boiling noodles for the rest of her life.

"Okimi-san must have been fifteen or sixteen, but looked more adult," Akutagawa writes of his fictional waitress. "Her skin was white, her eyes cool and knowing, and even though the tip of her nose curved upward, she had a standard sort of beauty. Her hair was parted in the center and stuck with a forget-me-not hairpin." The narrator of "Scallions" reveals that Okimi-san was not an ordinary waitress in her private interests, either:

I suggest you peek into the second floor of a beautician's house on a nearby lane. . . . This is where Okimi-san dwells when she's not at the café. The second floor is a six-tatami room with a low ceiling. . . . There on the tea table she uses for a desk is a collection of not very new books in Western bindings— . . . *The Collected Poems of Tōson, The Life of Matsui Sumako, Carmen,* and some others. . . . I regret to report that I don't see a single one of my books there.

The narrator is not the only man to find Okimi-san noteworthy; a creative sort named Tanaka, based on the young and eventually well-known author Kon Tōkō, is thoroughly smitten: "The talented Tanaka writes poems, plays the violin, paints in oils, has worked as an actor, is good at poetry games, and can also play the Satsuma lute. But the problem is that no one knows which is his real occupation and which are hobbies." As for Okimi-san, she is ready to fall in love, and Tanaka, so abundantly blessed with arty gifts, seems the likely candidate. But Okimi-san has a cagey side, and at times—when gazing at the moon, or hearing her heart roar like the wind-swept sea—she senses "a dark cloud of uneasiness" passing over her soul.

Astute instincts finally lead her elsewhere, on the very day that Tanaka takes her out on a big date. He is dreaming of escorting her to an intimate dinner when the young couple happens to pass a vegetable stall bursting with turnips, scallions, potatoes, carrots. In a moment, Okimi-san is jolted back to reality; she sees that the scallions for sale that day are very cheap. "Okimi-san had until this moment been intoxicated with thoughts of love and art, but her real life, which dozed within this bliss, woke up in an instant." She thinks of all the money she could save and bolts for the stall: "I'd like two bunches of scallions, please." With this, Tanaka's romantic visions of an evening at a restaurant vanish: "What floated up before his eyes was a mountain of scallions, and a tag that said they were four sen a bunch."

Akutagawa's irreverent story goes a long way toward fixing the young Uno Chiyo's character definitively, for Okimi-san's alternately dreamy and clever voice can be heard in many of her writings. Like that fictional waitress, Uno usually had enough of her wits about her so that even at her most overwrought she could keep a lookout for bargains in scallions. Her men too are defined here; they tended to be handsome dandies like Tanaka—artistic, but extremely slow in their reactions to everyday phenomena. Like Okimi-san, Uno occasionally wished to be viewed as a lovely and ladylike force in the background, essentially a homebody, strong but pliant, forbearing, the epitome of a docile Japanese female. But her hardy personality got in the way time after time, and try as she might, her actions did not always coincide with the ideal.

In 1920, Uno and Fujimura moved to Sapporo, on Hokkaidō, Japan's northernmost island, but even in that snow-covered city she remained alert to possibility and never forgot the influential friends she had made in Tokyo. In Sapporo, "the winter came early," she writes in another memoir, *My Literary Reminiscences*. "The snow reached the house's eaves and throughout the day I could hear the sleigh bells." Although she says that she was absolutely content to be at home waiting for her husband's return each evening, domestic tranquility was never Uno Chiyo's forte. It is difficult to believe that only the Hokkaidō snowflakes were on her mind as she watched the blizzards blow outside her window. Eventually she took up sewing to earn money, and soon bought a rather Spartan house for herself and her flabbergasted husband. It was the first of more than a dozen residences she was to acquire or build over the coming decades. Among them were a simple mountain retreat suitable for Zen austerities, a Japanese estate with long corridors in the manner of Kyoto's finest villas, and a Western-style residence built along the lines of the Parthenon. "I always build a house when I start something new in my life," she has written. "That's my custom. I'm like a snail crawling along with a shell on its back. I build a house, and then I start roaming around. Maybe I feel that by building a house I'll stabilize the insecure life I'm about to embark upon."

While she was still sweetly cooking meals for Fujimura in Sapporo, she came upon a Tokyo newspaper that asked readers to submit short stories for a contest. She had started to weary of carting her sewing all over the countryside for her customers. She needed money, but she also wanted to be able to work at home. She decided to write. "Remember, I don't want people to think that I am a great literary lady, with many ideas about literature," she told me firmly. "I wrote for money, and, frankly speaking, I wish I had earned more."

She submitted a story entitled "The Powdered Face," and won first prize. Exhilarated by her success and stupefied by the amount of money a single short story could bring, she immediately set out

to write another, and sent it to no less a personage than Takita
Choin, the editor of *Chūō Kōron* magazine who had left her all
those fifty-sen tips at the restaurant. When she received no reply,
Uno resolutely set off for Tokyo in the spring of 1922 to find out if
anyone had even read it. She fully intended to return to her husband in a few days, she says, and left a heap of dirty clothes and a
stack of dirty dishes to be attended to upon her return. Once she
reached Tokyo, she headed straight for Takita's office. He
answered her question by showing her the latest issue of *Chūō
Kōron*, in which her story appeared.

"All people have one or two times in their lives that they look
back on and say, 'Oh, I was happy then,' " she wrote in "Tales of
My Youth." "Well, today I'll tell you the story of a time when I was
really happy. . . . I wasn't some miserable young girl anymore. I
was a woman writer!" Emotionally extravagant in joy as in disaster, Uno just had to go home to Iwakuni to tell her family the good
news. Even in her most jubilant moments she was still the beauty,
and beauties understand the importance of dressing for the part:

I spent a whole day running around Tokyo and bought a fancy kimono
outfit as dazzling as I could find, a flowing lace shawl, and a parasol. Ah,
that night I put on a resplendent kimono such as I had never pictured
even in my dreams, threw the flowing lace shawl over my shoulders, and
entered the train. My face was painted as brightly as a flower.

She got off at the station from which she had departed with so little distinction years before.

Please imagine what I looked like. When the train arrived, my mother
and five brothers and sisters were waiting for me on the platform, lined
up like sparrows. . . . "Okaka!" I called my mother just as I used to, long
ago. . . . I was so elated that I sashayed out to the front of the station like
a queen. . . . There were rickshaws lined up in front to pick up customers.
"Okaka! Get in!" I said. "Tarō-san, you, too, and Jirō-san and Hana-chan
and Saburō-san and Shirō-chan, get in. Let's all go," I yelled, calling for

seven rickshaws. In the countryside in those days, you didn't take a rickshaw only for convenience. (The station was very close to town and you could easily walk.) Brides took rickshaws. Or geishas hurrying off to their customers. And bands of actors who came to towns with their plays would ride around town in rickshaws waving banners advertising their performances. . . . Thanks to the way we rode home in our rickshaws like an acting troupe, overnight the whole town knew that its strange girl had returned home.

In the excitement of her success, Uno forgot the charm of Sapporo's sleigh bells and the husband she had left behind. There are accounts of telegrams, emergency visits by in-laws, grim silences, but she was obdurate. This was the end of her brief tenure as a respectable Japanese housewife. She has always had trouble justifying this sudden change of plans; when a heroine in one of her stories finds herself in the same situation, Uno blandly speculates: "She didn't think about her husband who was waiting for her. Was it because Hokkaidō was quite far from where she was in the countryside? Or maybe she had forgotten him because there was still snow on the ground in Hokkaidō but here the whole town was bursting with cherry blossoms."

How could she think of returning to Sapporo when in her mind's eye she was in the latest nest she had found for herself in Tokyo, using her manuscript money to pay for the repair of her shoji screens. She had gone to Tokyo intending to stay only long enough to find out about her manuscript, but once there she gave up her former existence and started afresh with gusto. "When I look back," she has mused with all the deadpan philosophical objectivity she can muster, "I see that the year and eight months of married life in Hokkaidō was the period of my life most filled with hope. That was the only time I ever lived a very regular life, just like everyone else."

Unlike most of Uno Chiyo's adventures, this abandonment of her first husband does not go down well with contemporary

Japanese women. Many applaud her verve and her psychological ruggedness. But leaving Fujimura behind without a gentle word bespeaks cruelty and that most heinous of Japanese character flaws—*wagamama*, or selfishness. In Japan, even a *tonderu onna*—a liberated, "flying woman"—is expected to have a kind heart. A young Japanese woman television producer who has taken an interest in Uno's life clucks her tongue over such behavior: "She would just leave the clothes hanging out on the line and go off with a new man. That kind of thing gets to be a habit."

The cause of Uno's new burst of energy was not difficult to find: she had met her next husband, the writer Ozaki Shirō. The facts of this particular romance have been blurred by fictional accounts that both principals inevitably contributed later; the literary evidence has it that she responded with total sympathy to his painful stutter, while he was absolutely disarmed when the sake she drank at dinner went to her head. Neither neglects to mention the bohemian allure of the Kikufuji Hotel, where Ozaki lived, up on Kikuzaka Hill near the University of Tokyo. Of the separate room he discreetly rented for her there Uno notes, "It was of no help in quieting the fires that burned between us." They soon moved to the then sparsely populated district of Magome, some distance from the center of the city. Their home was a small straw-thatched farmhouse, set in a radish patch. In those cramped quarters the two young writers spent their days together.

By the time Uno and Ozaki had set up housekeeping among the radishes, they had earned more than their share of publicity. In 1922 a Japanese wife did not leave her husband for another man, and their activities had made the newspapers. In an autobiographical novel, Ozaki reports that he decided to take the offensive by writing a newspaper article of his own, in which he challenged public opinion by proudly declaring, "I stole her like a wild dog!" Those were the years of "Taishō democracy," when foreign ideas like liberalism and internationalism had great influence in the big cities. Serious thinkers agitated for universal male suffrage and discussed the merits of socialism, Marxism, anarchism. More frivolous citizens investigated jazz, film, and the foxtrot. Among the most visible products of the era was a group of progressive women who came to be called *modan gāru* (modern girls)—or *mo-ga* for short. Their companions were *modan bōi* (modern boys) or *mo-bo*.

According to the literary critic Ozaki Hotsuki, the *mo-bo* was always something of a fop, commonly associated with fancy clothing, but the more daunting *mo-ga* appeared to have grave intentions behind her up-to-date looks. It was suspected that she sought nothing less than the collapse of the old, repressive Confucian attitude toward women and their role in society. Famous *mo-ga* like the actress Matsui Sumako (whose biography was on Okimisan's tea table) captured the imagination of the timid and the trapped. Matsui's extraordinary life (her shocking stage roles, her various marriages, her very public alliance with a married man) had stirred much controversy, and her boldness was still felt even after her death. "I have decided to join my teacher after all," Matsui had written matter-of-factly in her suicide note. "I ask only that you make sure that we are buried together."

It is no surprise that the *mo-ga*, at times shedding her kimono for short-sleeved Western-style dresses and high heels, cut a terrifying figure. Uno Chiyo was of course well on her way to becoming a *mo-ga* supreme, in her rustic abode with her new husband. Soon like-minded literary figures moved in nearby. "My new husband had an open and sunny personality, and every day many guests would come to our tiny home," Uno recalls in *My Literary Reminiscences*.

It was all very pleasant and amusing—you might say that we ran a small, fashionable salon there. If we had been living in the middle of town, I am sure that the neighbors would have complained, but we held our small village salon every night until late, and the chanting of the old historical ballads and Bon dance songs rang out loud and clear across the radish field. . . . In every house there was dancing, which was then in great fashion, but no one had Western-style rooms. So we would roll mats out over the tatami flooring and the men and women would take each other's hands and dance. Since we danced on mats, our feet would get caught along the edges, and I'm afraid we didn't dance very gracefully.

But Uno Chiyo's transformation into a bona fide *mo-ga* was not to be complete until she abandoned the old-fashioned long hairstyle, fastened in the back, which Japanese women had traditionally worn with their kimonos. Beyond everything else, Ozaki Hotsuki writes, "the trademark of the *mo-ga* was her bobbed hair." To be strictly correct, the scandalous hairstyle had to be short at the back and on the sides, with Dutch-boy bangs in front. It was not a haircut to be undertaken casually. Uno writes that she decided to take this huge step in order to look more attractive alongside her new husband, who was a trifle younger than she. "I very seriously thought that if I could just get up enough courage to cut my hair I would definitely look not one, but three or five years younger than Shirō. When I finally screwed up the courage to cut my hair, I looked not three or five years younger but seven years younger."

At times, this daring *mo-ga* haircut produced just the results predicted by dour supporters of the status quo. For example, Ineko, the wife of the poet Hagiwara Sakutarō, took a look at the bobbed Uno and decided to take ten years off her age in the same way. Ineko unfortunately got carried away by her newfound youth and eloped with an eighteen-year-old student. Her husband, left to care for their two young children, was forced to return to his hometown of Maebashi. He surprised no one when he took the time during the train ride to write a poem called "Returning Home" that described, among other things, certain pitfalls of modern Japanese life: "I have not yet seen Jōshū Mountain. / In the faint light on the night train / the motherless children cry in their sleep."

After several years on the frontiers of change, Uno too began to pay a price. Her life of married bliss in the radish patch began to pall, and she grew increasingly restless. "Our amusing, interesting life continued for some four years, and during that whole period of our marriage we never quarreled," she relates in *Living in Search of Happiness*. "We didn't even exchange harsh words. . . . But although I had this charming, lovable companion, we both started to sense boredom creeping in, even as we enjoyed ourselves." One assumes that the conflicts hovered above the Magome breakfast table and were endured in tense Japanese silence for some time. Uno and her various companions were evidently unaccustomed to sitting down to discuss the state of their relationships, and favored indirect modes of communication, at least at first. This cut down on arguments but also led to misunderstandings, since both sides had to decode the ambiguous messages transmitted by the silences.

Uno began to frequent a spa on the Izu Peninsula to get a change of air and to work on her manuscripts. Her trips away from home grew longer as she joined the literary crowd already taking the waters there. Most notable among her circle was Japan's future Nobel Prize winner, Kawabata Yasunari, who in a 1929 photograph stands posed with a group of writers in front of an inn. Artistically draped in an inverness cape and sporting a cane, he looks astonishingly young, while to the side is a brooding but bobbed Uno Chiyo in a gaily patterned kimono. Uno's faltering marriage became the subject of gossip. She insists that she did not think her alliance with Ozaki was over; it was just that they were living apart. "Living in just two rooms of a house that was like a small hotel, two people could not both work at their writing," she observes. Monogamous felicity was a concept she could revere only after she had packed her bags to move out. Perhaps she had started to see her husband more objectively than was advisable for an adoring wife. She complains, with uncharacteristic scorn, of his sluggishness—in particular, of his behavior during a fire that had started on a mountainside. "He didn't even say, 'Wait a minute! I'm coming!' Ozaki just scooped up the water from the flume and walked over to pour it on the fire. . . . It was like watching a slow-motion movie, the way he lumbered up to help me." To judge from the killingly deliberate pace of Ozaki's fiction, there may have been some justification for Uno's annoyance.

Back in Tokyo, Ozaki was not idle; he was already employing the details of their breakup in his next literary work. He creates a cold portrait of himself, while depicting Uno's distress over this failed marriage as enormous. "Next time we see each other," pleads the frequently absent though penitent wife to her writer husband in one of his stories, "I'll be like the sweet young girl I was when we first met. It'll be just the same as when we slept together in Ueno. I'll do my hair in an old style, long and fastened properly. And I'll put on a good kimono and wear all the proper undergarments." In triumph, the hero yells back at her, "What does it matter to me where you go? Go wherever you like. You can take yourself to a garbage heap, or look in some crowd, for all I care, to find yourself someone new to quarrel with."

Ozaki was understandably piqued about Uno's friendship with the novelist Kajii Motojirō, who, despite tuberculosis that was soon to kill him, braved the evening vapors to visit Uno in her Izu inn. Uno paid return visits, it is said, by climbing up a back roof and through a window, since the proprietor of the establishment where Kajii stayed was not sympathetic to nocturnal literary gatherings.

By the time the marriage to Ozaki ended in 1929, both parties' fictional hostilities had been amply set forth in the pages of the literary magazines. There is no agreement about exactly whose infidelities served as principal catalyst. Ozaki had found a new love, and this relationship was encouraged by his friends, who were incensed by the way Uno had treated him. Uno, now a scorned wife, was in the meantime having second thoughts out at the hot springs, and sought a reconciliation. But Ozaki, at least in his stories, stood firm against her entreaties. "Since we broke up I haven't been able to sleep," the crazed, naughty wife tells her wronged, noble husband. "I'm taking both Adapin and Calmoden. I don't know whether it's the drugs or because of my cold, but I've had a bad fever for two days and been in bed. My feet and hands and face are swollen like a pig's. . . . I want to return to you. I want to return."

Uno resented Ozaki's descriptions of her anguish and swiftly took the most appropriate revenge possible. A character in one of *her* fictional works is soon muttering that her former husband is ungallantly writing things like "When I threw her out, she simply lost control of herself and went to pieces." Uno's fiction from this period crackles with pain. Her writings are raw and frankly autobiographical—just what her curious fans were eagerly waiting for. She had no compunction about revealing her delicious secrets to meet publishing deadlines. "So sensual, so provocative, was the life Uno lived and wrote about that she was soon dubbed 'a writer of illicit love,'" the American scholar Rebecca Copeland notes in a recent issue of *Japan Quarterly*. "Although admired, she was not always taken seriously. She was a legitimate member of the *bundan* (literary world), but something of a curiosity, at times even an embarrassment."

The stories Uno wrote after parting from Ozaki make it easy to see why she gained a loyal following. She may have lived beyond the bounds of propriety, married too often, or untied the sash of her kimono for too many men, but she never lost her homey touch. Her devoted readers were women locked into traditional lives, women consumed in daily combat with their mothers-in-law, women whose only excitement was killing the rats and frogs scampering around the kitchen (the trick was to twist their necks with a dish towel), even women in the countryside who squatted for hours before their earthenware stoves tending the dinner fires. Uno brought the adventures of the metropolis to these women but at the same time seemed to retain the good, simple instincts of a Japanese country girl. Though a trifle wayward, she still showed respect for the old virtues. "A tremor of joy as delicate as a spider's web made the moment all the more poignant," says one of her warm and guileless heroines in describing a meeting with her estranged husband. "I looked at him just like a young girl, smiling through my tears. 'Look,' I said. 'See how long my hair has grown.' 'Don't cry,' he told me. 'Don't cry like that.' "

Alone after the separation, Uno determined to get along without the burden of a man in her life. Like many an exhausted woman before and after, she taped a list of imperatives to her wall: "Be economically independent. Be emotionally independent. Ah, independence! To stand on one's own! Definitely don't fall in love with anyone." Although she wrote much during this period, she was miserable. She had not been born to undergo the rigors of being single, and eventually solitude proved too taxing. Before she had time to write even a paragraph about her intentions, Uno went to consult with Tōgō Seiji about the love-suicide scene she wanted to include in her newest work, *Why Are the Poppies Crimson?*. Astonished tale-tellers were soon reporting that the two were living together in the suburbs.

In Tōgō, Uno found a real soul mate, for he, perhaps more than anyone else in the entire Japanese archipelago, came trailing heartbreak and could match her, scene for high-pitched scene, in a history of personal disaster. Tōgō was by 1929 a well-known Western-style artist who, like many of his Japanese colleagues of that time, had lived in Paris for years. His paintings are on permanent exhibition in the lavish museum of a Tokyo insurance company (the same company that recently acquired van Gogh's "Sunflowers"). Tōgō, who died in 1978, is remembered for his murals, many of which adorned public buildings, and for his efforts to convey the essence of the female, writhing and white. At the start of his career, he could not decide whether to become a musician or an artist until a mentor advised him to express the music in his soul through his painting. To the contemporary eye, his style seems to derive something from Marie Laurencin and the rest from all the cubists who have ever lived, but he brought exotic hints of the West to Japan and became extremely popular. "The kind of colors women like," one connoisseur recently objected.

By the time Uno met Tōgō, he had earned as much fame for his love life as for his cubist rendering of "A Woman with a Parasol." He had married before leaving for France in 1921, but upon his return to Tokyo seven years later he fell in love with a tall, fair woman named Mitsuko. She was long of neck—a crucial mark of beauty for Japanese—and blessed with exquisite hands and feet. Since Mitsuko's father, who was an admiral in the Imperial Navy, objected to his daughter's romance with a married, unprosperous artist, Mitsuko was sent away; Tōgō, without officially divorcing his first wife, consoled himself by taking a second. After a while Mitsuko reappeared, and in March 1929 she and Tōgō embarked upon the suicide attempt that kept the journalists busy for weeks. ("You have to remember how it was then," Uno told me, offering her own recollection of that period. "No lovers attempted suicide in those days. It was a big event. The newspapers went wild. Now Japanese lovers kill themselves all the time. No one gets excited about it.") Several weeks later, the lovers had recovered, Tōgō sufficiently to write an article about the episode ("Notes of a Failed Love Suicide") for a women's magazine. He shared his reflections with readers longing to hear the story straight from the source: "We sadly did not die together, but the absolute purity we felt on the brink of death proved that our fates would be utterly entwined from then on, and we placed great faith in this. . . . I will never stop waiting for her. She is the eternal sun for me."

Uno's liaison with Tōgō began soon thereafter, and despite the buzz of gossip they were at first extremely happy. Since both had been through tremendous upheavals, they relished the peace of their life together. Uno let her hair grow longer and, at Tōgō's urging, wore Western-style dresses. Tōgō, the Westernized Japanese gentleman, sometimes donned kimonos. Uno stopped using makeup and applied face oil, the way Tōgō liked. They danced together, and collected thin, fleet dogs, as was expected of the most exciting of Tokyo's couples. "Maybe this is not a discreet way to talk, but I felt as if I were reading a novel and wanted to get to the next installment quickly," she recalls in *My Literary Reminiscences*. "Tōgō and I were as different as night and day in our tastes, but we were alike in readily adopting unconventional behavior."

The strains showed, however, after they began to build a house that was beyond their means. It was to be a residence somewhat in the manner of Le Corbusier, with atelier, salon, and fancy bedroom. Uno had to travel around selling Tōgō's paintings to raise the cash this project required. But they could not meet the expenses and were frequently harassed by creditors. "Sometimes there were notices pasted on the building announcing that our goods were being seized because we couldn't pay the construction fees," she writes. "In spite of this, the brilliant sun shone down upon the lawn of our big garden, and, while we did not have white cranes, our foreign breeds of dogs frolicked there. It was during this period that you could smell something criminal and shady behind this show we made of an 'elegant' life."

The romance waned. Uno was left with no time for her writing, and Tōgō had cause to suspect that she had become intimate with some of the buyers of his paintings. He himself confesses that he was "prodigiously fickle." It was only when they had almost finished paying for the house—a serene period Uno likens to the aftermath of a lengthy war—that she began to record Tōgō's reminiscences. The tale of his great romance with Mitsuko, the admiral's daughter, took him a year to relate and eventually became *Confessions of Love*.

There is a splendid photograph of Uno as she was in those days, her hair sleek and pulled back, face gleaming. Wearing a long chic dress fresh from Paris, she stands upon the magnificent tiled terrace just off the atelier of their estate in Setagaya. A dachshund, a greyhound, and an English bulldog loll about in the sunshine. Few other *mo-ga* in Tokyo and its environs could boast of fashionable dogs, a cubist lover, and silk stockings. But the days of Japan's lighthearted infatuation with Western ways were coming to a close as grimmer times settled over the country. In *Essays on Women Writers*, the literary critic Okuno Takeo explains, "The years 1933 through 1935, when *Confessions of Love* was being written, marked the very height but simultaneously the finale of capitalism and liberalism in Japan after the First World War." Japan had already begun to occupy Manchuria, and the brutal suppression of liberal elements among the Japanese was well under way. Fanatical nationalists maneuvered for positions of greater power.

Confessions of Love reflects the bleakness of those days. The novel, which was first published in magazine installments, takes the form of a monologue related by Yuasa, a well-known Western-style artist just returned from seven years in Paris. Yuasa has difficulty settling down to work, for in the course of many pages he hardly has a chance to get near the turpentine to clean his brushes. His charms overpower women wherever he goes, and they will not leave him alone. On the train ride home to Tokyo, he has kindly come into a young girl's compartment to return a fan she left in the dining car. "This is yours, isn't it?" is all he has to say to win her affections. The girl is clearly an autobiographical novelist in the making, because she is soon besieging the famous artist with notes begging for a rendezvous. When he finally deigns to meet her, she efficiently arranges a trysting spot. She loses courage at the last moment, however, and although Yuasa is willing to do her the favor of consummating their union, the lady swoons on the hotel bed. For Yuasa, feverish days ensue as he pursues this young woman, who disappears. By the time he finds her, he has shifted his interest to her friend, the beautiful Tsuyuko. Unfortunately, Tsuyuko comes from a strict Navy family, and they object to her consorting with an artist who is, as it happens, short on cash, married, and a father. Tsuyuko is sent away by her parents, and Yuasa follows close behind. In the course of his obsession there are violent rainstorms, a bout of pneumonia, and several more fainting fits. The prize continues to elude Yuasa. Tsuyuko is again shipped off by her parents, this time to places unknown, and he finds someone new to marry. The marriage is as brief as the flowering of Ueno's cherry trees in the spring, for Tsuyuko is soon back in Tokyo inviting Yuasa to die with her.

Uno claims that she didn't change one word of Tōgō's narrative—that she wrote down exactly what he said, only urging him on occasionally by asking what happened next. "Tōgō once told me, 'I think the real reason you lived with me was so that you could make a novel out of my story.' This was not so, but I exerted myself in writing the book as if it really were so." She gives full credit for the book's success to Tōgō's skillful way of telling his story. She is too modest, for finally in *Confessions of Love* her own sufferings served her well. "One of the finest love stories in modern Japanese literature," Okuno Takeo calls it.

Tōgō would surely have fashioned a more attractive picture of himself had he been the one to write his reminiscences. As Uno slyly presents him, the hero has a way with women, but his allure is accompanied by a terrible passivity. Weak, selfish, yet somehow irresistible, he manages to ruin the life of every woman he as much as sips a cup of sake with. Yuasa is a character Uno knew well: she had just finished spending years of her life in thrall to men like him. In form, *Confessions of Love* is one of those auto-biographical Japanese sagas in which a man relates the story of his private problems. Since honesty is essential in these stories, the male authors are obliged to reveal their basest motives, their cruelest moments. But a reader may feel that the narrator of *Confessions of Love* has flaws enough for several confessional Japanese novels. His indecisiveness, which is exceeded only by his vanity, keeps his female companions in limbo for many pages. He becomes dizzy—or faints—at critical junctures, leaving his women to their fates while they wait for him to recover. Yuasa can't even commit suicide properly. Although he has bought a medical handbook to guide him, he slashes his neck in the wrong place. His description of the suicide is especially famous for its high drama and comedy:

The sun went down, and although we couldn't see each other's faces clearly in the faint light seeping through the curtains, Tsuyuko was apparently staring at the scalpel she held in her hand. "Maybe now's the time . . . ?" I said, and just at that moment what seemed like a burst of hot water came fountaining out, soaking through my thin shirt. Tsuyuko had cut her throat first, and I could see the blood gushing from the wound as I called out to her. Thoroughly agitated, I gathered up her limp body and laid her down on the bed. I had wanted to remain calm, but a frenzy shook through me. "I can't die in a shirt that's soiled like this," I told myself in all seriousness. I got out of bed and took a fresh shirt from the bureau, removing the shirt that had been drenched in Tsuyuko's blood. I was so flustered that I didn't stop to think that if I was going to do the same to myself, the new shirt would become even more bloody. I carefully fastened the buttons and rushed to Tsuyuko's side, where I took up the other scalpel. My heart was pumping hard from the whiskey we had drunk earlier, and when I brought my hand to my throat I could feel the prominence of a large blood vessel pulsing with the heavy flow. I pressed the blood vessel with one hand and, praying that my strength would not fail me, pierced my throat with a single hard thrust.

Uno had already rented separate quarters for herself by the time *Confessions of Love* was published in book form, in April 1935. She was astounded when she learned that Tōgō had returned to Mitsuko. Upon hearing this news, Uno confesses, she went temporarily berserk and for the first time in her life felt real hatred. But her equanimity was soon restored. By early summer she possessed enough serenity to write the story "Parting Is Also a Pleasure," in which the heroine's former artist lover drops by for a friendly visit. Unappreciated still, he complains that he just can't communicate with his new companion: "I don't know what she's feeling, and she really doesn't understand me." Our heroine smiles and utters a few sage words about everyone's essential isolation.

In several of her reminiscences, Uno expresses gratitude to Tōgō for those years and for his painterly instruction in color combinations—a knowledge she would later put to use in her kimono business. ("He was a very fine person," she said to me.) Until Tōgō, Uno had been known chiefly as an accurate chronicler of her own eventful life. She had only to live dangerously and survive to set down the details. But works like *Confessions of Love* got her beyond her life story at last. "Speaking through a man's voice gave me a real sense of freedom," she says.

Somewhat at loose ends after the breakup with Tōgō, Uno leaped at the suggestion that she try her hand at publishing a magazine for women. In 1936 she started Japan's first fashion magazine, *Sutairu* (the Japanese pronunciation of "style"). She also found time to cultivate an attachment to Kitahara Takeo, a dapper novelist and critic ten years her junior. He was warned about keeping company with such a dangerous woman. Uno's friends, for their part, suspected that she had taken leave of her senses when the wedding was announced. Some of the literary luminaries who received invitations to the April 1, 1939 gala could not believe that she intended to marry again; they suspected an April Fools' joke. (The skeptics on Kitahara's side had reason to fret, for his professional reputation was eventually diminished by the glitter surrounding this union.) With Kitahara in tow, Uno focused her energies on making a success of *Sutairu*. The magazine featured full-page photographs of actresses and geishas, in smart layouts new to Japan. Kitahara thought up chatty surveys ("What do you do at night when you can't sleep?").

Kitahara, who had been devoted to French literature from an early age, was not universally admired; detractors came to see him as pretentious. His personal vanity became the butt of jokes, and to this day (he died in 1973) Japanese editors delight in recounting a rumor about how he used to spread black shoe polish on his head when he started to go bald and the problems he had when caught in the rain. The charge of affectation dogged his fiction as well. Kawabata Yasunari, commenting brutally on the novella *My Wife* (1938), found its mixture of influences confusing—"much like being fed sashimi with mayonnaise on top." Others have justifiably risen to defend the work (one critic has called Kawabata's remark "slanderous"), for Kitahara's story of a dying wife and her imperfect husband beautifully evokes a sense of life's emptiness and, in the grand manner of Japanese literature, gathers power from griefs that are never fully expressed.

Shortly after the war began, Kitahara was conscripted and sent to Java to write for the Military Information Corps. He returned in 1943, and the following year he and Uno left the dangers of Tokyo for a comfortable stay in yet another hot-springs resort on the Izu Peninsula. Uno prided herself on her ability to acquire white rice, chicken, yellowtail, and other hard-to-find items for the household. When the war grew fiercer, they were forced to evacuate again—this time to his family home, in Tochigi Prefecture. There she traded her clothes for honey and other supplies. Sometimes the attacking American planes flew so low that Uno could see the faces of the pilots. In August 1945, the family gathered around the radio to hear the Emperor's broadcast announcing Japan's surrender.

MODERN GIRL Never prolific, Uno wrote little in those chaotic times, but while the war was still on she fell under the spell of a Bunraku puppet that belonged to her publisher and went off to Shikoku, in the countryside, to interview the dedicated craftsman who had carved its superb face. "The Puppet-Maker Tenguya Kyūkichi," published in 1942, is another record of a man's reminiscences— this time those of an eighty-six-year-old master who had spent every day since his sixteenth year seated on his tatami floor quietly carving puppet heads for the Bunraku plays. "Art is a person's whole life," Tenguya explains in a humble endorsement of his own single-mindedness. "Once you start feeling that you've achieved enough, that is the end for you. . . . While you are alive you must think in various ways and put your mind to seeing how you can improve your work."

Uno says that Tenguya's example inspired her to return to her neglected writing. She spent a total of ten years working on *Ohan*. The novella's narrator, Kanōya, who must rank as one of the most irresolute heroes in world literature, is racked by love for his self-sacrificing, saintly wife, Ohan. He deserted her years before for Okayo, a savvy and brash geisha bent on keeping her man. Which woman should he choose? Related in Kanōya's colorful dialect (there is an English translation by Donald Keene), the lovers' conflicts and the atmosphere owe much to the old Bunraku plays, but the tart view of human psychology is unmistakably that of the postwar period. Rickshaws transport visitors to their destinations in the geisha quarter, and the clattering wooden clogs along

Kajiya Street distract Kanōya's already disorderly thought processes. The cherry-blossom petals flutter down upon the geisha's gaudy robes, Kanōya procrastinates further, and Uno happily dissects another fainthearted hero.

Publication of *Sutairu* was resumed after the Japanese defeat, when Tokyo was in ruins and food scarce. This slick magazine tantalized the stricken country by promising better days to come, and when the first issue appeared (with a sophisticated cover by a Japanese artist returned from Paris) the line of customers twice circled the building housing the magazine's offices. Because of the riches from *Sutairu*, Uno could dance in Ginza while many other Japanese faced starvation in bombed-out hovels. She built a palace for her entourage on choice Tokyo real estate. The cash flowed in and out—"like water," she has said—and the magazine was not always careful to pay its taxes. Finally an envious publishing colleague wrote an anonymous note to the tax office about these irregularities. Uno and Kitahara were ruined. They had to borrow to pay the taxes, and she used income from her recently founded kimono enterprise to stave off the loan sharks. They published a serious literary magazine between fiscal emergencies. For many years, they worked desperately to pay off huge debts. It was a shared burden that would keep them married until 1964, but they had drifted apart long before; by then, Kitahara was involved with another woman.

The passing years had left Uno battered but still on her feet, and it is not surprising that she found new applications for her life experiences. She began to see prudent patterns in her own youthful unruliness, and she became old enough to sound wise. Uno was a natural for the role of agony columnist. The titles of several of her later works place her solidly within the ranks of the Japanese self-help experts. In *I Am Always Busy*, "A Woman Can Get Married at Any Age," and *Living in Search of Happiness*, among others, she comes out in favor of a Japanese mixture of spiritual fortitude, useful activity, and finicky eating habits. Taking a grandmotherly "I have been there, Setsuko!" approach, she has at times advocated woefully conservative positions in her advice to the lovelorn. She urges blind loyalty to husbands and—lowest of blows—has also written on behalf of *gaman*, the ancient Japanese virtue of forbearance. In sections of "My Guide to Marriage," however, she does stand up for contemporary social mores. She includes the following admonition in her Ten Commandments for Avoiding Divorce: "When a wife discovers her husband's first infidelity, she must become insanely jealous. She must not even dream of telling him 'Dear, you have my permission.' " The seething, wordless stare—a variant of *gaman*—simply does not suffice to get the point across: "First, cry as loud as you can, then make a great show of screaming, 'I can't stand it! I can't! I just can't!' Don't think about what you look like. At that point, start heaving whatever is handy all over the place, or just start clawing at his face." In a mellower mood, she has shared her recipes with readers, reminding them to use only the very best sake lees for pickling vegetables.

Uno has traveled abroad several times, and was once photographed wearing Japanese finery in front of the Eiffel Tower. In 1957 she took her kimonos to Seattle, where Americans modeled her designs. Later on, she wrote *To Sting* (1966), a fictionalized account of the melancholy end of her marriage to Kitahara. She also followed the activities of another errant male in *The Sound of the Wind* (1969), but this time let the patient wife serve as the narrator of his dreadful exploits. Her writings have won many literary prizes. In November 1985, at an Imperial Hotel celebration of her eighty-eighth birthday, she emphasized her refusal to fade into demure old age by appearing in a *furisode*, the long-sleeved kimono reserved for young unmarried girls.

Some say that Uno Chiyo has gone too far in keeping her wild reputation alive. Japanese reporters have been only too eager to take advantage of her willingness to discuss the details of her love life in public. Even her fondest admirers cannot help wincing at the sight of a hard-of-hearing, heavily made-up ninety-year-old author responding to questions on television about whether there are any new boyfriends on the horizon, or airily describing one of her Buddhist statues as the spitting image of the late Kitahara, for whom it has been nicknamed. At such times, a Western observer might imagine that this is what Mae West would have been like if she had worn kimonos and gone on a tofu diet.

But Japan can be hard on women, and too many women writers seem to conclude their tales with the heroine staring moodily out into an unchanging landscape. They make a convincing case for a constricted world where lakes are silent, the black pines still. It is therefore cheering to read a story like Uno's "Happiness," written in 1970, when she was seventy-three. The elderly heroine has built a house on a snowy mountainside and lives there alone. Her assorted husbands have sought solace elsewhere, the heater isn't working, the cold seeps through the cracks—yet she remains unperturbed. She even considers herself blessed by her bad eyesight: when she looks in the mirror after her bath, she is pleased to see a beauty like Botticelli's Venus. "In this manner," Uno writes, "she collects fragments of happiness, one after another, and so lives, spreading them throughout her environment." The old woman refuses to think about whether her water pipes have frozen, and instead imagines herself skiing down the snowy slopes. As she studies the blizzard swirling outside her window, she offers hope to those not as pretty or as plucky as herself: "The snowflakes dance toward the sky, and the sun still shines. The winds have risen."

WHEN *FLOATING CLOUDS* WAS BEING filmed, in 1954, Takamine Hideko had still not shed the effects of a long stay in Paris. Camembert cheese and fresh croissants had been a serious part of her overseas experience, and by the time she returned to Tokyo she had put on weight. Since Yukiko, the character she portrayed in *Floating Clouds*, was supposed to be starving in impoverished postwar Japan, artistic sacrifice called for a diet. Not only Takamine was thick in the hips; but her co-star, Mori Masayuki, was also having trouble conveying an image of undernourishment. "There we were, supposedly as emaciated as stray dogs, scrounging around the black market looking for food and clothing . . . and Mori's stomach was sticking out," Takamine recalls in her autobiography. The two made a secret pact, pledging to reform their eating habits. Takamine may have dreamed of a lavish feast, but on the set she broke her fast only for a hard-boiled egg or something equally meager at lunchtime. Abstinence was rewarded; Takamine's Yukiko soon took on a truly haggard and desperate appearance. No one could have doubted the hunger of this heroine who had to sell tattered futons to pay for a winter coat. By the time Yukiko breathed her last, on a rainswept Japanese island — and her lover felt moved to apply lipstick to her corpse — Takamine herself was not in the best of health. "About halfway through the shooting," she wrote, "I would be saying my lines and feel so weak that I thought I was really going to pass out."

With Naruse Mikio directing these dieting principals, *Floating Clouds* makes its way among the freezing sake shops and tuberculosis infirmaries of a ruined, defeated Japan. The film is, beyond matters of survival, a love story — the saga of Yukiko and Tomioka, who meet when both are working in Japanese-occupied Indochina during the war. Yukiko is gifted in love and suffering, while Tomioka is handsome and charming but also cowardly, faithless, selfish, and constantly on the verge of financial ruin. Yukiko, among others, cannot resist him, and she follows him from the tropical forests near Da Lat to Tokyo shacks without heat, on to a hot spring and later to the island of Yakushima, and through his alliances with his own wife and somebody else's, sticking by him through scandal, lung disease, and the failure of a lumber business.

Everyone has a favorite section of this prizewinning film, and some Japanese especially relish the couple's *waruguchi* — their reproachful arguments ("Ah, the *waruguchi* is wonderful!" one critic happily exclaimed). The mad love of Yukiko and Tomioka does not always require dialogue, though, for Takamine and Mori display a magisterial command of sighs, grunts, and silences. When they do talk, they try not to waste a word. Their conversation about whether to die together upon Mt. Haruna is as hot as the steamy Japanese bathtub in which they are soaking.

With the release of *Floating Clouds*, Takamine Hideko was widely proclaimed a great actress. Critics agreed that the picture spoke of the grand and terrible nature of life, and one reviewer wrote, "This film has opened up a territory never before touched upon by Japanese cinema." The Takamine of *Floating Clouds* is an unforgettable sight. Wearing a sweater and cotton work trousers, with only wooden *geta* on her feet, she rushes through the bedlam of Tokyo, hardly pausing to notice the oddness of seedy alleys where Japanese might be eating traditional meals of noodles with bamboo shoots while listening to "Jingle Bells" on the radio. Her round face and troubled eyes make her seem to be always asking why she can't just find herself a little peace and quiet, and she communicates much emotion through her very expressive eyebrows.

201

Takamine moves through extremes of mood with splendid ease. When Yukiko encounters Tomioka for the first time after the war, she gives way to lovesickness ("Remember the first time I came to your room barefoot in the middle of the night and your door was unlocked?"), but a few scenes later, when she has been forced to take up with an American soldier in order to stay alive, she finds less reason to swoon over her wishy-washy Tomioka. Here we see a debating champion fed up with the verbal imprecision of a dim opponent: "Listen, I wouldn't underestimate women if I were you. Don't you dare look down on me when you can't do anything properly yourself!"

Takamine's voice can come as a surprise, for the emphatically nasal sound does not seem to match the big, round face. When I sought comments on it in my local Tokyo drinking establishment, a Japanese man said, "I'd call that voice charming, and very friendly, like the girl next door." But a female patron rose in dissent: no, no, the noise winding through Takamine's nose was "irritating and *becha-becha*." I needed clarification of that word, and the woman explained, "She sounds like what happens when a piece of candy gets stuck in your throat. You try to get it out, but it sticks—*bechaaaa.*" *Becha-becha* or not, Takamine's voice has modulated into the clear, authoritative tones of a tour-bus guide (she has portrayed one on two occasions), the affectionate bellow of a young girl calling across fields to her pet pony (in *Horse*, 1941), and even the plaintive cadences of a blind Chinese waif in pigtails singing in an opium den of how the wind blows off the sea and she can't find her sister (in *The Opium War*, 1943).

But this voice has served Takamine most effectively in her *waruguchi* scenes, when her complaints about the man of the moment hover around her vocal cords longer than normal. She puts a lot of misery into a word like *iya* (loosely translatable as "No, that's not for me"), as in "*Iya*, I don't need your money. I came here with only one thought in mind, to meet you, and now you . . ." Richer still is her extended rendition of *datte* ("but")—a word that even under ordinary circumstances has more syllables in Japanese than one might suppose. Taken in combination with Takamine's heavily knit eyebrows, a sentence like "*Datte* I'm suffering, and you won't pay any attention to me" goes a long way toward confirming the swinishness of whatever man she is reproaching.

Takamine's voice was most memorably heard during the golden years of Japanese cinema, soon after the war. "In 1951, when Kurosawa Akira's *Rashōmon* won the Grand Prix at the Venice Film Festival, the Japanese film industry turned its eyes outside the country for the first time," she writes in *My Professional Diary*, her autobiography. "Everyone ran around in high spirits: 'Just wait until I show them—I can do that too!' " Takamine was the favorite actress of Naruse Mikio and Kinoshita Keisuke, two of the most esteemed directors of the period, but she also found time to appear in the films of other notables, as a nineteenth-century mistress, a trapped housewife, and an advertising barker. For many Japanese, she was as much a part of postwar Japan as the strange-tasting powdered milk distributed by the American military.

Takamine's way of speaking was strictly her own, but the restlessness of the characters she portrayed originated in the misfortunes of many other Japanese film heroines. In those days, women on the screen were often noble and long-suffering, facing hideous abuse in a harsh male world. If hardship was women's lot, then steadfast endurance enhanced their inner and outer beauty. The heroine played by actress Tanaka Kinuyo, for instance, suffers terribly in the 1952 film *The Life of Oharu* (directed by Mizoguchi Kenji). Her lover is slaughtered and her child taken from her, but she soldiers on to face still more tragedy. Westerners in comparable dire circumstances plot murderous revenge, but makers of such Japanese films prefer to offer only the milder consolations of Buddhism. Time and again, actresses had to portray the ordinary Japanese woman as having the simple goodness to forget her own trials for the sake of others. Self-sacrifice could create extraordinary moments onscreen, as in *The Sound of the Mountain*, when a wife played by the adored and idealized actress Hara Setsuko tries to turn her mind from a philandering husband by speaking rapturously of the moon.

Takamine Hideko became known for suffering in a more modern way. She was at her best when her heroines, on sensing imminent disaster, indulged themselves in outright complaint rather than a study of the evening sky. In postwar Japan, where Takamine's films were often set, her heroines did not lack for encounters with bone-crushing disappointment. "Many of Takamine's heroines were typical of the women who had grown up after the war," the film historian Donald Richie told me. "Like so many Japanese women then, they wanted more out of life but couldn't get it. The war may have been over, women found, but they weren't better off. They were still fairly unhappy. So the kind of roles Takamine played fit the zeitgeist, may have even made that zeitgeist."

Many Japanese say they never tire of seeing Takamine play Kiyoko in the 1952 *Lightning*, also directed by Naruse. Kiyoko's mother has had four children, each by a different father, and they have been brought up in a déclassé section of traditional Tokyo. Kiyoko, who has ambitions to better herself, broods through much of the film about how to get away from the sordidness of her family and the clutter of noodle shops in the neighborhood. "You have to think about how things were then," a friend told me. "After the war, we thought we were going to have democracy, like the Americans. We were dying to get out of the house, just like Kiyoko, but we still had the strict Confucian family system to contend with. We were still trapped by the old obligations, duties, customs. We had to go along with our elders' wishes." Kiyoko does manage to leave her turbulent home and move to the more civilized suburbs, and there she meets a brother and sister whose conversations focus upon piano lessons instead of the unrefined topics she is used to hearing about in her own home. But in the film's final scene Kiyoko's escape seems less than assured: her endearing, unfashionable mother visits this haven of bourgeois harmony to remind her of family ties. Earlier in the film, Kiyoko and her mother have a startling exchange at home one afternoon. Chatting on the veranda, they come fearlessly to the heart of the matter. "Mother," Kiyoko asks, "you married four men, didn't you? Tell me, were you happy?" Her mother does not require even a moment's pause before replying, "Happy? Now, where do you get such fancy ideas?"

When *Lightning* appeared, Takamine Hideko was twenty-eight years old. One might assume that she was then in the early stages of her career, but the fact is that Takamine had already been a movie star for twenty-three years. She has often told the story of

how when she was five, in Tokyo, her uncle took her on a sight-
seeing trip to Shōchiku, one of the major film studios, carrying
her on his back in the Japanese style. She was dressed in plain,
everyday clothes, but there happened to be an audition that day
for a child's part in a new film, and on a whim she and her uncle
joined the line of gorgeously attired aspiring child stars. Hideko
was selected for the role, and *Mother*, the film in which she made
her debut, broke booking records when it was first shown in 1929.
Her talents as an adorable little girl established, she began playing little boys as well, benefiting from her extremely slender hips.
Takamine says that she took to these sex changes without alarm.
"If you put me in a girl's costume, I was a little girl. If I wore shorts,
I was a little boy. No problem."

Along the way, she acquired the nickname Deko-chan, and it
stuck much beyond her years as a little girl/boy star. She became
everybody's sister/brother, or the kid next door. It was the engag-
ing young girl weeping over a horse who remained in the public's
mind even after Takamine became an adult beset by more subtle
anxieties. Since mysteriousness is apparently part of feminine
allure, a child who had driven the entire Japanese nation to tears
by reciting an essay about a pair of rabbits, and whose big, healthy
teeth had first appeared in Lion Toothpaste advertisements when
she was eleven, was obviously going to have difficulty establishing
herself as an adult female idol.

Takamine could not compete with the enigmatic Hara
Setsuko, who is known in the West for her starring roles in many
of Ozu Yasujirō's films. Hara was called "the eternal virgin" or
even "the eternal Madonna" because she seemed to possess the
purity of a heavenly emanation. "After seeing a Hara Setsuko
movie," the novelist Endō Shūsaku writes, in a typically reveren-
tial response, "we would sigh or let out a great breath from the
depths of our hearts, for what we felt was precisely this: Can it be
possible that there is such a woman in this world?" Endō is one of

several men I know who dream of meeting Hara just once before they die. Hara was so refined, so moral, so beautiful, so representative of all that Japanese men valued in women that she remained excitingly out of reach for the hordes of males who adored her. Her appearance too—her long face and broad shoulders—did not seem completely Japanese to the scrupulous native eye, and rumors of foreign blood flowing in her veins only fed the fantasies. Hara added to this air of mystery when she abruptly retired in 1962, at age forty-two, and though persistently sought by eager paparazzi, she has never emerged from her seclusion in the Tokyo suburb of Kamakura. Some say that she did not wish to show her aging face in public; others speculate that she had problems with her eyes. Hara herself has remained silent on the subject, and unapproachable—the Garbo of Japan.

It is still said that Takamine was never able to match this immaculate white lily. During the recent sumo-wrestling season, when the jargon of the sport was current, a Japanese professor soberly took me aside to remark that Hara remains the *yokozuna* (champion), while Takamine will always be the second-ranking *ōzeki*. Takamine, with her round face and excellent teeth, struck her Japanese fans as cute and lovable but at something of a remove from the sublime. While the Hara of Ozu's films carried the Japanese tradition of feminine grace on her wide shoulders, Takamine, in the only Ozu film she made as an adult (she was in his *Tokyo Chorus*, among others, as a child), played a tomboy who liked to stick out her tongue. Her portrayals of the kind of genteel upper-middle-class women who were Hara's specialty had an awkwardness about them. In particular, Takamine's hearty appetite threatened to disrupt the decorum of austere Japanese sitting rooms; she looked as if she might at any moment help herself to double portions of sweet cakes or seaweed-covered crackers.

Takamine was more at home with Japan's *shomin*, the people of the lower middle class. She could munch at her leisure among the revelers at street festivals and catch up on the gossip at the public baths. She took to *shomin* roles as if she had been playing them since she could talk, which was almost the case; and her fans always believed her to be one of their own. "If Takamine turned up here tonight, she wouldn't mind serving drinks to help me out," the owner of my local bar said. "You'd never find Hara Setsuko doing that." Even Takamine's walk, with her hips sometimes following slightly behind the rest of her body, has a hale aspect, as if she had just finished hauling a heavy object behind her, perhaps a rickshaw. The closest she came to this activity, however, was in *Rickshaw Man*, in which Mifune Toshirō, as her devoted admirer, played the title role.

Takamine more easily finds a place beside the actress Tanaka Kinuyo, who was born in 1909 and died in 1977. Although Tanaka came from an established middle-class family, she had no difficulty living among the less elegant *shomin* in her films. As a brothel keeper, a maid in a geisha house, or a ticket hawker at the bicycle races, Tanaka could put a surly edge into a Japanese sentence that ensured her survival in any rough neighborhood. Tanaka treated Takamine like a younger sister, and often invited her out to her palatial Kamakura home. When they appear together in films, their camaraderie amid the bean-cake shops is obvious. But there was almost a generation between them, and when Tanaka's characters suffered, their distress came to seem old-fashioned. In Tanaka's films the men had too much power and could spurn her for a richer girl; the family system kept her taking care of her children alone while her husband wandered off to seek his fortune or the fast woman next door. The enemy loomed as clearly as the rising sun itself, as Tanaka joined the ancient female struggle against feudalism, unequal pay scales, and Confucianism.

When Takamine stepped forward to complain, the same samisens may have twanged in the background, but the enemies she faced were too disparate to be so easily categorized. In *Where Chimneys Are Seen*, a 1953 film directed by Gosho Heinosuke, Tanaka and Takamine occupy the same house in wretched postwar Japan. Downstairs, Tanaka has problems with a slow-witted husband and an abandoned baby who won't stop crying; her situation is further complicated by a family-registration system that had its beginnings many centuries ago.

Upstairs, in equally drafty quarters, Takamine is getting ready to wreck all her chances for happiness without the help of customs left over from premodern civilization. Next to her lives an attractive and intelligent young man who adores her. Takamine, however, is not one to settle into contentment without putting up a fight. She harangues her would-be lover about his character flaws or the nature of the human struggle while the baby bawls downstairs. In her desire to eradicate all traces of sloppy thinking from the world at large, this Takamine can be a wearying presence. Were her boyfriend not so enamored of her, he would see that living with a woman like this could take years off his life. In the final scene, he must chase her down the street while she leads a discussion on the likelihood of his being able to predict accurately whether or not he will be an unfaithful husband.

A woman who puts such a fine point on things will not have to look far to find imperfections in life. The banter of *Where Chimneys Are Seen* led to more somber ruminations in other movies. Takamine's heroines often found themselves in contemporary quandaries that went beyond disputes with the old Chinese sages. With an intensity that makes you gasp, these women ask the largest, most painful questions: Why am I working? Why am I suffering? And, in *As a Wife, as a Woman*, Takamine dares to pose the most extreme of these: "Can you tell me," she inquires of her professor lover, who won't leave his wife, "why I am living?"

I met Takamine Hideko for the first time in October 1989, at the Kawakita Memorial Film Institute in the Ginza section of Tokyo. The late Kawakita Nagamasa began importing foreign films to Japan more than sixty years ago. (He also showed a Mizoguchi film to Berlin audiences in 1929—more than two decades before any Westerner ever dreamed of pronouncing a word like *Rashōmon*.) Kawakita Kashiko,[*] his widow, has continued his work, and the institute now organizes Japanese-film screenings for film-festival directors, scholars, and journalists. Noteworthy foreign films are also shown in its screening room for the enlightenment of Japanese buffs.

Takamine made her last film—*Oh My Son!*, directed by Kinoshita—in 1979, and considers herself retired. She joined me for a screening of the 1964 *Yearning*, which was directed by Naruse from a script by her husband, Matsuyama Zenzō. In this film, she plays a capable war widow who lives with her late husband's mother and her young brother-in-law. The widow runs the small family shop, but the lower prices of a new, modern supermarket down the street threaten her business. She furrows her brow and considers discounts.

Although Takamine has complained about her face ("My face, my eyes, my nose are all round, my upper lip is too short; it's a child's face, and there's nothing I can do about it"), to a Japanese her soft features and full cheeks are the very picture of a *shomin*. A more aristocratic Japanese face needs sharper features and angles—something along the lines of Meryl Streep's face. To movie audiences in Japan, an upper-class Japanese Meryl Streep would look odd running a grocery store, but tie an apron around Takamine Hideko and you're in business.

Trying to remain competitive during an egg-price war, the widow must also contend with relatives who are plotting to sell

[*] Kawakita Kashiko died in 1993.

the store out from under her. Egg prices do not distract her from her devotion to her work and to her husband's memory, but she does get flustered when her brother-in-law declares his love for her. The widow cannot bring herself to accept the sincere advances of this very appealing young man. She refuses him, he resigns himself to the rejection, she shows signs of weakening, and he decides to take over for the delivery boy, just to be on hand in case she wants a private word.

Finally she cannot bear the strain of dealing with her relatives and with her admirer's importunate glances. Renouncing shop and in-laws, she gets on a train to return to her own family. No sooner has the train started, however, than her brother-in-law comes down the aisle to take a seat next to her. What follows is one of the most emotionally complex train rides in the history of cinema. No, she cannot sully her love for her dead husband by taking up with the attractive relative sitting so close to her. No, it is unthinkable. But then, a couple of box lunches later, the unthinkable appears more tempting. After a few more train stops, her resistance vanishes. The widow and the brother-in-law get off together at a hot-springs hotel. When they are at last ready to put an end to all wavering, she again rejects him. The distraught young man goes on a drunken binge and is later carried in, dead, on a stretcher, having thrown himself off a nearby cliff.

The Japanese title of this film is *Midareru*, which means "confusion"—highly seasoned with anguish. In the Japanese classics, love-wracked heroines are often found in this state of *midareru*. On the train, Takamine's face, registering dozens of nuances between fastidiousness and passion, offers superb *midareru* that is every bit a match for the ancients. She can take you to the brink even on such frail material.

When the lights went on in the screening room, I found Takamine crying in her seat. She explained that until then she had seen only parts of the film, in daily rushes. "But it's a Naruse film," she said, wiping her eyes. "So it's too long, too slow. And all that hesitating." Then she mockingly imitated the quivering chin of her screen widow and asked, "Do you think that's easy to do?" Takamine took a moment to compose herself while Mme. Kawakita, among others, came by to offer formal greetings.

At sixty-five, Takamine was impeccably dressed and coiffed. She favors smart black suits, without much jewelry. Although she likes to eat, both onscreen and off, she told me that, at about a hundred pounds, she can still fit into the wedding dress she wore thirty-five years ago. In any one of her tasteful outfits, she could be just another of the many petite matrons who are out shopping everywhere in Tokyo now, busily taking advantage of Japan's economic miracle. But unlike Takamine, the run-of-the-mill wife of a White Plum Heavy Industries executive does not have to fend off fans wherever she alights. As soon as the film ended, people began requesting autographs. After drying her eyes, Takamine showed none of the indecisiveness of the widow in *Yearning* but crisply begged off signing just then. Perhaps she caught the surprise that registered on my face when the contrast sank in. Her grin might have been asking me, "Didn't they tell you I can act?"

After the flurry of autograph seekers receded, we adjourned to a *shabu-shabu* restaurant down the street. "You know, that brother-in-law in the film was supposed to get drunk and die accidentally in the snow," Takamine said, once we had settled down on the restaurant's tatami floor. "That kind of thing happens all the time. But we waited and waited out there on location and no snow fell. So Naruse finally got tired of waiting for a snowstorm and had the brother-in-law kill himself."

Takamine's distinctive voice has lowered over the years to a smoker's tenor. The sound, when she is calm, is clipped and matter-of-fact, but when she is impatient she can easily shift into a more tart mode. In this country of subtle modes of discourse, where you can lose sleep trying to figure out exactly what someone really meant to tell you that morning, Takamine Hideko has gained a reputation for extreme forthrightness. Her admirers find her pleasantly open and honest in her opinions, a welcome relief from the ordinary obfuscations of polite conversation. Her detractors say they wish she would let people finish their sentences before she cuts them off with her sharp tongue. Even in Japan, where psychological probing isn't customary, there are those who like to refer to childhood experiences in explaining adult character. Such analysts speculate that this manner of speaking frankly started when Takamine was made to play naughty, outspoken little boys so long ago. I was told that while her blunt style can pass in Tokyo, she would terrify a visitor from the Japanese countryside.

Shabu-shabu is a beef fondue cooked at the table with assorted vegetables. Takamine likes to cook, and expertly took over the job of swirling cabbage around in the steaming pot, meanwhile responding to my questions. Takamine has been interviewed since the start of her career, in 1929. Reporters have pursued her to the studio, to her home, to her koto lessons. Hunted down a few times too many, she told me, she has come to suspect that journalists are in search of her very self. Boundless enthusiasm is therefore not her principal response to yet another question-and-answer session. Nevertheless, she leaned forward stalwartly to start coping with the ordeal.

Because Takamine began working at such an early age, she has had, to her regret, very little formal education. She studied at the studio during free moments and read whatever came her way. She has written a number of books, however—besides the autobiography there are books on her travels, a book on the artist Umehara Ryūzaburō, and, of course, a cookbook—and their strong, candid style has won considerable praise. It must have pleased this intense autodidact when, some years ago, an essay she wrote was cited as an example of excellent Japanese on the University of

Tokyo's entrance examination. "How did I start writing?" she mused as she cooked our meal. "I didn't think anything of it. Oh, it just came to me naturally, like writing a letter. When I was young, I would write for some of the publications they put out at the studio. Then, when I was twenty-seven, I went to Paris for half a year and wrote a diary, and it was later published as a book."

Takamine does not like to take herself seriously, and her eyes start rolling if she is asked to make weighty pronouncements about her acting career. "I'm telling you, acting is no different from being taught to do tricks, like a cat or a dog," she said. There is, of course, much Japanese modesty in her unwillingness to utter a single positive word about her more than four hundred screen appearances, but Japanese reticence goes only so far. Takamine has not failed to let it be known that a pack of increasingly greedy relatives destroyed her childhood by turning her into a "money-making machine" in the film world. For decades, she has struggled with a substantial supply of anger and bitterness. In an interview she has said:

When I was a child, my mother would put on my makeup. In those days, the face makeup came in a hard compound that was the devil to apply. You had to heat the makeup over the fire or else the thing wouldn't soften. So my mother would put this stuff over the flame and then paint it on my face, spreading it out all over. That hurt, really hurt, I hated it. That's why I didn't like working in films. I was miserable all the time. I can't remember a single instance when I thought I liked my work. It's all the aftereffects of my childhood.

On talk shows, in interviews, in her books — even while downing a hamburger with me — she has been consistently frank in informing the public about her attitude toward her profession. She has written:

Every time I finished a film, I would feel that being an actress was a hateful occupation. A script I had treated as reverently as a god during the shooting—I would feel like ripping it apart page by page and then stomping on it. That's how much I hated it. Because I had the feeling that I was being bullied while I was working, I would feel a sense of liberation but, at the same time, this strange desperation. And then, just when it was over and I thought I could breathe a sigh of relief, go out to have a good time and relax, I'd have to prepare for the next film. Tell me, do you think the film world is the only place I can live?

From these pronouncements Takamine can effortlessly arrive at outspoken appraisals of the most famous names in Japanese cinema.

On Kurosawa: "He can make his actors miserable, twisting them around, trying to get them to do what he wants. Directors like that make me very nervous." On working with Ozu Yasujirō: "Ozu was very particular. Me, I can be pretty shameless about not letting things like that bother me, but others on his set would be quivering with fear. Ryū Chishū—why, he shivered and shook all the time. I'd take a look at him and start shaking myself."

On Naruse (she has more than once entertained audiences with her routine about this formidable director): "He never spoke to me. Not once. When I went over to him, I'd get so nervous that I felt I couldn't breathe—as if there weren't enough oxygen in the room. I really wondered if I should carry a portable oxygen tank around with me. It was that awful. I never did have a real conversation with him, even though we worked together for decades. I suppose you could call this a little odd." Takamine and Naruse worked at the same studio when she was a young girl. "When we were filming *A Wanderer's Notebook*," she recalled once at a public interview, "I thought I'd better say something to him, and so I asked him, 'Naruse-sensei, what kind of kid was I?' 'You were too smart for your own good,' he said. You can see that from there the conversation isn't going anywhere."

Naruse, who died in 1969, was, like Takamine, in his element among the struggling *shomin*. His view of the world was bleak at best. It was his conviction, after years of reflection, that all the energy spent seeking happiness brings no more results than would sitting absolutely still until the end came. "I have thought that the world we live in betrays us," he has been quoted as saying. "This thought still remains with me." Nonetheless, the stymied bar hostesses and typists in his films never cease scurrying forth on errands of self-improvement. Takamine Hideko fashioned magnificent heroines from these wiry, doomed women: she does not flinch at catastrophe, even though Naruse heaps every misfortune imaginable upon his protagonists. When she's in charge of a character, she doesn't hesitate to wring truths from heartbreak, lingering illness, insolvency, betrayal—the stuff of melodrama in lesser hands. Toward the end of his life, Naruse suggested to her that they make a film together without props or color, just a stark white background. He was well aware that Takamine did not require a well-appointed movie set to get to the heart of things. The taciturn Naruse's communication with his actors relied heavily on silences, and Takamine does not deny that those wordless exchanges conveyed sufficient meaning. She has written that she felt Naruse's death so keenly that she has never been able to bring herself to visit his grave.

As we started our meal, Takamine launched into one of her favorite stories. "As I told you, Naruse and I hardly ever talked," she said. "So this is how our days went. I would go to the set every day and just stand there where the lights and the camera were. But Naruse, he was out there somewhere in the dark, and so I thought it was affected to shout out into nowhere, 'Good morning!' And I'm nearsighted, you see, so I thought that instead of my trying to find him it would be easier for me to stand in front of the lights, where he could easily find me. Then he would surely say something. So I'd do that, but then there'd be only a voice from somewhere saying, 'OK, let's start.' And I'd say, 'OK.' We'd go on like that until evening, until he said, 'That's it for today.' I thought it was too much trouble to go looking for him to say good-bye, and so there were many days when I never saw his face at all. There would just be this voice coming from somewhere. But you know, I heard later that Naruse told one of the producers, 'Hide-chan comes to the set and doesn't even say 'Good morning.' '" Can you believe he said that?" When pressed, she admitted that Naruse could express himself if necessary. "I suppose that he didn't talk in public, he talked through his films," she says. But she feels more comfortable in her ironic vein. "When we were shooting *Untamed*," she often recalls in interviews, "I asked him, just to make conversation, how the heroine Oshima should behave in a particular scene. He said to me, 'Before you realize it, you'll be finished.' Now, is that any way to talk? 'Before you realize it, you'll be finished.' "

Takamine conceded that with actors who could not respond so intuitively to his ideas Naruse was not all that opaque. "If he didn't like something, he could spend the whole day on it," she said, animated over her chopsticks. "Once during the filming of *When a Woman Ascends the Stairs* he was late. Usually, if he said we would start at nine in the morning, by nine he'd be working on the first cut. When I asked where he was, they told me that he didn't like the actor who was playing the bartender. In that film I'm the mama-san of a bar, and there's a scene when I come in to work, before any customers have arrived, and the bartender is wiping a glass. The bartender looks over at me and says, 'Good morning.' Well, Naruse didn't like the way he said 'Good morning.' He had the bartender repeat it through that whole day and night, but he still wasn't happy. When I got to the set the next day, there was another actor playing the bartender. I could see from that what a frightening person Naruse was."

Soon after Takamine had regaled me with this story, she and I walked back to the Kawakita Institute for tea and more talk, and then she excused herself so that she could catch the last showing of a film that was playing at a theater around the corner. As she prepared to leave, well-wishers appeared, eager to help her to the door, into the elevator, onto the sidewalk, out to her car. Determined to elude these volunteers, she quickly gathered her possessions together. Since, as she has often said, fate works in mysterious ways, the moment she was ready the elevator arrived to take her down. She bowed a firm, solitary farewell to all of us as the doors closed.

Takamine has had good reason to call fate mysterious, for no one could have predicted that she would one day be ranked, along with salmon, as one of the most famous products of Hokkaidō, Japan's northernmost major island, where she was born in 1924. Her grandfather was enterprising, but his fortunes were subject to wild fluctuations, and at the time of her birth he owned a *soba* (noodle) restaurant in Hakodate, a coastal city. Geishas served their guests on the second floor, and Takamine remembers being taken upstairs as a baby to attend their sake-drenched nightly festivities.

Before Hideko was born, her mother had produced only sons—three of them—and when she became pregnant again the prospect of another male offspring did not stir great interest, so her husband promised to give the new baby boy to his childless younger sister, who lived in Tokyo. The parents' delight at the birth of an adorable girl was diminished by the arrival of this sister, who exhibited a tenacity and hysteria that were to blossom in later years. The cute baby, she argued, belonged to her. She gave the baby the name Hideko and kept traveling to Hakodate to demand that the goods be handed over. "She would come for me, and my father would just disappear from the house, carrying me on his back," Takamine recalls.

Finally the family grew tired of this harassment, and Takamine's real mother formally told her sister-in-law that the couple intended to keep their daughter. But soon afterward Takamine's mother developed tuberculosis and died. The father, never a strong presence in Takamine's chronicles, decided that Hideko, then four years old, should be given over to his sister's care. "My new mother was delighted when my real mother died, because she got me," she told me. "If my real mother had lived, I'd still be in Hakodate. You can see how mysterious fate is."

Takamine moved to Tokyo with this new maternal influence, who was to bedevil her through the years to come. "My new mother became consumed with trying to convince me that she was my real mother," she recounts. "Even though I was only four years old, I knew exactly what had happened — that my real mother had died and I had to go with this new woman. But my new mother insisted that she had always been my mother. I think that's when I started to distrust people." Nevertheless, Takamine soon began to address, and refer to, her aunt as her mother, and has usually done so ever since.

The new mother and her husband (from whom she later separated) had both worked as *benshi* in the countryside. *Benshi* served as narrators in Japan's movie theaters during the silent-film era; they adopted stage names, and some were so gifted that they surpassed the actors in popularity. Actors apparently had nothing to fear from the talents of Hideko's new mother, and her ambitions were to find expression elsewhere. After Hideko was "discovered" on that outing to the Shōchiku film studio, her new mother, ominously, changed her child's family name from Hirayama to Takamine — her own stage name. "I think my mother sometimes really believed that she was me," Takamine often says.

The five-year-old Hideko entered films at a time when a truly pathetic child could go far. Dramas about unlucky, self-sacrificing mothers and their sorrowful children were bringing throngs into the movie theaters. Films called *A Stepmother*, *A True Mother*, and *A Foster Mother*, among others, drew upon a tradition of problems including widowhood, child-care problems, slave wages, and tuberculosis. They belonged to an artistic genre loosely known as *Onamida chōdai*—"Your tears, please!" But by the time of Hideko's debut these melodramas had lost some of their maudlin vigor and needed a boost. "In the old Kabuki plays, children had always been portrayed as sad and unfortunate," the film critic and historian Satō Tadao told me. "Films had continued this trend. But at the end of the 1920s, at about the time that Takamine Hideko made her debut, American films with very playful, happy children started to be popular in Japan. Here were these kids from *Our Gang* comedies, and they were mischievous and wonderfully innocent. That's when you started to see carefree, happy children in our own films."

Takamine appeared in about a hundred films as a child; many of them have not survived, but there are photographs of this tiny film star grinning out from the laps of her kimono-clad movie mothers. Her hair was short, cut in the shape of an inverted noodle bowl, and with the plump, healthy face that was not quite male and not quite female, she seemed entirely capable of pilfering snacks from the local sweet-potato vendor. When portraying little boys, Hideko was especially rambunctious and might, if provoked, challenge adults many feet taller to a boxing match. "Takamine was representative of a new type of child star," Satō says. "She was cute, very cute—that's what people always said when they saw her in films. Before, the children in films followed the Confucian ethic that they should be good and obedient to their parents even if they were given a hard time. But Takamine was very lively and irrepressible. Even if you treated her badly, she didn't cry. And she was very energetic, able to hold her own with the little boys. This was a child who had broken free of the old Confucian strictures."

A Takamine film sometimes played on the same bill as a film starring Shirley Temple, who was very popular in Japan. "But I didn't sing or dance, like Shirley Temple," Takamine told me. "They didn't build shows around me. I think I behaved more naturally, like your child star Margaret O'Brien. The problem with Shirley Temple was that she had this big head, and the rest of her body didn't grow." At first Hideko's lines were taught to her, but later, when she could read, the clever Hideko memorized her own part and everyone else's as well, in order to know when she was supposed to speak. She followed the directors' instructions without thinking—like an organ grinder's monkey, she has said. "I didn't really understand for a long time what they were asking me to do," she told me. "I didn't know what it was to act—I just thought it was strange that I was supposed to stand there in front of everyone and repeat dialogue or laugh or run. What I did understand from the first was that if I didn't say the lines they wanted me to say, the filming session wouldn't end. That I understood. So even though I didn't want to cry, I had to, or else they wouldn't let me go home. I gradually realized that I was doing something called acting."

Around the studio, she was considered highly precocious, and very astute when it came to reading the emotions of adults. She was also way ahead of her age group when it came to suspecting her fellow human beings. "I was just a child, but I could sense that the adults were not to be trusted," she has said. "I could see how they lied all the time. I started to become a really unpleasant child." Even so, by the time she was six her pinup posters were selling well across the nation. Her mother, sensing that Hideko had a film destiny beyond performances as a winning tyke, kept up the girl's strength by plying her with Chinese herbs and garlic. Unlike other stage parents, who were given to starving their toddlers to keep them small fry as long as possible, Takamine's parents tried to stretch out her legs at night to hasten the growing process. Takamine attended primary school sporadically, but education was never part of her mother's plans. "In those days, almost all the actresses had been waitresses in coffee shops around Ginza or Shinjuku or were former 'chocolate girls'—models for the candy companies," Takamine has written. "All the studios wanted was beauty. Acting skills were not an issue, and of course no one cared if the women hadn't gone to school."

Takamine still fumes about the neglect of her education. "I didn't know whether I was appearing in movies during breaks from school or going to school when there were breaks between films," she once said. There were no rules then about the education of children or about the hours they worked. Kept on the set day and night, Hideko was accompanied by her mother, who was always lugging several scripts around. "My mother had never been to school at all," Takamine told me. "She could just barely read and write the simplest things. She was a very bad, very bad stage mother. She didn't hire tutors for me, as the other mothers did. So I had to learn to read by myself."

One of her teachers at school took pity on the exhausted child. He saw that no one in her home cared about her studies, so every time Hideko was about to go off on location this teacher hurried to the train station with a pile of children's magazines. "I don't know why, but I never tried to appeal to my mother's sympathies by telling her how I really felt, that I was tired or that I found the work unpleasant or hard," Takamine writes in her autobiography. "And similarly, not once in my whole long acting career did my mother ever ask me if I found it unpleasant or difficult, or if I wanted to quit." Many adult colleagues, aghast at her situation, wanted to adopt and educate her. "There were dozens of people who said that they would take me into their house as an adopted daughter," she has said. "I suppose it was because I was so cute. And then they saw the stepmother I had and felt sorry for me."

The most persistent of these would-be foster parents were Shōji Tarō, a popular singer, and his wife. Shōji had spent eight years working in a library of the Southern Manchurian Railroad Company. After returning to Japan, he made his reputation with a record of a lugubrious song called "The Lullaby of Akagi," about an outlaw named Sentarō leaving on a journey with a child on his back ("Don't cry now, hush, hush, go to sleep"). "Shōji-san had two sons by another wife, but his new wife thought that the boys were too rowdy and she had no use for them," Takamine explained to me. "She wanted a girl like me. They simply adored me. Shōji-san was very busy touring the country with his act. But no matter how busy he was, when he was in Tokyo he and his wife would come to visit me every day, even if I had already gone to bed. They would come sometimes just to see my sleeping face." After his many offers of adoption were refused, Shōji promised to send Hideko to school and give her singing lessons and piano lessons. Finally it was decided, in 1934, when Hideko was ten, that both mother and daughter would move into Shōji's fine house.

Takamine described the situation: "Please—imagine how it was. We moved to Shōji-san's place, but my mother became one of the maids. She lived in the servants' quarters, and I was treated as the pampered daughter. It was very confusing to me. Shōji-san and his wife were crazy about me. I was like their little pet, and they fought with each other about who was going to take me out every day. They were a strange couple, in that they slept separately, one upstairs and one downstairs. I would sleep with one or the other. And I remember that I had this pillow. I would wait with my pillow near the staircase until they decided where I was going to sleep that night." From a green hat down to green patent-leather-and-snake-skin shoes, Hideko was often dressed in Shōji's favorite color. The shoes and the fabrics were frequently just like his. When he went off to sing "The Lullaby of Akagi" yet again ("Don't cry now, hush, hush"), he liked to take his cute, all-green doll along.

Takamine spent about two years in the Shōji household, during which her acting career tapered off and she could have attended school in her free time. But Shōji and his wife, caught up in their passion for their darling's company, forgot their promises about her schooling and her music lessons. "I started to feel very nervous," Takamine told me. "The maid left, and that meant my mother had to do all the work in that house. Whenever I got something good to eat, I would sneak it to my mother. Then there was another problem. Shōji's wife ignored his two boys, and so they started going to my mother whenever something went wrong. Imagine the situation in that house! At last, I just couldn't stand it any longer, and we moved out. Now I can see that adopting me would have never worked out anywhere. I was cute, you see, but my mother wasn't."

In 1936, mother and daughter rented an apartment near Shōchiku's new studio. There Hideko became acquainted with a more banal variety of covetousness. Her salary proved insufficient to support a contingent of relatives from Hokkaidō who, having lost everything in a fire, had turned up in Tokyo demanding assistance. Confucius, Takamine soon discovered, had declared that it was her moral obligation to support those strangers. She was twelve years old. "I hadn't seen this so-called family since I left Hokkaidō for Tokyo, when I was four," she has written. "The only person I remembered was my grandfather, but the others—it was as if I were meeting them for the first time. The more my mother kept saying that it was a child's filial duty to support her relatives, that it was the path of righteousness, the more I kept wondering, Why in the world do I have to work to support these people?" In an essay called "Even Famous People Have a Lot of Problems," she reflects:

There were my parents, brothers, cousins, cousins' cousins, and other relatives, a slew of them, but I had been adopted into another family and since I was four I had never lived with them. Funny thing, but when I started to make money they all stopped working. . . . They took such a lot of my money and when I said I didn't have any more one waved a knife at me. That's pretty frightening. . . .

Really, I got to the point where I couldn't even stand to look at people. When I met someone, I'd just want to avert my face. I started disliking all human beings. . . .

I was treated differently from other people. That was my biggest worry. I don't really know what normal is. Even though I wasn't good at studies, I would go to school and immediately be made the president of the class. I would try to do some shopping and they would charge me extra. Even though we were poor, I always rode around in a car. I never rode on the subway or the train. It was a crazy kind of life. I didn't know what it was to be treated with the kindness people showed to an ordinary human being. People always treated me as if I were someone special, and so I started suspecting that everyone had an ulterior motive. I didn't trust anyone or anything.

To earn more, Hideko modeled for advertisements—for chocolate and other foods as well as for toothpaste. In an old photograph, she smiles pertly above a pyramid of cans of Meiji corned-beef hash, tomato ketchup, and adzuki beans. She did not enjoy appearing in these ads, and cringed at the thought that her photograph might be used to stuff up a hole in the window of a public toilet, but a dazzling smile above the canned goods meant income for the horde of relatives. For this reason, the child's incisors and canines were always a matter of great interest to her mother. Takamine tells unsettling stories about her childhood dental work, but her mother's efforts in this area did not pass unrewarded. In years to come, movie cameras often paused to admire Takamine Hideko's big and perfect white teeth.

By 1937, Takamine was too grown-up to go on winning the hearts of her fans by adorably addressing pleas to a dead mother up in the clouds, as she had done at nine, but she was not mature enough yet to embark upon a proper love affair. Nearly thirteen, and with the treacherous transitional period upon her, she left

Shōchiku when a rival film studio promised to pay for her education. More candy advertisements supplemented her income there. She began to attend a progressive school, which did not require the uniforms that Japanese students usually wore, but Takamine saw this interlude as her only chance to put on the costume of a normal child. She had a school uniform made for her and, as one sees in a touching photograph, tried to play the part of an ordinary Japanese girl of thirteen. But no sooner had she been outfitted in her uniform than she became so busy at the studio that she had to withdraw from the school.

At least she had the opportunity to shine in her studies onscreen: she became a 1938 teen sensation in *Composition Class*. Playing the daughter of a poor tin dealer, Takamine wins the admiration of her teacher for superior essays about stingy neighbors and the personalities of her rabbits. Poorer filmgoers, flocking to the movie houses, responded to Takamine's spunky personality as she brought life's sunshine to the wearying chores being performed around the local well, and more prosperous viewers were delighted by the vivacious young girl who darted down alleys in a kimono that was too short. Since Deko-chan, as she was now fondly known throughout the nation, was still not ready for a full-fledged romance, her next triumph concentrated on her devotion to a horse. Yamamoto Kajirō, the director—with his assistant director, an unknown named Kurosawa Akira—spent four years working on *Horse*, which was shot in the remote Tōhoku district.

By the time of the film's release in 1941, Japan was mired in a war in China. Takamine was a young woman of seventeen. *Horse* shows her battling life's tribulations in a harsh northern climate. Her father drinks too much; she adores horses; there are village festivals and the moving birth of a colt. In a blizzard, Takamine struggles out to a distant snowbank one night. As fervent as Kurosawa's future samurai, she will not rest until she has dug

225

through the snow for the fresh green grass that will cure her sick horse. Eventually the horse is auctioned off to the Army. In teenage roles like this one, Takamine gave audiences Japan at its sweetest; a war was surely worth fighting to improve the life of such a girl.

She must have been a far better actress than she realized. Audiences saw her as a healthy, happy adolescent, whereas at fourteen—overworked and depressed—she had once walked by the railroad tracks, contemplating suicide. "It was clear to everyone that she didn't have a good mother," Yamamoto once said. "But Deko kept saying and writing things like 'I have my mother to thank for everything.' She even hid the fact that this was not her real mother."

Things were at their worst during the years while *Horse* was being filmed. The work proceeded smoothly until, one day, Takamine lost consciousness. "You have to remember that I was very busy then," she explained to me. "I was making several films at the same time, and I hardly ever had time to go outside the studio. Then, when it came time for me to appear in *Horse*, I had to take a long train ride out to the location site. I was very tired and too pressured by work. And also, I was suddenly outside in the sun. Remember, I had been living like an owl, always in the darkness of indoor sets. Then they brought in this big, big horse, you see." Telling this story, Takamine lengthened her face to mimic an equine shape. "It was the first time I had ever seen such a big, big horse up close. Very long face too. And what a smell it had! I don't really remember what happened next, but I had to work the plow with the horse in front. I think maybe it was all that sun in my eyes. Or else I was tired. Or I was afraid of the horse. Anyway, I fainted, and the next thing I knew, I was lying in bed. I had appendicitis, which I must have been ignoring for a long time, and also some lung trouble—that's what my real mother died of. Kurosawa-san was very nice. He got me to take my medicine."

Takamine became enamored of Kurosawa, who was in charge of much of the location shooting. Although the extent of his response is not clear, he did not rebuff her. Accounts differ about what happened next. According to Takamine, her mother stormed into an innocent private meeting between the couple, took her home and locked her up, and then brought all her fierce energy to bear upon the studio officials, who feared a loss of business if the innocent Deko-chan should become involved in a grown-up relationship. The romance was squelched. But gossip about an engagement had appeared in the newspapers, and Kurosawa was appalled by the vulgar focus on his private life. Takamine writes in her autobiography that he priggishly refused to speak to her after she was finally released from house detention. Though heartbroken, and enraged by her mother's interference, she was willing to be helpful. During studio auditions in 1946, she did Kurosawa the favor of calling his attention to a promising young actor named Mifune Toshirō.

In the middle of that November of 1989, while I was attending screenings of Takamine's films at the Film Center of Tokyo's National Museum of Modern Art, I spent many hours pondering whether I could ever muster a stoicism to match that of the Japanese. The screening room was extraordinarily cold, and the heat was not to be turned on until December 1. Takamine herself came by for one of the screenings, and the schedule skipped ahead seventeen years because she was interested in seeing the 1958 film *The Chase*. She was bundled up in several layers of clothing, for she had been warned about the bracing temperatures, but even so, she expressed surprise at the conditions inside the building. "Cool, very cool, I'd call it," she mordantly observed as she hurried by a fluttering of greeters. Fortunately, *The Chase* was set in torrid summertime Kyūshū, in Japan's south, and the sweating country people onscreen, waving their fans to cool off, cheered up the audience.

In this film, two detectives maintain a watch on Takamine as she keeps house for her stingy banker husband and his children from another marriage. The police suspect that this woman's former boyfriend, wanted for armed robbery and murder, will travel down to Kyūshū for a visit. ("Hey, here she is!" Takamine happily announced when her younger self appeared as the housewife.) The woman goes about her daily chores with a daunting regularity, and with no suggestion of a tempestuous romance in the background. ("But she looks a little fat, don't you think?") She has about her the atmosphere of a dormant volcano, and the film is a long wait for the moment when she will explode. Finally her old lover does arrive, and a detective, after a few slapstick interludes, follows the couple to a hot-springs rendezvous. Here Takamine kisses her (tubercular) lover beside a stack of logs in the hot springs' glade.

"I made so many films with Kinoshita and Naruse, but not once in any of their films did I kiss a man, embrace, even hold hands," Takamine has complained, with some exaggeration. "Not in a single film. I guess they thought that I wasn't the type." In *The Chase*, under the direction of Nomura Yoshitarō, she reveals her aptitude for such encounters. "I ruined my own life by not marrying you," she tells her lover so tenderly that it breaks your heart. "Every day is empty, and I don't see any reason to live." The couple decide to run off together but are captured by the detectives at the inn where they go to bathe. The boyfriend (coughing) is led away by the police. Takamine, who has such a quiet way with sadness, stands, devastated, in her robe. When she starts to weep, it is clear that the young girl who could cry so convincingly about her horse grew up to be an authority on adult sorrow.

"You know, the director of *Mother*, my first film, was Nomura Hōtei," Takamine said later, when we were warming up over a cup of green tea. "He was a big, fat man, a good director—I remember him very well. But when I appeared in his films I was still almost a baby and used to get bored on the set, so he would have his son come and play with me. The boy was in primary school, I think. We'd play Ping-Pong. Or he would carry me around on his back. I urinated on him, I'm afraid, but look, I was just a little girl. That son was Nomura Yoshitarō, the director of *The Chase*. He went to a lot of trouble to get me to appear in it. When we met again, it was after almost thirty years. Just to break the ice, I said to him, 'Listen, I'm sorry that I urinated on you. You'll forgive me, won't you?' "

Takamine interrupted her reminiscence when an admirer came over to ask for her autograph. Autographs in Japan require more than just some scribbled characters, and this time she was asked to write a few poetic words about *The Chase*. An amateur painter, Takamine dashed off an ink drawing of a weeping-willow tree with a snail beside it to decorate her impromptu comment ("Saw *The Chase*—felt very nostalgic") and the characters for her name. When her fan pronounced this acceptable, Takamine raised her eyebrows in mock relief.

Certain aspects of acting theory inspire Takamine to emphatic comment, and she can never resist a droll consideration of the Japanese critics' fondness for *netsuen*, the intense display of emotion onstage. "Ah, *netsuen*, *netsuen*, they really like it!" she said. "In the film today, I could have gone overboard with overacting, especially in that scene when she meets her lover again. But it's better to be reserved when you act, don't you agree? This *netsuen*—people get tired of it. Do you think people could have looked at me on the screen for so many years if I gave them *netsuen* all the time? It embarrasses me and overwhelms all the other actors. I'd rather be more controlled and natural. Actually, I try to be like the people who appear on the newscasts. A plane crashes and the survivors are interviewed. Those survivors, they're not acting. It's all perfectly natural. That's what I try for." She refrained from making any other formal pronouncements on her craft, since, she said, she grew conscientious about her work only after many years in films.

However, Satō Tadao has found early signs of artistic seriousness in her autobiography—particularly where she credits Yamamoto Kajirō with tuning up her professional sensibilities for the first time. That happened when she was fourteen, during the shooting of *Composition Class*:

It was a misty winter morning, and the girl I was playing was building a fire outside in back of her house with her brother Minoru. Director Yamamoto, who'd been stirring the blazing fire with a dead branch, came over to me, his eyeglasses gleaming, and said, "Deko, I'm adding a few lines to the script. I want you to say, 'These winter mornings smell nice, don't they?' And then Minoru will sniff the air and say, 'I don't smell anything special.' Then you should sniff the air and say, 'No, you're wrong, of course there is something.' That's all. You understand, don't you?" . . . And when I thought about it, I saw that he was right—those winter mornings did have a special smell. It was a clean, sharp, piercing smell, the kind that reminded you of a fresh field high up in the mountains, that filled you with nostalgia, like the scent of a distant fire.

Two years later, Takamine happened to see the actress Sugimura Haruko (best known to Westerners as the selfish daughter in Ozu's *Tokyo Story*) in *Spring on Lepers' Island*. "She played a leper and there was a scene where a nurse came to visit her," she writes. "Probably because she didn't want to expose her ugly, disfigured face, Sugimura kept her back to the nurse and the camera during the whole scene as she took down the laundry from the line. What great acting! I couldn't believe how wonderfully talented she was! Then I just groaned to myself and thought, damn, why, this really is acting! . . . I'd never realized that such a great actress even existed!"

Sugimura's example incited Takamine's competitive spirit, and she decided to exert herself more in appearances before the cameras. She also decided that something had to be done about her peculiar film voice. "In those days, the equipment was bad," she has said, "and even though I thought I was speaking properly, when I heard myself afterward, with all that garbled sound coming out, I sounded like some female Mifune." Formally taking up the study of operatic technique, she gave her attention to deep breathing and control of the diaphragm. In prewar films, singing and dancing were commonly interpolated to spice up stretches of dialogue, and after the lessons Takamine's voice had more élan in her duets about the blue sky over the rice fields.

By the summer of 1945, however, she was flagging, and she recalled that as she was sulking on a veranda during a break in the shooting of another film, Yamamoto, once again her director, turned up for further conversation. "Deko, what are you thinking about here all by yourself?" he asked, and so began the day's discourse. "Look over there at that pine tree, will you?" he said. "Do you know why it bends in this direction?" He went on to point out a few of the mysteries of the universe to this petulant twenty-one-year-old: "I think the wind blowing off the sea makes it bend naturally. . . . You know, pickled radishes have a strong odor to most people, but an actor has to sense that smell two or three times as fully as ordinary people. . . . You should take an interest in something, never mind what. Ask yourself, Why? How? . . . Then you'll find that the world isn't that boring to you."

Takamine claims that those words stunned her, for bland Japanese sentences are often not what they seem. Yamamoto may have been literally speaking about vegetables soaking in a vat of miso paste, but Takamine heard other messages roaring from the porch shrubbery. "A fireball of shame burned up into my throat," she writes, "and with that shame came the recognition that for more than eight years, since the age of thirteen, when I started working at the Tōhō studios, I had been making from six to eight films a year and had never once thrown my whole self into my work." From then on, she resolved, she would put all her energies—absolutely, without qualification—into her professional appearances. She would respond to the odor of pickled radishes *ten* times as fully as ordinary people did. And indeed, Takamine learned to draw blood from the shortest pause. "As far as technique goes, Yamada Isuzu is the best," one director has commented. "When she moves, you really see how good she is. But Takamine Hideko is good even when she's not moving at all." She almost frightened a critic who observed her closely in the 1953 film *The Mistress*: "Takamine's full breasts were being embraced from the back by her patron and what passed over her face was a look of utter misery and revulsion that took my breath away. . . . It was the overwrought response of a woman who thought of human beings as nothing but beasts."

Yamamoto Kajirō's acting lesson did not come in the tranquility of temple ruins at twilight, where a Japanese would undoubtedly prefer to set such an epiphany. Rather, it happened while he was shooting *Full Tilt Into America*, in the countryside, in August 1945. The production surely gained a sense of reality from what was actually occurring then: the crew fell behind schedule because U.S. B-29 bomber squads were conducting frequent raids overhead. Then on August 15, when Emperor Hirohito announced Japan's surrender, the film was canceled.

During the war, Japanese actresses had been relegated to the background, since films concentrated on extolling the valor of soldiers going off to defend the nation. Onscreen, a woman could do little more than tearfully look up at a squadron of kamikaze planes heading south. "Takamine pretty much kept out of the war effort," Donald Richie says. "She made some politically questionable films, but that was not her fault—she was under contract and had little choice. She was not like some others, who had gone all out for the war effort. And so, after the war, people still trusted her, loved her."

In 1943, Takamine appeared with Hara Setsuko in Makino Masahiro's *The Opium War*, an exceedingly odd adaptation of D. W. Griffith's *Orphans of the Storm*. It replaced the French Revolution and the Gish sisters with China's Opium War, Takamine, and Hara. Makino apparently assumed that enforcement of copyright laws would not be uppermost in the minds of the enemy while the war was in progress; he therefore appropriated a few cuts from *Lives of a Bengal Lancer* and pinched some footage from *In Old Chicago* for his film's last big scene, the great fire in Canton. A screed against British imperialism, *The Opium War* has Takamine arrayed in silly pigtails and Chinese silks. She plays a blind young woman (the Dorothy Gish role) who is led around a made-in-Japan China by her sister, the even more foolishly attired and elaborately pigtailed Hara (in the Lillian Gish role). Opium, imported by the evil British, has broken the spirit of the Chinese people, and they writhe from the horrors of their addiction in the streets of Canton.

"The only thing I remember about that film is that I couldn't blink my eyes, since I was supposed to be blind," Takamine told me. "I don't know if you've ever tried not to blink, but it's very hard." Her memory has mercifully obliterated the bizarre moment when Hara performs a ridiculous Chinese fan dance—cymbals galore—while balancing upon her head an ornate Empress-of-China hairdo. During breaks in the opium intrigues, great throngs of Chinese—addicts, women, children, rickshaw bearers—rush from one end of the movie screen to the other.

Takamine had no major roles during this period, but her pinup posters bolstered the war effort. These pinups, known as *buro-maido* (bromides)—after the silver bromide used in the developing process—were packed, along with soap, candies, amulets, and cigarettes, in *imon-bukuro*, "cheer-up bags," sent to soldiers at the front. Once the hostilities had begun, her friendly, girl-next-door face consoled countless soldiers far from home. "In my *buro-maido*, I'm always smiling, as usual," she has written. And, in accordance with military regulations, she was usually waving a flag. She received bundles of fan mail from the front, many addressed simply to "Takamine Hideko, Japan." One soldier wrote that he hoped to stay alive in order to marry a girl like her. Another said that his war buddy had been carrying her photograph in his pocket when he was killed. She also received a letter from the mother of a dead soldier, who returned the soiled, wrinkled pinup that had been among her son's belongings.

Throughout the war, Takamine sang for the troops up and down the country. When the war ended, she quickly began to sing for American Occupation troops at a Tokyo theater newly renamed the Ernie Pyle. "You will wonder how she could do it— one day entertaining the Japanese troops, next day the Americans," a Japanese friend said to me. "But you should have seen what went on here just after the war. People who had been ready to die for Japan were suddenly coming out in full support of the Americans. Overnight, they changed completely. They had to, in order to survive. So Takamine was like everyone else. It shows you that she was a real *shomin*." Takamine memorized the incomprehensible English words of popular songs (she sang me a few very sultry bars of "Sentimental Journey"), and soon she was a star attraction on the GI circuit. After her performances, Yankee soldiers would come to her dressing room bearing gifts of chocolate, chewing gum, and peanuts, and greeting her with an exuberant "Hello, Miss Takamine!" A brand-new Cadillac was always waiting to take her home.

The early postwar period, when she was in her early twenties, found Takamine Hideko at the peak of her popularity and in many forgettable films. She became a genuine movie *aidoru* (idol) at this time, because she helped distract her audiences from the distress of facing Japan's defeat, erratic food supplies, and the oversized Occupation soldiers in their midst. A cultivated *cinéaste* might have complained that she had overcome the jinx of a child star and become a grown-up success, but to very little purpose. The masses, however, savored Takamine's well-fed ebullience in films like *Ginza Can-Can Girl*, which sends her and a noted boogie dancer around Tokyo with a bouncy variety show. Occupation authorities encouraged films that showed women freed from feudal bondage, and they must have been delighted with the wholesome Takamine in the liberated, "democratic" outfit of overalls and beret she wore in that film. With one of the male members of the cast seriously overweight, it is a film entirely free of urban starvation and other postwar suffering.

An American admirer can still take pleasure in a zesty Takamine rollicking across the screen with her dog, but for a Japanese *Ginza Can-Can Girl* has all the artistic significance of an Annette Funicello saga. While families were hoping against hope that meager backyard vegetable patches would produce enough food for their households, Takamine and her dancer friend were singing the film's catchy title song:

That cute one, she's the Can-Can Girl.
She's wearing a red blouse, with sandals on her feet.
Wonder who's she waiting for on that Ginza street corner?
She's looking at her watch, grinning, all excited.
That's our Ginza Can-Can Girl.

As winter was settling into Tokyo, I had tea with the director Kinoshita Keisuke in his penthouse. Takamine appeared in a dozen of his films as an adult star. For more than a decade, beginning in 1951, she alternated between Kinoshita and Naruse — "like a Ping-Pong ball," she has said. Takamine, who has been asked for comparisons of the two directors more times than anybody could reasonably bear, dutifully notes in her autobiography that, in contrast to the inscrutable Naruse, "Kinoshita, whose every feeling showed all over his face, was much easier to work with." She adds, "If Kinoshita was really pleased with a cut, he'd be beside himself with emotion—'Just take a look at that! What a great director I am!'"

The Kinoshita I met was seventy-seven, and spry, dapper, jovial. His living room, filled with art objects from around the world, was far removed from the usual Japanese glamour of solitary vases and empty space, and there among his treasures he seemed the benevolent potentate of a kingdom that could tolerate a little clutter. "It's a coincidence, but my first job, when I started working as a camera assistant at Shōchiku, was to shoot a close up of Hideko in *My Cheek Near Yours*," he told me. "It was 1933, and she must have been about nine. Oh, you should have seen her! She played a chauffeur's daughter. There was a scene when she had to cry outside a church, and I'll never forget what a wonderful little actress she was even then. I was shocked. Such a sensitive child! She looked so sad and so cute."

Kinoshita had the grown-up Takamine play a schoolteacher, a widow, a medieval mother opposed to war, a stripper, and a student suicide, among other roles that happened to occur to him. "At the beginning of a film, I'd give her a little advice, but after that she was quick to understand a character," he said. "I'd just stand back and enjoy myself, waiting to see how she'd interpret the role. That's the most charming thing about her, her intelligence. More than her face, more than anything, it's her intelligence. She's so smart that sometimes she gave me trouble." In dozens of interviews on the subject, Takamine has taken a wry view of Kinoshita's abundant energies. In one, she said, "When I worked on a film with Kinoshita, he'd say to me, 'So tell me, Hide-chan, what do you think we should do this time?' Really, he could come up with the strangest ideas, just like that. . . . I'd be physically exhausted working on his films."

Although on any list of important Japanese directors Kinoshita would face stiff competition in matters of elegance, swordplay, and psychological depth, few would fail to grant him top honors when it comes to earnestness. In describing Kinoshita's dramatic works Japanese use words like "honesty," "sincerity," "intensity" — great praise in a country where purity of emotion is the highest virtue. Westerners, however, frequently find his dramas shamelessly sentimental, turning, as they may, on the home life of a simple lighthouse keeper or on the plight of a woman forcibly married off to the landlord's evil son. "You can't judge Kinoshita's films by Western standards," a Swiss specialist in Japanese films has explained. "Japanese go to a movie to feel. To cry. The happy ending, for example, is a Western concept. If you have a happy ending, then you can't cry. Japanese critics like Kinoshita's films because they make you have good feelings. The films are judged not on their artistic merits alone but on the depth of the humane feelings they inspire."

Kinoshita reached a similar conclusion when he spoke to me about Ozu Yasujirō, whose works have traveled abroad more successfully than his. "Ozu was not the type of director who entered the lives of the people, who suffered with them," he said. "He seems to stand above them and observe their lives. I am more involved with hoping for the happiness of the people. In my films, I become at one with their dreams."

While a Western audience may balk at a Kinoshita scenario that concludes with the whole cast weeping in various rooms of a city dwelling, only the dourest of us can resist his comedies. Kinoshita Keisuke can be very, very funny. "After that film I shot when she was a little girl, I didn't have a chance to work with Hideko for a long time," he told me. "Even when I became established as a director, I always had to settle for admiring her from afar. It was not until 1950, after she went freelance, that we were able to work together for the first time as adults. By that time, of course, she was a big star and had appeared in many films. So I wanted to make her happy—to have her appear in a kind of role she'd never done before. I thought about it for a while and finally decided that I had just the thing for her: since she's so smart, such an intelligent woman, I'd have her play someone who's plain dumb."

The first dumbbell that Kinoshita created for Takamine was Lily Carmen, stripper and artiste, magnanimous daughter, and brooding philosopher, in the 1951 color film *Carmen Comes Home*. "You know," Kinoshita continued, "at the time *Carmen* was written, Japan was still occupied by Allied troops. And the Americans, in particular—in order to make us Japanese feel happier—started encouraging strip shows here. Before that, of course, it was considered immoral for women to do anything like display their breasts in public, and so more traditional people felt that something extremely disagreeable had become popular in our country. I too started to worry about these new, looser morals. So I wrote this story about a girl born out in the countryside who, because she was kicked in the head by a cow in her youth, is a little on the slow side mentally. She leaves to make her way in the big city and, in Tokyo, turns to stripping. Actually, in the world of stripping she's something of a star. But Carmen believes that by becoming a stripper she's now a great artist. The story is about her return to her country home with a stripper friend."

From her first appearance at the country train station, where she greets the locals in sunglasses and a radiant orange dress, Takamine's Carmen reveals to the Japanese provinces just what mischief American influences can wreak upon a refined civilization. Carmen and her stripper friend have their own ways of demonstrating their urban sophistication while nostalgically renewing their ties with nature. They revel in the fields by singing and dancing and removing their clothes. Even as spectators, they cause a stir; a public function is interrupted when the skirt on

Carmen's friend falls off. Takamine, aglow in this, her first satire, spares no pains in giving us the full sweep of Carmen's coy vulgarity. She is impossible to ignore in her garish red lipstick, and bursts into a lusty song from her Tokyo revue, punctuated by thrustings of her breasts, while riding through the village fields in a horse-drawn cart. The school principal, a man regularly driven to tears by the first bird's cry in spring, struggles hard against this prophet of social change, but the raptures of nature don't stand a chance beside women who appear before an audience of villagers in little but the roses clenched between their teeth.

Carmen Comes Home stirred the crowds when it was released, and a professor friend of mine shudders to recall one of its most exhilarating moments: "I saw it when I was still living in the country, and you know, when Carmen's friend's skirt fell off I just couldn't believe what had happened. I was so shocked that for a long time, I tell you, I couldn't even move."

Carmen Comes Home was Japan's first color film, and because of the primitive state of the technology, most of its scenes were shot outdoors. "The people from Fuji Film themselves didn't know how the color would come out," Kinoshita recalled. "So they advised us to film as much as possible outside. As the day wore on, the colors changed, so we had to film everything very quickly. If a parasol was opened or closed, the colors of the actor's face would change."

Though Kinoshita evidently had a good time playing with his new equipment, Takamine remembers the experience as something less than a jolly adventure. "At one point, I really thought that this film would kill me," she has written. "Since I was playing a stripper, I couldn't just wear makeup on my face. I had to put makeup on everything that wasn't covered by my clothes, from my breasts to my back, my arms down to the backs of my legs. They mixed powder with greasepaint and used that to stuff up my pores. Over and above the heat of this encasement, there were the hot lights blazing down strong enough to make you dizzy. It was really more than I could bear. . . . Then, one day, while I was doing my best to hold out in heat that tested my endurance, I could feel some smoke rising in a misty trail out from the top of my head. I say smoke, but I don't mean that my hair caught fire and my whole head burst into flames. What happened was that the hair oil I was wearing was getting cooked in the hot lights. It was the same thing that happens when you overheat tempura oil and it starts giving off a purplish haze. I was, as you can imagine, very much surprised."

In 1951, being particularly despondent about her life—fed up with her mother, movies, men, reporters—Takamine left her film career behind to spend six anonymous months in Paris. There she felt lonely enough to buy a doll to keep her company in her *pension*. In the book she published about her stay in France, *Alone in Paris*, she did not dwell most on her enjoyment of French cuisine. Rather, she exulted in the primitive state of international communications systems, which kept intrusions from Japan at a minimum. On her return to Tokyo, she had no time to ponder whether her mental health had taken a turn for the better. A tax official met her at the airport demanding money, and her mother had turned the family home into a boarding house and began charging Takamine for her room just like any other customer. Finally abandoning the house, which she had bought with her own money, Takamine put up in a hotel where, she says, the rate was lower.

In short order, it became clear that Takamine required no further coaching in fury and despair. "After she returned from Paris, you could see a steel core in her acting," one analyst writes. The high-strung behavior of some Takamine heroines in the next decade cannot be attributed solely to Japan's postwar turmoil; these women possess feverish nervous systems that would find chaos even in paradise—women such as the desperate student in Kinoshita's *The Garden of Women* (1954), who is driven to suicide by a rigid social system and her own dangerously acute insights. For bringing the romantic obsessions of Yukiko to the screen in *Floating Clouds*, Takamine received many of the year's acting awards, to add to a growing collection. When a reporter had the temerity to ask how she had created this ardent heroine, she replied, "For thirty years, I've suffered with her kind of sadness. And I certainly don't think the path I took from time to time was a mistake." Her anxious, trapped Otama in Toyoda Shirō's *The Mistress* (1953), who longs to fly off like the wild geese but languishes as a moneylender's kept woman, showed that Takamine could take her special psychological vibrations back to a nineteenth-century setting. This film also gave visual proof of her other endowments. "Before I made *The Mistress*, I'd never really exposed much of anything onscreen," Takamine has recalled. "But in the scene where Tono-san embraces my breasts from the back Toyoda-san kept telling him, 'Go down just a little more,' 'Just a bit more,' 'A little more,' and before long you could see almost everything." While Takamine's unlucky bar hostess in Naruse's *When a Woman Ascends the Stairs* (1960) again brings to mind a volcano, this time it is Mt. Fuji—majestic, cool, and, as every climber knows, simple-looking from a distance but highly complex up close.

Wafting in and out of these films is the usual collection of Japanese film heroes: philanderers, liars, weak-willed parasites; the irresponsible, the haughty, the cunning, the steadfastly married. These males manage to distract, disrupt, or destroy the heroine in question, yet finding a good man appears to be only part of her problem. In many roles, Takamine does not require love so much as a respite from those who pick away at her finances and plague her every waking moment. This sensation—of being eaten alive—Takamine understands well, and her women sigh, grimace, and despise marvelously. Suffering mars the face that could belong to the rice-shop owner next door, and its familiarity only makes her distress more compelling to the audience.

In *Lightning*, Kiyoko is revolted by the dismal relatives collected in her sordid household—one surely reminiscent of the actress's own. Hysteria in Japan, as Takamine demonstrates memorably in this film, usually has certain limitations: a proper tantrum is impossible when the doors are made of paper and no one has any concept of privacy. Heroines like Kiyoko don't subscribe to the beliefs that have traditionally tamed women's lives. "Takamine's women were not willing to wait patiently until the next life for their rewards, as Japanese heroines used to do," a Japanese-film historian told me. "Her women had an urgent need to do everything, settle everything, in this life. Takamine symbolized this for us." When Kiyoko confronts her mother with her grievances in the film's radiant final scene, she reaches with a vengeance for the rewards of the here and now.

Takamine also had critical failures during this period. For example, the writer Yasuoka Shōtarō was not alone in complaining about her unflattering portrayal of Hayashi Fumiko, a well-known author, in the film *A Wanderer's Notebook* (1962). "I may be overstating this," he wrote, "but if Hayashi Fumiko were to see this film in the other world, she'd probably be so furious that her tombstone would shake." Takamine squeezed in other kinds of roles, just in case anyone had forgotten about her range: Carmen the stripper once again, in a sequel, *Carmen's Pure Love* (1952); a nutty, scheming daughter-in-law in *A Candle in the Wind* (1957); and the most virtuous of Japanese housewives in Kinoshita's big moneymaker *The Lighthouse* (1957).

Most important to Japanese audiences, Takamine Hideko became Ōishi-sensei, the schoolteacher in Kinoshita's 1954 antiwar epic *Twenty-four Eyes*. "When Japanese think of Takamine Hideko," Satō Tadao told me, "most will think of her as Ōishi-sensei." It must be acknowledged that this film does not affect Americans so profoundly. Here is Japanese sentimentality undiluted and unafraid, and even some Japanese find it hard to swallow.

Twenty-four Eyes tells the lengthy story of a young woman who goes to teach school on an island in the Inland Sea. Her twelve students (with their total of twenty-four eyes) are in primary school when the film opens, and the action follows them and their teacher over the next quarter century. During the film, one of Ōishi-sensei's students must give up her studies because of money problems, another dies of tuberculosis, and, when the Second World War begins, many of those formerly adorable little boys leave home to fight overseas. Ōishi-sensei herself loses her husband to the war, and she stops teaching when she cannot tolerate new, militaristic education policies. She knows what she is saying when she tells a sick child, "There aren't many happy people in this world, so believe me, you're not alone."

The film score, arranged by Kinoshita's brother, is taken from school songs every Japanese learned in childhood, and the familiar melodies help to keep the audience's tears flowing. In one particularly weepy scene toward the end, when the surviving members of the class gather for a reunion with their teacher, a student blinded during the war lovingly fingers an old school photograph, pointing out from memory each member of the class, dead or alive.

Satō Tadao had heard complaints about the film's sentimentality many times, and he was ready for me when I approached him with my reservations. "Yes, I'll agree with you, it's sentimental, but remember, *Twenty-four Eyes* is an extremely important film for the Japanese," he said. "When it came out, people were tired of war. We had been through so much suffering. It really expressed how much we disliked war. Every class of society, people of every political persuasion were moved by it. And I would guess that ninety percent of the population had no trouble with the sentimentality of this film. You know, the famous advertising slogan they used was that even the Minister of Education cried when he saw *Twenty-four Eyes*. The Ministry of Education usually supports an extremely conservative kind of thinking in this country. It tries to get people to venerate the emperor system, to be nationalistic. Other antiwar films were made at about the same time, but the Minister of Education cried only at *Twenty-four Eyes*."

Satō conceded that the film is not without flaws: "You see, Kinoshita really wants to say, 'Look how awful war is—it made these cute children go off to die.' But the fact is that they did not die in the war as cute little kids, and the film doesn't tell you what kinds of terrible things they did as soldiers." Satō paused, and went on, "All right, so all he's saying is that it's sad, so sad, that Ōishi-sensei's students died in the war. But at that level almost all Japanese agreed with this emotion. *Twenty-four Eyes* is not a radical movie. Ōishi-sensei is no radical. She doesn't start an antiwar movement. That's why so many Japanese could be moved by the film. It's important that you understand this feeling. And by the way, for a sentimental movie, it's very well made. Everyone cried."

Takamine alone, with her intelligence, her cynicism, her melancholy, kept the film from absolute surrender to bathos. Her Ōishi-sensei not only stood firm through tragedies but also showed a particularly Japanese sensitivity toward people and the natural world. To her fans Takamine became Ōishi-sensei offstage as well, and along the way, a national icon. Kinoshita told me, "During the filming of *Twenty-four Eyes*, Hideko must have been about thirty, and the role called for her to age—from nineteen years old to about forty-five, I believe. Other Japanese actresses don't like to show aging faces to their fans. They don't want to think about how they'll look in the future. Hideko must have been the first actress to have the nerve to show herself as an aging woman. I keep telling these other actresses that if they just have the courage to show their faces as old ladies it'll be easier on them in years to come. After all, their fans will have seen what they will look like later. Take, for example, your Lillian Gish or Bette Davis. They weren't ashamed to show themselves when they grew old. But in Japan you have someone like Hara Setsuko, who refuses to show her face in public now. 'The Eternal Beauty,' they call her."

Among the other benefits of *Twenty-four Eyes* was Takamine's romance with Matsuyama Zenzō, who was then Kinoshita's assistant director. Having been credited with much behind-the-scenes plotting to effect this union, Kinoshita now takes a modest view of his role as matchmaker, but there is little doubt that he was eager to get his directing protégé and his troubled star safely married. "What happened was that Matsuyama asked me to intercede for him," he told me. "He wanted to marry her, and he asked me to talk to her about it. I said to him, 'Look, she's a big star and you're just an assistant director. You probably don't have a chance.' He still said he wanted to marry her. So then he asked me just to tell her that he liked her. That I did for him. I thought she would refuse him, but no. She said, 'You know, I might not meet another man who thinks so much of me, so I'll go out with him for a while and see how it goes.' And you can see what happened after that." They were married in 1955.

I next met Takamine for lunch at Tokyo's International House. Anonymous among the overseas guests there, she looked tidy and professorial in her usual black suit. A large diamond ring was the single touch of the movie star. She swept me into the restaurant, and there our meal was organized in no time. Once the menu negotiations were over—she told me that she wasn't in the habit of counting calories—I asked about an essay of hers that had just appeared in *Notebook for Living*, a popular women's magazine.

"Oh, that, it's the silly kind of writing I've been doing lately," she said.

"Zenzō-san's Meals," written in impeccable Japanese deadpan, details her husband's dental problems (he's having work done on his gums) and gives advice about preparing food for husbands with similar afflictions. Besides providing recipes for soft-textured dinners ("Buy the medium-size tapioca at the Chinese food store"), Takamine reveals that she spends about three hours in the kitchen each day preparing their meals. Out in my Tokyo suburb, I told her, public opinion was running against this excessive catering to a husband. My cronies believed that the man was getting too much service, and I had been delegated to tell her that he should at least be prevailed upon to boil the water for his tea.

Takamine, as she brooded over her hamburger steak, was accepting none of these admonitions. "Look, think about it from my point of view. When he does try to do something in the kitchen, he just gets up, makes a mess, and leaves the microwave door open. I'd rather do it myself." In her essay she dryly describes domestic arrangements with her spouse, who has been ill frequently since their marriage. "The person who gets sick has his own problems, but the nurse (that is to say, me) is kept on her toes doing the invalid's bidding and so doesn't have the time to get sick herself." Takamine, a meticulous woman famous for never being late for a shooting, takes no casual view of her daily schedule, and her husband's meals have received her formidable attention. She writes:

My husband is basically a very gentle person. And as the years go by, he becomes even gentler. One day, he said to me very gently, "You know, you've really got to take care of yourself. If you die before me, I'll really be in trouble."

"Why?"

"Don't you see that from the day you die I won't know what to do about my meals?"

Over the years, Takamine and Matsuyama have made films together—most notably *The Happiness of Us Alone* (1961), about a deaf-mute couple, which he wrote and directed. They have also written books about their travels. If a situation comedy were to be made from the published accounts of their marriage (and I see potential here), it would be about an affectionate, impossible pair from Japanese movieland—the wife a highly charged retired actress who whips up a Chinese banquet for sixteen on a low-energy day, and the husband bookish, hypochondriacal, a scriptwriter-director of immensely kindly dramas, who nevertheless is prone to bursts of choler at taxi drivers in Hawaii, where the couple have a second home. (Unused to American ways, Matsuyama was thoroughly provoked by the assertion "I'm the one doing the driving, buddy," from a speeding cabbie.) Takamine and Matsuyama have no children, and at the time of their marriage Takamine considered motherhood a frightening prospect. She writes that when her husband announced a wish for six boys ("to make a basketball team") her shock may have been so severe that she didn't have even one child.

Takamine's mother died in 1978, and after their many years of conflict, Takamine has attempted to make peace with her memory. In a recent talk she gave at a luncheon in a downtown Tokyo hotel, it was apparent that she was still trying to understand this woman's behavior:

When I was a big star, my mother became very proud of being my mother. Once, she decided that people of our status needed a new house, and since I was so busy I didn't know about her plans. One day when I came home from the studio, my key didn't fit into the front door. Soon I found a map left there for me, showing where the new house was. My mother, of course, had bought it with my money without letting me know. This kind of thing happened all the time. And maids—we had seven of them. And they weren't the seven samurai, either. . . .

When I talk about my mother like this, you may think she was an ogre. But later on I thought about my mother's situation and started to see things from her point of view. Now I see that she realized that some-day—she didn't know when—this daughter of hers was going to flee beyond her reach, and the thought made her very anxious. Taking money from me and trying to keep me tied to her was her way of allaying her anxiety. And as for me, I simply didn't have the psychological strength to real-ize that she was so worried. It's sad that a mother and child should have been like this.

Since her mother's death, Takamine has not written about her. "When my mother died," she told me, "my friends said to me, 'It's good—finally she's gone.' When so many people talked like that, I felt very sorry for my mother, whom I used to hate." She says that the financial demands of other relatives continued to plague her for many years into her marriage and beyond her mother's death. She fully expects that after her own death some family members will be scrambling to make legal claims upon what will be her considerable estate. (From 1955 until her retirement, Takamine says, she was Japan's highest-paid actress. Her house is in one of Tokyo's most expensive areas, and her art collection includes pre-cious Asian ceramics, paintings, and antique furniture.)

Since the actresses Yamada Isuzu and Sugimura Haruko, both older than she, are still performing, I asked Takamine whether she regretted retiring from films so early. Leaning back with a ciga-rette, she delivered her response in that sure, gravelly voice. "Actually, I wanted to quit long before *Oh My Son!*, in 1979, but Kinoshita-san came all the way out to our place in Hawaii with red roses and begged me to take the part," she said. "I couldn't refuse him. I thought I would quit when *Floating Clouds* was released, in 1955, after I got married. After all, I had been working in films since I was five. But once I realized how little money Matsuyama had, I kept on working. We had a big household to support. At the time, there were three maids, a dog, birds, a chauffeur. So, while I said I wanted to stop acting, I had to continue; I couldn't afford to quit then. But gradually, as Matsuyama made more money, I appeared in fewer films. I don't like to appear on television. I was in Japanese films during their best, most extravagant years. Why, back then, if the cameraman wanted some clouds he would wait for days until the right clouds came along. Now, even if it rains or snows, those television people have to shoot. I was able to work with the best directors — Kinoshita at Shōchiku and Naruse at Tōhō. Because of that, I don't want to appear in those mixed-up things they put on television. But I've been in about ten dramas on television. People I know ask me to, and I can't refuse."

The organizers of a conference began to take over the part of the restaurant where we were seated. Then the participants streamed in and announcements about the afternoon's schedule started coming over the microphone. Turning conspiratorially in my direction, Takamine persevered above the commotion. "Being a movie star meant that I had to make many public appearances outside the studio, have my picture taken, meet people. It was hard on me — that lack of privacy. I like making things, whether it's a movie or anything else. I say that I disliked acting, but you've got to understand that I didn't just slough my work off. I put everything into it. I disliked doing it, but that's why I had to work so hard. If I had enjoyed acting, I would have found it easier. Whether I liked it or not, I worked hard. But I wanted to preserve my privacy. I wanted people to go to see my films, that was all. I was happy if fans enjoyed my films and then wrote to me about it. But some fans wanted more — they wanted to look inside me, learn things that others don't know."

We lingered for a while as members of the crowd bowed themselves in and out of meetings. By the time we were ready to go, the sun was setting over the bushes in the hotel's formal garden. Since she and her husband were soon leaving for Hawaii, Takamine said her final good-byes to me now, at the front door. Her canny, reckless way of talking has become a part of my consciousness, and were I to hear her speak the briefest word anywhere I'd jump to my feet immediately, knowing it was Deko-chan, from the movies. "I worked very hard, for fifty years, in films," she said in parting. "I wasn't like ordinary people who work at their jobs for a while and then go on a little vacation. No, I worked and worked. So now I am relaxing. This is the happiest time of my life."

ACKNOWLEDGMENTS

THE RESEARCH FOR THIS BOOK WAS supported by two fellowships from the Japan Foundation; I am very grateful for this generosity. Robert Gottlieb, former editor of *The New Yorker* and enthusiastic Japanophile, first suggested that I try writing these biographical essays. He and Sara Lippincott, my other editor at *The New Yorker*, have been great sources of guidance and encouragement. Teruko Ugaya Craig has given me immeasurable help in checking these essays and answering my many questions. She has done this with grace, gusto, and efficiency, and I cannot thank her enough. Haruko Aoki Iyer has also served as my tireless adviser, and I will remember the summer afternoons we spent together reading Yanagiwara Byakuren's poems on her back porch. Janine Beichman helped me select some of my subjects; her communications—in person, over the phone, and via e-mail—have helped me clarify my thoughts about these five women. Best of all, she agreed to translate Byakuren's poetry for this book. Mary Few, who knows only a few words of Japanese, read various drafts of my essays while burdened by a very hectic schedule. She sometimes had to call before dawn to discuss her impressions and suggestions, which have been an important influence on my writing.

Professor Asai Kiyoshi has helped me with much practical advice and much kindness.

Many others have assisted me along the way and I would like to thank some of them, if only by name: Nancy Andrew; Albert Craig; Janet Goff; Hayashi Kanako and the Kawakita Memorial Film Institute; Jon Husband; Iwanaga Emi and her family; Miyazaki Fuki and Tomoo; Mori Kazu; Nina Raj; Donald Richie; Hiroaki Sato; Victoria Skurnick; Takechi Manabu; Torigoe Bunzō and the Tsubouchi Memorial Theatre Museum of Waseda University; Yukawa Yukiko and Seki Yōko of Chūō Kōronsha; Watertown Public Library.

Special thanks to Jennifer Crewe and Leslie Kriesel, my editors at Columbia University Press.

BIBLIOGRAPHICAL NOTE

LISTED BELOW ARE THE MAIN SOURCES of these essays. I have also made use of other newspaper and magazine articles, miscellaneous books, and personal interviews. I will be happy to supply exact references to anyone who contacts me.

For information about Matsui Sumako in English, Sharon K. Nolte's *Liberalism in Modern Japan: Ishibashi Tanzan and His Teachers* (University of California Press, 1987) is an excellent study of intellectual life in that period. There is a brief introductory essay, "Matsui Sumako: Actress and Woman," by Brian Powell in W. G. Beasley, ed., *Modern Japan: Aspects of History, Literature, and Society* (University of California Press, 1975). In Japanese, Matsui Sumako's autobiography *Botanbake* (Shinchōsha, 1919) gives her side of the story. Toita Kōji's *Matsui Sumako* (Bungei Shunjū Bunko, 1986) is good for general information, but three other works, informative and also splendidly opinionated, make for much livelier reading. These are: Tanaka Eizō, *Shingeki sono mukashi* (Bungei Shunjū Shinsha, 1957); Kawamura Karyō, *Zuihitsu Matsui Sumako* (Seiabō, 1968); Kawatake Shigetoshi, *Shōyō, Hōgetsu, Sumako no higeki* (Mainichi Shinbunsha, 1966).

BIBLIOGRAPHICAL NOTE

The quotations from *A Doll's House* are from *Four Great Plays* by Henrik Ibsen (Bantam, 1981); those from *Magda* are from Hermann Sudermann, *Magda*, trans. Charles Edward Amory Winslow (Samuel French, 1899); *Monna Vanna* from Maurice Maeterlinck, *Monna Vanna*, trans. Alexis Irinie Dupont (Harper and Brothers, 1903); *The Dream of a Spring Morning* from Gabriele D'Annunzio, *The Dream of a Spring Morning*, trans. Anna Schenk (*Poet-lore* vol. 14, no. 1, 1902).

All quotations from Takamura Kōtarō's *Chieko-shō* are from the Shinchōsha Bunko edition (1994). I consulted two English translations: Hiroaki Sato, *A Brief Period of Imbecility* (University of Hawaii Press, 1992) and Furuta Sōichi, *Chieko's Sky* (Kodansha International, 1978).

Kanai Mieko's essay, "Takamura Chieko," is in volume 10 of *Kindai nihon no josei-shi* (Shūeisha, 1981). Another provocative work is Kurosawa Ariko, *Onna no kubi* (Domesu Shuppan, 1993). Informative biographies are Gōhara Hiroshi, *Shijin no tsuma* (Miraisha, 1983) and Matsushima Teruaki, *Takamura Chieko— sono wakaki hi* (Nagata Shobō, 1977). In addition, *Takamura Chieko* (Nihonmatsu Kyōiku Iinkai, 1990), a work published by Chieko's hometown, has many photographs and reproductions of her beautiful paper cutouts, as well as biographical information. Satō Haruo's novel *Shōsetsu Chieko-shō* is available in a Kadokawa Bunko edition (1993).

Yanagiwara Byakuren's poetry is mainly from *Tsukushi-shū* (Banrikaku Shohan, 1928) and quotations from her novel, from *Ibara no mi* (Shinchōsha, 1928). The most readily available biographical source is Nagahata Michiko's *Koi no hana: Byakuren jiken* (Bunshun Bunko, 1990).

Hayashi Mariko's novel is *Byakuren renren* (Chūō Kōronsha, 1994). Other biographical and autobiographical works about Byakuren are scattered and hard to find. I am extremely grateful to Yukawa Yukiko and Seki Yōko of Chūō Kōronsha for allowing me access to the wealth of materials in their archives. Miyazaki Fuki and Tomoo, Byakuren's daughter and son-in-law, also have valuable materials that they have shared with me.

Uno Chiyo is the best source for information about herself in her reminiscences and autobiographical fiction. These include: *Ikite yuku watakushi* (2 vols, Mainichi Shinbunsha, 1983); *Watakushi no okeshō jinseishi* (Chūō Bunko, 1984); *Shiawase o motomete ikiru* (Kairyūsha, 1987). *Watakushi no bungakuteki kaisōki* and *Irozange* can be found in *Uno Chiyo zenshū* (Chūō Kōronsha, 1977). My translation of *Irozange* is *Confessions of Love* (University of Hawaii Press, 1989); my translation of her short story "Kōfuku" appears as "Happiness" in *Rabbits, Crabs, Etc.* (University of Hawaii Press, 1982). Donald Keene's translation of *Ohan* can be found in *The Old Woman, the Wife, and the Archer* (Viking, 1961). Rebecca Copeland's translation of "Ningyōshi Tenguya Kyūkichi" is "The Puppet Maker" and appears (along with other translations of Uno's works) in *The Sound of the Wind* (University of Hawaii Press, 1992).

The primary source for information about Takamine Hideko is her autobiography, *Watakushi no tosei nikki* (2 vols., Asahi Shinbunsha, 1980). There is also Satō Tadao's excellent essay in *Fumetsu no sutā: Takamine Hideko no subete* (Shuppan Kyōdō, 1990).